modest part in the contemporary process of renewal. But if I have lived to see the day when laborers in the theological vineyard are not without honor, I must bear witness that later fruits were made possible only by earlier planting, and watering, and God-given growth.

In the pages that follow Professor Tracy is offering an introduction to my thought. He believed an introduction was needed because my work has been highly special-ized, because it occurred outside the frame-work of the American university, and because the vastly increased audience for theological discourse implies a demand for information on what had been going for-ward in the past.

For this task Professor Tracy is notably qualified. He has read my books, followed the various courses I gave when he was a student in Rome, studied my notes and un-published papers, and wrote his doctoral dissertation on the development of my thought on theological method up to 1965. In our many conversations he has let me experience Schleiermacher's paradox, namely, that an intelligent interpreter will know the process of a writer's development better than the writer himself."

THE ACHIEVEMENT
OF BERNARD LONERGAN

THE ACHIEVEMENT

OF BERNARD LONERGAN

DAVID TRACY

HERDER AND HERDER

1970
HERDER AND HERDER NEW YORK
232 Madison Avenue, New York 10016

Nihil obstat: Leo J. Steady, Censor Librorum
Imprimatur: ✠ Robert F. Joyce, Bishop of Burlington
October 24, 1969

CONTENTS

To

Frederick E. Crowe, S.J.,

with respect and thanks

FOREWORD

The attention accorded theologians in the latter part of the twentieth century is due, I think, less to themselves than to their times. For theology is a function not only of revelation and faith but also of culture, so that cultural change entails theological change. For over a century theologians have gradually been adapting their thought to the shift from the classicist culture, dominant up to the French revolution, to the empirical and historical mindedness that constitutes its modern successor. During this long period there has been effected gradually an enormous change of climate. It crystallized, burst into the open, and startled the world at Vatican II. Earlier contributors to the movement made their mistakes and were denounced. Later contributors despite their mistakes not only are acclaimed but even have books written about them.

For twenty-five years I was a professor of theology, first in Montreal, then in Toronto, and, finally, for twelve years in Rome. I turned out the usual notes and handbooks, contributed to periodicals and wrote a long book on methods generally to underpin an as yet unfinished book on method in theology. In so far as I have been alert to what has been going forward in Catholic thought, perforce I have had my modest part in the contemporary process of renewal. But if I have lived to see the day when laborers in the theological vineyard are not without honor, I must bear witness that later fruits were made possible only by earlier planting, and watering, and God-given growth.

In the pages that follow Professor Tracy is offering an introduction to my thought. He believed an introduction was needed because my work has been highly specialized, because it occurred outside the framework of the American university, and because the vastly increased audience for theological discourse implies a demand for information on what had been going forward in the past.

For his task Professor Tracy is notably qualified. He has read my books, followed the various courses I gave when he was a student in Rome, studied my notes and unpublished papers, and wrote his doctoral dissertation on the development of my thought on theological method up to 1965. In our many conversations he has let me experience Schleiermacher's paradox, namely, that an intelligent interpreter will know the process of a writer's development better than the writer himself.

BERNARD LONERGAN

AUTHOR'S INTRODUCTION

In some of his earliest thoughts on methodical activity, Bernard Lonergan set down the following five very general rules: first, understand; second, understand systematically; third, develop positions; fourth, reverse counter-positions; fifth, accept the responsibility for judgment. This work is initiated in the hope that these rules have been fruitfully employed for the present case of understanding the achievement of Lonergan himself. But all of them have been developed within the context of the limited aim and the projected audience of this work. Indeed, the aim of the present work can be stated very succinctly: it intends to expose to a general theological audience the work of that increasingly more influential thinker, Bernard Lonergan. Its principal aim, then, is exposition, not criticism. All explicit criticism, therefore, will be kept to a minimum; it may, in fact, best be observed in the footnotes. Implicit criticism, on the other hand, will be obvious from the structure of the work itself: the themes chosen for development, the characteristics of Lonergan's thought emphasized here, the comparisons and contexts set up for analysis. Moreover, the audience intended for this work can also be determined in more detail: it is that "general" if not easily definable audience which the publishers of this series on major contemporary theologians had in mind when they initiated the project. Negatively, then, the addressee is not meant to be the person who is already an expert in Lonerganian analysis, although it is hoped that they too may benefit from this comprehensive, structural introduction. Nor is the work addressed to experts in the philosophy of science, or of language or of symbol even though, once again, it is hoped that some of Lonergan's suggestions for those disciplines may prove helpful. The book is written, in short, from the only vantage point from which the present author may claim any professional competence, viz. theology. And it is addressed, therefore, to the general theological community in the hope that the often-mentioned but too seldom analyzed theology of Bernard Lonergan may receive more careful study and more deliberate criticism.

Secondly, the emphasis of this work is more formal than material, more structural than determinate. The wisdom of that choice is, I believe, an entirely defensible one: for Lonergan's major contribution to theology, in my judgment, does not lie so much in his often original and important solutions to particular theological questions as it does in the reflective attitude and structural forms which ground all his individual achievements. That attitude may accurately be named a theoretic, indeed, a critical one. That structural emphasis may be called heuristic and thematic. Indeed, the structure of the present work is one which exposes in the first chapter and employs in all the remaining ones some of the principal Lonerganian thematic categories (horizon, conversions, worlds, exigencies, etc.) in order to use those same categories to thematize Lonergan's own performance over these many years. Whether that attempt has been successful my critics will have to decide. At the very least, one hopes that the demanding criteria exemplified in Lonergan's own work will find some resonance within the present theological context. Beyond that, one also hopes that the exact categories and exacting concerns of his work will find the critical audience they deserve. In a later and more technical work on contemporary theological methods, the present writer will initiate some of the criticism he believes to be needed. In the present work, however, he will be content to expose as accurately as he is able the meaning and the achievement of Bernard Lonergan.

It remains for me to offer my gratitude to the many persons who have made the present work possible. It would be impossible to mention all of them. For over the last two and a half years and in the midst of several quite distinct tasks of teaching and research, this book emerged as a result of the prompting and criticism of several friends and colleagues. I should especially like to thank Father Lonergan himself for the many hours of discussion, for his ready response to any and every question and for his willingness to make available the many materials (especially unpublished) needed to complete this work. I should also like to thank Father Frederick Crowe, S.J., and Mr. Justus George Lawler, who together asked me to undertake this work and who singly endured (and in the detached, pure and disinterested manner worthy of students of Lonergan's work!) the series of questions and delays which ensued. And, among many others, I should like to thank publicly the following for their valued advice and criticisms: David Burrell, C.S.C., Joseph Flanagan, S.J., Joseph Komonchak, Matthew Lamb, Frederick Lawrence, Robert Richard, S.J., and John Huckle. I need hardly add, of course, that no one of the above shares the responsibility for the final interpretation; still, their advice, questions and criticisms have helped me to structure or to revise several sections.

I should also like to express my thanks to John Bosworth, Stephen Happel and Gordon Truitt for their exacting construction of the index.

Finally (but certainly not least of all), I would like publicly to express my gratitude to my mother and to Mr. William Baskin and Miss Doyle McCarthy for their painstaking labors in typing this manuscript.

THE ACHIEVEMENT
OF BERNARD LONERGAN

1. INTRODUCTION: HORIZON-ANALYSIS

A. INTRODUCTORY CONTEXT

Of all the major figures in contemporary theology, Bernard Lonergan still remains the least known. There seems to be a widely-held if somewhat vague suspicion that his work is of major import for theology. Still the precise nature of that importance too often sinks beneath atmospheric, indeed sometimes mythic, discussion (as in *Time* magazine some years ago) of his growing Wittgenstein-like "underground legend." That he has profoundly influenced a number of the most creative philosophical and theological younger figures in contemporary American Catholicism (Burrell, Dunne, Lawler, Novak et al.) is generally recognized. That what Lonergan himself often refers to (one trusts with some irony) as his "little book" *Insight* is a major creative philosophical achievement is granted even by his most ardent critics. But precisely what all this might mean for contemporary theology and contemporary culture is, to many observers, at best vague and at worst a re-emergence of a whole set of procedures, categories and methods which they instinctively distrust. For the questions continually recur: is there not simply too much to be done concretely and now with long-overdue structural changes, too much psychological re-orientation to be endured, too many specific issues crying for resolution to afford ourselves the seeming luxury of Lonergan's concern for explanatory method? And anyway, and perhaps more devastatingly, science and scientific concerns no longer seem of major interest to many students of religion.

1

Yet Lonergan's own re-emergence on the American scene in the last two years (following his year of recuperation from his illness) seems to have re-stimulated interest in his work even among the most hardened anti-theoreticians among us. Indeed, his lectures delivered throughout the country, the dual publication of the *Verbum* articles and the number of articles in *Collection,* combined with the several articles devoted to his thought in a number of journals (especially *Continuum*) have surprised many previously wary observers with the relevance of the legendarily rigorous and abstract Lonergan to the contemporary context. And yet, although impelled to interest by those lectures and writings, the observer still quite understandably continues to ask a number of questions: Yes, but what exactly is this methodological problem he speaks about so often? What implications are to be drawn from his analysis of the contemporary Catholic shift from classical to historical consciousness? What, when all is said and done, may one really say any longer about religion and theology which would free us from the confines of a classical culture without allowing any too-easy retreat into yet another mythic consciousness?

The occasion of this work, then, is the attempt to communicate to a general audience a basic outline of Lonergan's long and intricate theological career. Accordingly, the intention of this book will be to expose some of the principal concerns, procedures and categories which emerged during those years. The final expression of those interests, of course, will have to be Lonergan's own in his forthcoming book, *Method in Theology.* In the interim, however, this brief communication of those interests may serve at least the minimal function of allowing his influence to enter more immediately (and less mythically) into contemporary discussion.

Nor should that influence be unwelcome. Unless, of course, the introduction of the exigencies of reason, of theory and of science into the present almost traumatic American and Catholic cultural scenes is already considered useless (read, too "dispassionate") to be able to deal with the modern contexts of ambiguity. But many participants of that same scene may well agree with the present writer that our "post-ecumenical," "post-existentialist," "post-Marxist," "post-Freudian" and post-, it almost seems, everything else situation is such that the Christian people in general and theologians in particular need not feel obliged to create any new myths but might profitably return again to some strictly theoretical and critical work. Nor is this to argue for some blessed return to "neo-Thomism" or "neo-Kantianism" or neo-anything else. It demands rather something at once more radical and more imperative: a call to theologians to examine themselves, their operations, their worlds of meaning, their horizons. It calls for them to give up the search for new myths (even such *"tremens et fascinans"* ones as Thomas J. J. Altizer's "death of God" or Rosemary Reuther's Spirit-theology) and enter critically into a critique of all myths and, more important still, of all myth-makers. To assert this, moreover, does not imply an attack on myth. For need one really have to add at this stage of the modern discussion that myth is not intended here to be a pejorative term but rather a referrent to the first, and in one sense, richest meaning of that coming to self-consciousness which has always defined great cultural transition periods and certainly defines our own?[1]

In such a context what Lonergan demands is not obscure at all but devastatingly clear: the constant and presently almost desperate need for a critique of the self—a critique, moreover, that is as rigorous, as disciplined, and indeed as theoretical as the present development of the various natural and human sciences and of philosophy and theology will allow. And is it not precisely this exigence which seems most obviously lacking in the present American and Catholic cultural contexts? For in either context the options so often presented today as the only authentic ones are either a classicism that is dying or a romanticism that is, at first, fulfilling and exhilarating but ulti-

1. Amidst the vast literature on the subject, for a brief conspectus, cf. Rollo May (ed.), *Symbolism in Religion and Literature* (New York, 1960).

mately disappointing. For no sooner does Leslie Fiedler or Susan Sontag or Andrew Kopkind or the entire New Left announce the end of American innocence and the death of American liberalism than someone is bound to ask: Very well, but then what values do you propose for us? How can you express them intelligently, reasonably, theoretically? How can we incorporate them into structural forms that might define our society? And no sooner does the theological world allow itself to rest content with a "salvation-history" approach in one decade or become exhilarated by the passions of the new Romantics in the next, when a James Barr or a Daniel Callahan is bound to emerge and ask one or two pointed and inevitable questions demanding an intelligent and reasonable (and non-mythic) reply.

Perhaps the Catholic reader might gain some helpful perspective by recalling the recent history of Protestant theology. For the present shift of Catholic thought from classical to historical consciousness is not without its historical parallel in Protestantism. Indeed, at a time when Catholic thought (except in isolated figures like Newman or Möhler) was content to live a ghetto existence, Protestant theology had already witnessed the breakdown of classical Protestantism in the wake of the romantic, critical and historical movements of nineteenth-century Germany. And only in this century has Protestant theology been able to remove itself thoroughly from its classical context and enter wholeheartedly into the various possibilities and difficulties of the modern period of historical consciousness, i.e. of man's full acceptance of his responsibility to transform himself, his worlds, his meanings. And the fact that many of the younger and more determined Protestant theologians in this country (e.g. John Cobb, Schubert Ogden, James Robinson, Langdon Gilkey) are becoming even more and not less theoretical should be of major interest to those Catholic thinkers tempted to an age of theological romanticism. In short, might not the "transcendental" imperatives "be intelligent, be reasonable, be responsible, be loving, develop and, if necessary, change" once again

4

find some resonance in the contemporary American Catholic? If they do, then—but only then—the foundational (and seldom applied but highly applicable) work of Bernard Lonergan on the nature of theology will begin to make sense as a question. Furthermore, it might also help to recall that the key moments in the history of any culture or of any discipline come about not when a new answer (classical or romantic) is proposed, but when a radically new question is articulated. Such a question (more exactly, series of questions) has been proposed, in the author's judgment, in the work of Bernard Lonergan.

Let us speak, then, more specifically of that work: No theological discussion is more important at present than that of the theoretical models which the theologian employs for any "God-talk" or "salvation-history-talk" or the like. The time is now past when one may use such phrases as "redemption" or "God acts in history"[2] or even "God" without trying to articulate theoretically just what such language might mean. In ecclesiology, for example, the enthusiasm accorded the genuine gains of Vatican II in its richer, more biblical images for the church is beginning to wane.[3] In fact, many theologians (Protestant and Catholic alike) realize anew the need for more rigorous definition and more technical theoretical defense of their too often loose language. The gains of the radical theology debate and,

2. The works of James Barr are the best-known critique of the "salvation-history" approach. For a short summary of Barr's position, cf. "Revelation Through History in the Old Testament, and in Modern Theology," *Interpretation,* 17 (1963), 193–205; for a fuller study, cf. Barr's *Biblical Words for Time* (Naperville, 1962) and *Semantics of Biblical Language* (London, 1961); for a helpful introductory bibliography on the "God" question, cf. Frederick Herzog, *Understanding God: The Key Issue in the Present-Day Protestant Thought* (New York, 1966), pp. 175–188.

3. For example, much of the theological dissatisfaction and cultural ineffectiveness of the recent pastorals of the American hierarchy stem, in this writer's judgment, from the authors' apparent failure to recognize the present need for something more than a commentary on a part of one constitution of Vatican II; by way of contrast, cf. L. K. Shook (ed.), *Theology of Renewal* I–II (New York, 1969) for some post-Vatican II possibilities.

5

for this writer, the still greater gains of the positions outlined in the *New Frontiers in Theology* series[4] represent only the beginning of a theoretical enterprise in contemporary theology which already makes the debates of the forties and fifties and, indeed, of the aggiornamento seem like an age of theoretical innocence attractive, no doubt, but also no longer possible.[5] In essence, then, the real problem of contemporary theology is not simply to continue its engagement in a "return to the sources" but is, rather, to locate the conditions for the possibility of any such return, of just what such a return might mean and of just what language might be available for it. The problem, to use the excellent phrase of the practitioners of the "new hermeneutic," is to "bring to speech" once again the Christian fact. And once one enters that problematic, there is no exit other than that of attempting to ground critically and order methodically the language[6] one chooses to employ—whether it be the Hegelian and Nietzschean language of Altizer, the Whiteheadean language of Ogden and Cobb, the late-Heideggerian language of Ott, Ebeling and Fuchs, the Wittgensteinian language of van Buren or

4. Viz. *New Frontiers in Theology* (New York, 1963–67), I *The Later Heidegger and Theology;* II *The New Hermeneutic* (Ebeling and Fuchs); III *Theology as History* (Pannenberg).

5. One occasionally wonders whether Protestant observers of Roman Catholic theology are familiar with the work of Catholic theologians on hermeneutic (especially Lonergan, Rahner and, more recently, Schillebeeckx); or would so fine a critic and practitioner of the "new hermeneutic" as James M. Robinson still consider the discussion of *sensus plenior* representative of advanced Catholic thought on this central question? Cf. James M. Robinson, "Scripture and Theological Method," *The Catholic Biblical Quarterly* (January 1965), 6–27.

6. Indeed, the discussion of the primal nature of language—following the work, principally, of Heidegger, Wittgenstein and Merleau-Ponty—is one of the central studies of contemporary philosophical theologians as the discussions of hermeneutic, method and development of doctrine amply indicate. For a useful introduction to the problem, cf. John Macquarrie, *God-Talk* (New York, 1967); for the more theoretical issues involved in the German discussion, cf. Hans-Georg Gadamer, *Wahrheit und Methode* (Tübingen, 1962), and J. Derrida, "La structure, le signe et le jeu dans le discours des sciences humaines," *L'Ecriture et la différence* (Paris, 1967); for a recent American contribution, cf. Ray L. Hart, *Unfinished Man and the Imagination* (New York, 1968).

any of the other "languages" of others, even of the less rigorous practitioners of the contemporary theological task. This present work, moreover, will merely be a brief exposé of another and rather generally unknown theological language, viz. what we shall call the horizon-analysis method of Bernard Lonergan. This first chapter will initiate that discussion by introducing a certain heuristic and schematic possibility, viz. horizon-analysis as a viable theological method and language. It will attempt to expose some of the key categories developed in Lonergan's later work in order to employ those same categories through this present study of that work. Such a procedure, it is hoped, will allow the reader to use these categories for holding together as tightly as possible the wide range of diverse material to be found in Lonergan's work over the years.

First, then, let us consider that heuristic and schematic possibility, viz. Lonergan's horizon-analysis as a viable theological approach. All three of those words, moreover, are important: "possibility"—i.e. not a proof of Lonergan's method but an exposé of its basic features and its possible usefulness; "schematic"—i.e. not a detailed account but an outline of the main lines of the approach (and, therefore, some necessary brevity on certain key words such as "mediation" and "constitution"[7]); "heuristic"[8]—i.e. an outline that will cumulatively head towards an unknown (viz. horizon-analysis) whose main features, at least, may become known to those not familiar with them.

By way of background to this discussion, one might recall that horizon-analysis or intentionality analysis refers generically to that group of methods associated with such names as Husserl, Heidegger, Merleau-Ponty, de Waelhens, Ricoeur, Coreth,

7. Cf. Bernard J. F. Lonergan, *Collection* (New York, 1967), pp. 240–269; idem, *De Methodo Theologiae* (privately printed notes; North American College, Rome), pp. 13–14; idem, *Insight: A Study of Human Understanding* (London and New York, 1957), pp. 341, 373; for the distinct Husserlian use of the key word "constitution," cf. R. Sokolowski, *The Formation of Husserl's Concept of Constitution* (The Hague, 1964).
8. For Lonergan's important use of "heuristic notion," cf. *Insight*, esp. pp. 36–37, 63, 541–42, 683–84.

Rahner, Lonergan and many others.[9] More generally, it refers to the efforts of two principal movements of contemporary thought: the phenomenological movement and the movement of transcendental method. Moreover, it finds interesting and important parallels in distinct but allied movements of thought, such as, most recently, the attempt of Wolfhart Pannenberg to establish a hermeneutic equal to the historian's (and theologian's) problem (in his words, following Gadamer) of "merging horizons."

Now, quite clearly, one cannot argue to any easy and ultimately disreputable "concordism" from the mere use of a common word (horizon) by a number of quite different thinkers. In fact, the differences among any two of the thinkers listed above are too significant to allow for any such synthesis (more exactly, syncretism). However, one can begin to see in all these thinkers certain shared concerns; shared, if variously articulated, conclusions, and, to a more limited extent, shared approaches.

That sharing can be exposed in its basic positive and negative features: On the positive side, a basic and common concern lies in what Karl Rahner has called "that turn to the subjective at the beginning of modern times."[10] Briefly, they share an insistence upon the need to investigate, through some species of a critical philosophical method, the subjectivity-intentionality-meaning-possibilities of man as questioning being. More specifically, in reference to the widely used word "horizon," a common origin may also be found: viz. Husserl's attempt to analyze and ground philosophy as *the* basic horizon by means of his transcendental phenomenology. One need hardly add, of course, that the various horizon-analyses need share neither Husserl's presuppositions nor his conclusions. Negatively, one might note the common strain against extrinsicism of any kind,

9. Cf. Patrick Heelan, "Horizon Objectivity and Reality in the Physical Sciences," *International Philosophical Quarterly* (September 1967), 375–412.

10. K. Rahner, *Theological Investigations*, IV (Baltimore, 1966), p. 324.

against positivism, against the critical foundation (or lack thereof) of pragmatism and, generally speaking, against idealism.

The main body of this chapter, however, will not try to expose and compare all the horizon analysts but will attempt a more modest and perhaps more necessary task: to expose the method of horizon-analysis employed by Bernard Lonergan. One must note, however, that the Lonergan in question in this chapter is not the Lonergan of his early works on Aquinas (*Gratia Operans* and the *Verbum* articles) nor the Lonergan of his speculative treatises *De Deo Trino* and *De Verbo Incarnato* nor even the Lonergan of *Insight* but rather the Lonergan of his post-1957 work: that work in which the categories of historical consciousness and constitutive meaning have become his chief interest, methodology his chief question, and the technical category "horizon" one of his chief theoretical tools. In short, to add yet another neologism to an already overloaded theological vocabulary, the work in question here is principally that of the "later Lonergan."

B. DESCRIPTIVE ENTRY INTO HORIZON

The first and perhaps most significant area of agreement between these various thinkers is the importance they attach to the fact that knowledge is essentially in process.[11] The process referred to, moreover, at least in the case of Lonergan, is the process of raising and answering questions: what, why, how often, etc. At any stage of that process, furthermore, a threefold division appears: First, the known, i.e. the range of questions I can raise and answer. Second, the known unknown, i.e. the range of questions I can raise, find significant, find possible ways of solving but, in fact, cannot as yet answer. In more traditional vocabulary this is the area of *docta ignorantia*. Third, the unknown unknown, i.e. that range of questions that I do

11. This entire section represents a summary of Lonergan's 1957 "Lectures in Existentialism and Mathematical Logic" at Boston College.

not and, in fact, cannot raise as they lack significance for me—are literally meaningless to me. Traditionally stated, this is the area of *indocta ignorantia*. As a first approximation, therefore, horizon may be called the limit or boundary between my *docta* and *indocta ignorantia*. As a second approximation, it is to be noted that what lies beyond my horizon consists not principally of answers but of *questions* that are meaningless and insignificant to me.

A further problem, however, soon reveals itself: how is one to approach the question of one's own horizon? In a direct approach, in fact, horizon-analysis is rent with difficulties—for I cannot have any clear picture of either the boundaries or the limitations of my present horizon until, as a matter of fact, I have already surpassed it. Its boundaries are obscure and hazy to me. And what is outside it I simply cannot see.

For that reason, then, Lonergan throughout his work pays great attention to an indirect, i.e. a historical approach to the problem. For such an analysis, he examines certain key historical figures or periods in which a horizon-shift has clearly taken place. He turns, for example, to the history of empirical science, more specifically to the horizon-shift involved in the seventeenth century scientific revolution against the Aristotelian scientific ideal in favor of the more empirical approach of Galileo and Kepler.[12] More contemporaneously, he elsewhere analyzes the collapse, in the twentieth century, of the Newtonian horizon following the rise of relativity theory and quantum physics.[13] Still later in his own development, he studies the horizon-shift involved in Dilthey's attack on historicism and his concomitant insistence upon the basic distinction between the *Natur-wissen-schaften* and the *Geistes-wissenschaften* (or of Heidegger and

12. Herbert Butterfield, *The Origins of Modern Science* (London, 1957); more recently, and yet more helpfully, Thomas S. Kuhn, *Structure of Scientific Revolutions* (Chicago, 1962), and Stanley L. Jaki, *The Relevance of Physics* (Chicago, 1966).

13. Cf. Patrick Heelan, *Quantum Mechanics and Objectivity: A Study of the Physical Philosophy of Werner Heisenberg* (The Hague, 1965), esp. pp. 25–54.

Gadamer's horizon-shift from the romantic hermeneutic of Dilthey and Schleiermacher).[14] Or, as in the parallel cases of Karl Rahner and John Baptist Metz,[15] Lonergan re-interprets Aquinas' achievement as, in fact, fundamentally a horizon-change (from symbolic to theoretic interiority for Lonergan; from a cosmocentric to an anthropocentric horizon for Metz). In *Insight,* moreover, he critically investigates the meaning of the "Copernican revolution" in the transcendental philosophy initiated by Kant.

After an examination of such periods, Lonergan tries to impel his readers more directly into the question of horizon-shift by some realization of the meaning of the existentialist categories of *dread* and the *existential gap. Dread,* in fact, refers to that phenomenon experienced by anyone whose horizon has been radically threatened; i.e. whose entire present orientation, interest or concern has been challenged on some basic level. Two features of such dread are clear and commonplace: an anxiety in the face of such a threat and a spontaneous and ingenious (often sub-conscious) resistance to the demands for change now put upon one. In short, the only possible remedy, psychologically, is a new self-identity or, ontologically, a conversion, i.e. an entire shift of orientation, direction or concern; a radical transformation of myself, my operations and worlds of

14. Cf. James Robinson's introductory essays to the *New Frontiers in Theology* series (New York, 1963, 1964 and 1967), esp. vols. I and II; and Robert W. Funk, *Language, Hermeneutic and the Word of God* (New York, 1966), and Richard E. Palmer, *Hermeneutics: Interpretation Theory in Schleiermacher, Dilthey, Heidegger and Gadamer* (Northwestern, 1969).

15. J. B. Metz, *Christian Anthropology* (New York, 1969); it is to be observed, however, that Metz's interpretation of several Thomist texts is somewhat strained: the general interpretation, however, finds important support from Karl Rahner, *Spirit in the World* (New York, 1968); for a brief but helpful survey of some of the major interpretations of Aquinas, cf. Helen James John, *The Thomist Spectrum* (New York, 1966); for an excellent study of the horizon shifts from classical to medieval to modern and post-modern philosophy, cf. Thomas Prufer, "A Protreptic: What is Philosophy?" *Studies in Philosophy and the History of Philosophy,* II (Washington, 1963), pp. 1–19.

11

meaning. At the same time, the second and correlative existential phenomenon may be located: the much discussed *existential gap*—not simply in the sense of the usual gap between the master (e.g. Hegel or Aquinas) and the school which bears his name, but the yet more basic existential gap in the horizon-threatened subject himself—his alienation-through-ignorance-through-horizon-limitation from the reality of his true self, and through and because of that, of reality itself. This gap reveals not simply the self exposed by the sciences of biochemistry or depth psychology or sociology or even contemporary journalism (generation gap; credibility gap), but the still more basic self as the center of one's reasonableness, one's intelligence, one's freedom: the self, in short, revealed to anyone who has undergone a basic intellectual (indeed philosophic) conversion and quite literally beyond the horizon of anyone who has not.

In other words, one finds oneself, with Rahner, where we began "at that turn to the subjective at the beginning of modern thought." For, as is becoming increasingly clear in the contemporary debate, it is the reality of no single object or even series of objects (including the subject as object in introspection) which can ground one's horizon or one's critique of horizons. Rather, it is the reality, first, of the subject as subject: the subject, moreover, in all his concreteness: the one who lives and dies, loves and hates, rejoices and suffers, wonders and dreads, questions and doubts. It is, in Lonergan's words, "Descartes' 'cogito' transposed to concrete living. It is the subject present to himself, not as presented to himself in any theory of consciousness first but as the prior prerequisite to any presentation, as *a priori* condition to any stream of consciousness."[16]

C. LONERGAN'S TECHNICAL DEFINITION AND USE OF HORIZON-ANALYSIS

If the first descriptive section has explicitated the purely experiential meaning of horizon, it is the intent of this section

16. Cf. Boston College lecture notes, *op. cit.*

12

both to specify the discussion in the direction of Lonergan's more rigorous use of horizon-analysis and to supply an explanatory or technical definition to the term.[17]

Once again, however, a few basic directions and definitions are in order: First, if the descriptive discussion of horizon as an experience has been successful and the centrality of not new answers but new questions has been recognized, then perhaps the attempt of transcendental method to question (with Coreth) man's power of "questioning itself as the *a priori* condition for all knowledge" or the attempt of the Lonergan of *Insight* to explicitate "the meaning of meaning" and to expand that explicitation, in his later works, into a discussion of incarnate, historical consciousness may not seem as strange or ill-directed as they so often do to more classical thinkers. Secondly, although it is impossible in the present context to summarize the full argumentation of Lonergan in *Insight* and his later works, still a few key definitions must be communicated in order to allow some understanding of Lonergan's use of "horizon." Those definitions will be: consciousness, intentionality and presence or awareness.

Consciousness, for Lonergan, is a property or quality of acts of a given kind:[18] sensitive and intellective; cognitive and appetitive. In brief, operations are conscious inasmuch as they

17. For the briefest and clearest expression of Lonergan to date on horizon, cf. the oft-reprinted "Metaphysics as Horizon," *Collection,* pp. 202–21; for Coreth, cf. *Metaphysics* (New York, 1968); for a general and dependable survey of transcendental method, cf. Otto Muck, *The Transcendental Method* (New York, 1968); for a briefer presentation of the Rahner and Coreth positions, cf. Kenneth Baker, *A Synopsis of the Transcendental Philosophy of Emerich Coreth and Karl Rahner* (New York, 1967); for Lonergan's own position, cf. Frederick Crowe (ed.), *Spirit as Inquiry: Studies in Honor of Bernard Lonergan* (Au- *"Continuum"* tumn, 1964) along with Crowe's introductory essays in *Collection,* pp. vii–xxxv; in *Modern Theologians, Christians and Jews* (Notre Dame and London, 1967), pp. 126–52; and in *Theological Studies* (December, 1962), 637–43.

18. For a useful introduction to *Insight* on consciousness, cf. the essays in *Collection,* esp. *"Insight:* Preface to a Discussion," pp. 152–64; "Christ as Subject: A Reply," pp. 164–98; "Cognitional Structure," pp. 221–40; and *De Constitutione Christi, Ontologica et Psychologica* (ad usum auditorum) (Rome, 1961).

render the subject aware of himself and his operations. They are intentional inasmuch as they constitute an awareness of an object. The key word, then, is awareness; but awareness is itself an ambiguous term, for there is a presence of objects to a subject and, concomitantly but quite differently, the presence of the subject to whom objects (including the subject as object in introspection) are presented. Object is present as intended; subject is present as intending.

With these basic presuppositions in mind, therefore, one may speak of Lonergan's definition and use of horizon. A horizon, for him, is defined as a maximum field of vision from a determinate viewpoint. It possesses both an objective and a subjective pole, each one of which is conditioned by and conditions the other. The subjective pole refers to the intentionality-meaning possibilities of the present stage of development of the subject. The objective pole refers to the "worlds" of meaning achieved by or open to the subject at his present stage of development. His world, in other words, may be defined as that totality of objects with which the subject in his present intentional development can operate.

For example, the subjective pole of an expert in a particular field would be comprised of that set of scientific operations with which he is familiar, while the objective pole is the field or fields (worlds) that such operations may reach. More philosophically, the objective pole of a philosopher in the Christian Wolff tradition is all possible being. His subjective pole would be the logical operations of necessity and possibility establishing the relationships between possible and necessary "beings." Or, more to the point, the subjective pole of a philosopher employing transcendental method is that method itself; the objective pole is the being intended by and critically grounded in such method. Finally, in such a framework, one may recognize that any man at any stage of his life is open to at least refinement of his horizon, usually development and sometimes even conversion (i.e. radical transformation).

With that understanding of horizon, therefore, Lonergan next

14

attempts (by a highly personal use of the genetic child psychology theory of Jean Piaget and by his own analysis of intentionality in *Insight* and his later works)[19] to describe the basic expansions of the horizon of the meaning-seeking-constituting animal, man.

The first division, then, is the child's world. According to Piaget the basic mode of development for the child is as follows: from an undifferentiated state to a differentiation of operations (e.g. hand and foot) to an integration of differentiated operations (e.g. walking) to grouping groups of integrated operations (e.g. walking back). Furthermore, as the child develops he learns to move beyond the world of immediacy (sense, taste, sight etc.) to a world mediated by means of story or language to a yet further world mediated by technical language (math., science) until, usually as an adult, he moves to the possibility of abstraction on the highest level—i.e. a critical analysis of all his operations and, yet more basically, of the possibility of Being itself.[20] In short, he may become a philosopher. Moreover, if he reflects *critically* upon the actual human condition in the light of the Christian fact, he may also become a theologian.

On the adult level, however, most men find that their subjectivity possibilities reveal, ever more clearly and differentiatedly, yet further worlds. Lonergan locates at least six such worlds upon three basic antithetical possibilities of human consciousness: First, the dynamism of human consciousness,[21] if allowed

---

19. Cf. *De Methodo Theologiae*, pp. 2–5.

20. The language of "immediacy," "meditation of meaning" and "constitutive meaning" is Lonergan's, not Piaget's; cf. *Collection,* pp. 252–69.

21. For a schematic presentation of Lonergan's approach to transcendence, cf. *Collection,* "Openness and Religions Experience," pp. 198–202; also *Insight,* pp. 634–87. For two interesting Lonergan-inspired approaches to the question of transcendence, cf. David Burrell, "Aquinas on Naming God," *Theological Studies* (June, 1963), pp. 183–213; and Michael Novak, *Belief and Unbelief* (New York, 1965). The present writer continues to find difficulties in Lonergan's analysis of transcendence but will reserve an articulation of those difficulties.

full range and especially if brought to question its own grounds, may reveal the possibility of speaking of a world transcendent to and grounding man's world, viz. the sacred. If undifferentiated, these worlds tend to merge (as Eliade has documented). If not clearly differentiated (because, for example, of an important but as yet unabsorbed horizon-shift) the "reality" of one of the worlds will be called into question (as in the Enlightenment attack upon Christianity or as in the contemporary discussion of secularism). In some cases (as, for example, in the Augustinian-Aristotelian medieval dispute or in much of the contemporary German theological context) the very dynamism of consciousness can permit, in fact demand, the clear differentiation between the world of the profane (where a spade is just a spade) and the world of the sacred (whose "sacred grove," Heidegger warns, must not be profaned).

Secondly, the specialization possibilities of human consciousness reveal two other worlds: the "common sense" world and the theoretical world. For what is the world of common sense but an objectification of the specialization of human intellect's ability to deal with the concrete and the particular? And what is the world of theory but an objectification of the *logos*-specialization of human intellect's ability to understand and define in the light of exigencies of scientific reason? Indeed, if that differentiation is lost, "theory" becomes a pejorative term and Voegelin's "doxic thinkers"[22] prepare a culture for its eventual collapse. Common sense and theory differ further in their object: in theory the object is the relationships of objects to one another. In the world of common sense it is the relationship of all things to me, more exactly to my desires and fears, my present needs and abilities. To recall the two worlds as distinct we need only recall the classic confrontation of Thales and the milkmaid or the classic theological development from the *quoad nos* of the Scriptures to the *quoad se* of the councils.[23]

22. Cf. Eric Voegelin, *New Science of Politics* (Chicago, 1952), esp. pp. 1–27, 162–91.
23. Cf. *De Deo Trino* (Rome, 1964), esp. I, pp. 87–113; II, pp. 7–61.

16

Thirdly, the central differentiation of human consciousness reveals the presence of two further worlds—the interior and the exterior. The basis for such a distinction is the dual mode of awareness-presence referred to above: immediate awareness of myself and my operations and mediate awareness of objects other than myself (or even myself as object in introspection). It is, in brief, the distinction of worlds (and presence of worlds) discovered and brought to speech so eloquently by an Augustine in his *De Trinitate* and developed into a rigorously technical analogy of intelligible emanations by an Aquinas. More recently still, the world of interiority is the world of history, of self-constitution, of *Ex-sistenz:* it is the world one enters only by a noticeable shift, indeed, conversion of one's horizon. Or as Robert Johann would say, "When one leaves nature and enters history things become unstuck." Whether this discovery will lead to a radical immanentization of all reality or to a radical rediscovery of Being is at the heart of the problem faced by the contemporary philosophical and theological theorist.

Finally, it should be noted that these six differentiated worlds are not arbitrarily chosen. Rather they are based on three fundamental features of human consciousness: Its dynamism (sacred-profane); its differentiation of awareness (interior-exterior); and its specialization possibilities (common sense-theory).

Granted, then, the possibility for the adult of six differentiated worlds, what might be the hope of some integration of them? Surely one cannot hope for any easy synthesis or Piaget's child-like grouping of groups of differentiated operations for the mature adult. Still there are, historically, certain attempts at integration which present themselves for consideration.[24] Lonergan himself suggests five such integrative possibilities: First, *elimination.* This possibility is at once the easiest and the most common. It refers to the universal fact that a man can simply eliminate those worlds which cause him doubt or trouble. He can deny the possibility of other worlds or of any reality beyond

24. Cf. *De Methodo Theologiae,* pp. 7–13.

that which he immediately affirms. It is the method of the ideologue or of a certain kind of journalism; for example, if one eliminates the worlds of the sacred, of theory and of the interior, one is left with something very like the "world" of, say, *Time* magazine. Nor is such integration-via-elimination confined to the theoretically undemanding. In fact, it may and usually does overtake any genuinely original mind. That latter phenomenon may, perhaps, be most clearly observed in what might be termed the "One Great Idea" syndrome. A man has a valid, indeed, original insight, but claims too much for it; he uses it as a totally sufficient response to any question, e.g. Spengler, Freud or, more recently, McLuhan.

Secondly, *synthesis*. Another solution is the attempt to find some genuinely synthetic factor that will eliminate the opposition within the pairs of worlds, e.g. Hegelian dialectic; Rahner's *"Aufhebung"*; Lonergan's "higher viewpoints."

Thirdly, *oscillation*. This is integration by movement back and forth between worlds, a refusal to settle down permanently in any one of them. For example, the scientist must take time out to eat or sleep (theory and common sense); or, more theoretically, Toynbee's doctrine of "withdrawal and return."[25]

Fourthly, *transposition*. This is a radical change of context or problematic (e.g. the recent demands of the "New Left" on political values or of any romantic against all classicists).

Fifthly, *mediation*. Once a person or a culture has reached a certain level of development, the exigence for a still higher level is usually perceived. In that restricted sense, then, each development exigentially mediates the next. Moreover, a critical analysis of the basic operations involved in all development attempts to thematize this mediating performance (as in Lonergan's analysis of the systematic-critical-methodological exigencies). One example of exigential mediation should suffice: total fidelity

25. Cf. Erich Rothacker, *Logik und Systematik der Geisteswissenschaften* (Bonn, 1947); Eric Voegelin, *Order and History,* 3 vols. (Baton Rouge, 1956–58); and Karl Jaspers, *The Origin and Goal of History* (London, 1953).

to one world (e.g. the world of the profane) can, and in most cultures does, mediate movement into the next world (the world of the sacred). This is the problem of the relationship between contemporary secularization and transcendence (Cox, Bonhoeffer). But a basic problem revealed by every attempt at integration-via-mediation is: which world mediates which? For Husserl and Hegel, for example, religion mediates philosophy; for Lonergan, Rahner or Coreth, philosophy mediates religion. Only a genuinely critical analysis of the various differentiated worlds, their exigencies and their criteria may hope to resolve that problem.

In the technical analysis of horizon, finally, one further distinction is necessary, viz. that between relative and basic horizon. For in his most recent work, Lonergan has not remained content with his earlier analysis of man's differentiated worlds and possibilities of integration.[26] Rather he has attempted to formulate a basic theological methodology whose full complexity (e.g. the key concept of functional specialization) cannot be investigated here, but one of whose features merits attention for all theologians, i.e. the attempt to differentiate the notion of horizon into what he calls with increasing frequency relative and basic horizon. The distinction, this interpreter believes, is fundamentally the fruit of his deeper reading in the problematic of the human sciences (especially psychology, sociology and cultural anthropology) and in the contemporary philosophical movements of phenomenology and existentialism. But whatever its origin, the distinction itself is clear enough: Relative horizon is one's present horizon relative to one's psychological (education), sociological (society) and cultural (epoch) development. It depends for its articulation on the present stage of development of those varied human sciences. Basic horizon, on the other hand, is the horizon of any man in relation to the presence or absence of what Lonergan begins to call the four

26. An introduction to some of the categories may be found in Lonergan's "The New Context of Theology," *Theology of Renewal* (New York, 1968).

basic, i.e. transcendental, conversions (intellectual, moral, religious, Christian). The key word, of course, is conversion. As an operative definition of this central category, one may say that conversion is the actual transformation of the subject, his orientation and operations and therefore his world(s). While it is normally a prolonged process, it is often remembered as concentrated in a few key judgments and decisions. When Lonergan refers, moreover, to the four *basic* or transcendental conversions, he is referring to the horizon-factors that must be operative in any theologian: intellectual (or philosophic) conversion —i.e. (for Lonergan) the experience, understanding, affirmation and thematization of intellect in its invariant self-structuring process and normative procedures: in short, the "self-appropriation of one's rational self-consciousness" of *Insight;* moral conversion—i.e. the transformation, for Lonergan, involved in moving from the level of judgment to that of decision: in short, the question of value, of ethics, of self-constitution; religious conversion—i.e. the transformation of the subject when he is aware of himself as possessing an openness not merely as fact and achievement (self-appropriation) but as gift: it is the level of *Existenz,* of the self as gift of the self by God to the self; Christian conversion—i.e. that transformation-in-faith of the subject into the life of the Spirit, into the death-resurrection of Christ Jesus:[27] a transformation, moreover, made in the face at once of one's highest possibilities and of one's own recognized inability either to sustain indefinitely one's development or to avoid the reality of the surd, the irrational, the genuinely evil factor in one's own life and that of one's society and culture, one's own or other epochs.

But to communicate more accurately the full meaning of these basic-horizon factors of Lonergan demands a study of his own horizon-development. With that goal in mind, then, the

27. However, Lonergan's analyses of the law of the cross-resurrection and of the historical causality of Christ's *ex-istenz* bear important theoretical possibilities for a theology of eschatology; cf. *De Verbo Incarnato,* esp. pp. 332–416, 552–93.

following chapters were written. For if Lonergan's work on basic horizon is to receive the attention it deserves, his interpreters must be willing to understand the slowly evolving development of the contexts, questions and categories (i.e. the horizons) of Lonergan's own intellectual career before hoping to understand (or, *a fortiori,* to apply or transform) that horizon into more immediate contact with some of the pressing problems of this latter day.

2. *GRATIA OPERANS:* THE RECOVERY OF THE MEDIEVAL WORLD OF THEORY

In the context of the categories developed in the last chapter, the earliest period of Lonergan's work can best be described as a recovery of the theoretic horizon of the medieval period in theology, more specifically of St. Thomas Aquinas. In his own words, it represents his attempt to fulfill the Leonine adage, "vetera novis augere et perficere."[1] More exactly, it is his attempt to know precisely what the horizons of the "vetera" were before attempting to transform them in the light of the expanded horizons of the "nova." In retrospect, that attempt might more accurately be named the effort of the young Lonergan to re-originate the Catholic theological tradition by a return to and a recovery of its authentic intellectualist origins in Aquinas.

To accomplish this hermeneutic task took close to fifteen years and produced two major works of interpretation in St.

---

1. This "Leonine adage" (i.e. of Pope Leo XIII) is an important hermeneutic principle for recognizing the continuity between Lonergan's earlier work (on the *vetera* of the Catholic theological tradition, more specifically on St. Thomas Aquinas) and his later work (on the *nova* of the modern and contemporary periods, i.e. from the critical work of *Insight* on); e.g. "My purpose has been the Leonine purpose, *vetera novis augere et perficere,* though with this modality that I believed that the basic task still to be the determination of what the *vetera* really were. More specifically, my purpose has been to understand what Aquinas meant by the intelligible procession of the inner word" (*Verbum,* p. 215). For a further clarification of the importance of this adage, cf. Walter J. Burghardt, "From a Theologian," *Spirit as Inquiry,* pp. 308–10.

Thomas: the doctoral dissertation, *Gratia Operans,* and the much-discussed *Verbum* articles.[2] Both works demand close study of the precise theological problems at issue there: In the first case, the highly complex development of Aquinas' theorems on actual grace and transcendence; in the second, his still more complex thought on the nature of the analogy of intelligible emanations for Trinitarian theology. For present purposes, however, the principal interest of these works is not so much their precise positions on these important theological questions as it is the important horizon shift which this hermeneutic work allowed Lonergan himself to undergo. To understand that development accurately it will first be necessary to indicate the general intellectual context within which that work was initi-

2. The main sources for this chapter, therefore, will be "St. Thomas' thought on *Gratia Operans,*" *Theological Studies* (I) 2 (1941), 289–324; (II) 3 (1942), 69–88; (III), 375–402; (IV), 533–78; and (ed.) D. Burrell, *Verbum: Word and Idea in Aquinas* (London, 1968), originally published as "The Concept of *Verbum* in the Writings of St. Thomas Aquinas," *Theological Studies* 7 (1946), 49–92; 8 (1947), 37–79, 404–44; 10 (1949) 3–40, 359–93. The book version of *Verbum* is cited in the footnotes as more generally available for verification; the London edition is cited as it corrected some of the errors of the original American edition. For *Gratia Operans,* except for those sections of Lonergan's original doctoral dissertation not reprinted in *Theological Studies,* the footnote references will be to the latter as more generally available for verification (hereafter cited as *"G.O."* I, II, III or IV with proper page citations); for the former sections, citations will be verified in the original doctoral dissertation *Gratia Operans: A Study of the Speculative Development of St. Thomas of Aquin* (A thesis undertaken under the direction of Rev. Charles Boyer, S.J., and submitted at the Pontifical Gregorian University, Rome, towards partial satisfaction of the conditions for the Doctorate in Sacred Theology—1940).

The documentation for the interpretation of this complex period of the revival of Catholic thought would prove too cumbersome for the present work of Lonergan interpretation. The present writer is preparing a work for the *Catholic Theological Encyclopedia* which will attempt the genetic-dialectic historical study suggested here. For one unacquainted with this history, Helen James John's *Thomist Spectrum* (New York, 1967) would prove helpful, especially if combined with van Riet's masterful historical study *Thomistic Epistemology* (St. Louis, 1963); and (on a specific theological question but helpful for the wider view suggested here) Roger Aubert's *Le Problème de L'Acte de Foi* (Louvain, 1961).

ated. From the vantage point of 1968, that context can most helpfully be named the period of "the Thomistic revival."

A. CONTEXT: THE THOMISTIC REVIVAL

Because the work of St. Thomas Aquinas has by now become an accepted part of the theological horizon, it is sometimes difficult to recall that not so long ago at all this was not the case. Besides the general secular and Protestant mistrust of his "fideist" (from the former viewpoint) or "rationalist" (from the latter) leanings, Catholic manual theologians in the nineteenth and early twentieth centuries were not notably enthusiastic about Aquinas either. Pious tributes to the genius of St. Thomas, to be sure, were there. But that genius had either been so domesticated that it had become boring or so distorted that its Thomistic products arrived at the intellectual marketplace bearing such a manualist tone of defensiveness and sterility that they belied their inventors' affinity with the daring intellectualism of Aquinas. In Catholic thought the early years of this century were still the years of the theological "manuals" and the various "schools." Indeed, if one reads the manuals of that day, it almost seems that no one read Aquinas himself. Instead, each theologian seems to have enrolled in one of the prevailing schools and read about Aquinas through someone else—usually Suarez or Cajetan or Báñez or John of St. Thomas. It takes nothing away from the genuine accomplishments of the great commentators of Aquinas to insist that they were not—and are not—Aquinas himself.

But the correlative phenomenon of the Catholic "renaissance" of the late nineteenth and early twentieth centuries at last put the manualists on the defensive. Besides the authentic, if isolated, achievements of a Möhler, a Newman, a Blondel, there emerged —in the wake of a general Romanticism—a new found enthusiasm for the medieval period. Granted that this earliest medievalism was romantic in its tone and more than unfortunate in many

24

of its enthusiasms (Pugin's "Gothic revival" provides one ex- ample; the Chester-Belloc "medieval" distributism another). Still, its rich, if overdrawn, portrait of the medieval world allowed more serious scholars to discover the real Aquinas. The medieval Romantics had not, in fact, been able to prove their case. But they had at least brought into serious question that of the manualists. For the latter, with their now obvious inability to understand the Thomist horizon (due to the limitations of horizons formed by some kind of conceptualism) had at last become thoroughly suspect media for the communication of the intellectualism of Aquinas.

And if the literary revival extolling the medievals in general and Aquinas in particular revived interest in the subject, it was left to more serious historical scholarship and more philosophical minds to free Aquinas. Indeed, the Continental school of historians—of which Grabmann, Landgraf, Lottin, Chenu, Gilson, van Steenberghen and Fabro are merely the more outstanding members of a much larger group[3]—forged the needed criti-

3. It may prove helpful to note that this chapter was written only after an original draft comparing Lonergan's work to that of other medieval interpreters proved unwieldy. Besides the works referred to in this chapter as influential upon Lonergan's own interpretation, a comparative-genetic work still remains to be done of Lonergan's Aquinas' interpretation vis-à-vis (to mention only the most obvious figures alphabetically); J. Beumer, *Theologie als Glaubensverständnis,* (Frankfurt, 1953); J.-F. Bonnefoy, *La théologie comme science selon Saint Thomas d'Aquin* (Bruges-Paris, 1939); M.-D. Chenu, *La théologie comme science au XIII siècle,* (Paris, 1957); C. Colombo, "La metodologia e la sistemazione teologica," *Problemi e orientanenti di teologia dommatica* I (Milano, 1957), pp. 1–56; Y. Congar, "Théologie," *DTC,* XV, 1 (1946), 341–502 (ET *A History of Theology* [New York, 1968]); R. Gagnebet, "La théologie de Saint Thomas, science aristotélicienne de Dieu," *Acta Acad. Pont. S. Thomas Aquinatis,* 11 (1946), 203–28; A. Gardeil, *Le donné révélé et la théologie* (Paris, 1932); E. Gilson (*inter alia*), *La philosophie au moyen age, des origines patristiques à la fin du XIV siècle* (Paris, 1944), *Le philosophe et la théologie* (Paris, 1960); R. Latourelle, *Theologia, scientia sacra* (Rome, 1965); S. Mansion, *Aristote et S. Thomas D'Aquin* (Louvain, 1957); J. Peghaire, *"Intellectus" et "Ratio" selon S. Thomas D'Aquin* (Ottawa, Paris, 1954); A.-M. Pirotta, "De Methodologia Theologiae Scholasticae," *Ephemerides Theologicae Louvaiensis* 6 (1929), 405–38; P. Rousselot, *L'Intellec-*

cal editions, the interpretations and the histories which allowed a later generation secure entry into the world of Aquinas. Almost as an afterthought, they buried the manuals. For, given a certain amount of serious historical research, no one could any longer accept the easy talk about Aquinas' simply "baptizing Aristotle." As the repeated excursions into Aquinas' own work and his general context by Gilson or Maritain, or Fabro or Geiger made increasingly clear, Aquinas' philosophy was a wholly original creation dependent principally on his own metaphysical genius and his ability to transform the categories and exigencies supplied by the entry of the Greco-Arabian culture into the Christian interiority of the West. Aquinas' achievement gradually began to be understood not as one of essentialism but as a wholly original philosophy of *esse*. In short, Aquinas had constructed not a logic but a metaphysics. By his distinctive achievement on the differentiation of *esse* as the prime metaphysical category, he had established a principle of philosophical unity which previous philosophers had not been able to achieve and which his later commentators had never fully recovered. To read today the differing articulations of that discovery in the earlier works of Gilson or Maritain or Fabro or Geiger is to sense the freshness of those days of recovery. And even though, as

---

tualisme de Saint Thomas (Paris, 1908); G. Van Ackeren, *Sacra Doctrina: The Subject of the First Question of the "Summa Theologica" of S. Thomas Aquinas* (Rome, 1952); F. van Steenberghen, *The Philosophical Movement in the Thirteenth Century* (Edinburgh, 1955); P. Wyser, *Thomas Von Aquin* (Berne, 1950); B. M. Xiberta, *Introductio in Sacram Theologiam* (Madrid, 1949).

In the present writer's judgment such a comparative-genetic-dialectic study of Lonergan's interpretation in contrast to that of other major contemporary theologians is especially needed in the case of the interpretations of Aquinas of K. Rahner, *Spirit in the World* (New York, 1968), and E. Schillebeeckx, *Revelation and Theology*, I–II (New York, 1968). For two recent studies of some interest, cf. T. Tshibangu, *Théologie positive et théologie speculative* (Louvain, 1965), for a clear presentation of a major interpretation of the "Louvain School"; and V. Preller, *Divine Science and the Science of God: A Reformulation of Thomas Aquinas* (Princeton, 1967), for an interesting analysis from the viewpoint of Anglo-American analysis.

will become apparent shortly, there will be serious differences between either the Gilson-Maritain interpretation or the Fabro-Geiger one and the later Maréchallian, those differences cannot be used to overlook the greatness of the formers' historical achievement nor of the latter's debt to it.

It is time, however, to move from more general considerations of the Thomist revival's re-interpretation of Aquinas to more specific ones. At least two such factors merit consideration here: First, the Thomists rediscovered the penetrating deftness with which Aquinas was able to "distinguish-in-order-to-unite" the realms of nature and grace, of reason and faith, of philosophy and theology. To realize what an achievement this involved, one has merely to compare Aquinas' work with that of his predecessors Anselm or Albert or with his great contemporary Bonaventure. Secondly, it was Gilson's special merit to expose the importance for all post-medieval philosophy of the "Christian philosophy" and theology of the "Middle Ages."[4] Indeed, the introduction into philosophical discussion of the questions raised by Christian belief in a transcendent, personal God, in creation, in personal freedom, in the immortality of the soul and so forth freed Western philosophy from the more narrow confines of the Greek classical horizon. To realize the centrality of these "Christian" questions for later "secular" thought (as Gilson suggests) one has only to try imagining later Western philosophy (Descartes or Leibniz or Kant or even Nietzsche) without questions which emerged from the medieval period.

Such emphases are largely the legacy of the great neo-Thomists of the early part of this century. Others may and do disagree strongly (and, it will be argued here, correctly) with many of their views—on the exact meaning of *esse* and its relationship to essence, on the exact nature of the interdependence between metaphysics and epistemology, on the precise nature of the interrelationship of the world of Thomist theory and of Thomist interiority. Still the bulk of their labors was done well. So well,

4. Gilson, *Being and Some Philosophers* (Toronto, 1952).

27

in fact, that later laborers often forget to be thankful for it. Among such permanent achievements was the quiet funeral their work provided for the manualist approach. In fact—except for some remaining holdouts in a few benighted Catholic seminaries and colleges—the manualist approach to Aquinas is dead. Anyone still trying to collapse the horizons of Aquinas' metaphysics of Being into the narrow confines of a naturalism or a Wolffian rationalism or of a Lockean dogmatic empiricism or of any other variety of late-Scholastic conceptualism soon finds himself striving to justify his a-historical position by ever more strident arguments.

By the thirties and forties of this century, then, much ground had already been covered. The Catholic Romantic revival set the mood by means of which the true questions might emerge; the early scholarly work in history and philosophy routed the manualists and charted the area with an ever-increasing flow of historical and philosophical works. Yet many remained discontent. Inspired in England by the singular example of Newman, in France by Blondel and the influence of Bergson and everywhere by the questions raised in the German context, many Catholic intellectuals returned to their interpretations of Aquinas to see what possible help he could provide for the critical questions raised in the contemporary period. Above all, they wished to face the critical problem raised by Kant with something more than the dogmatic denials of the chief Neo-Thomists.

The central figure of the new controversy was the Jesuit philosopher at Louvain, J. Maréchal. The central work around which the controversy raged was his attempt to answer Kant through Kant, *Le point de départ de la metaphysique.*[5] His suc-

5. For the development of the Maréchallian movement, cf., among others, O. Muck, *The Transcendental Method* (New York, 1968); H. Holz, *Tranzendental-philosophie und Metaphysik* (Mainz, 1966); R. Heinz, *Französische Kantinterpretation im 20. Jahrhundert* (Bonn, 1966). Lonergan's own relationship to Maréchal is not as important as most of the French and German interpreters of Maréchal suppose; cf. his statement "what has come from Fr. Maréchal is, not a set of fixed opinions, but a movement." "Metaphysics as Horizon," *Collection,* p. 220.

cess—which not even his greatest admirers would claim as complete—depended largely on the novelty of his method. For he determined, from within a realist horizon, to take Kant's question on the possibility of metaphysics seriously, learn from it, and attempt to answer it not by a dogmatic affirmation of realism but by working out the negative and positive implications of what to Maréchal was Kant's basic flaw. For Kant, according to Maréchal's critique, had not been critical enough. In trying to discover the *a priori* conditions of the possibility of human knowledge, Kant had overlooked the central clue: the dynamic nature of intellect itself. By replacing that dynamism with a static conception of intellect's ability to create the categories Kant had unwittingly substituted that conception for the actual performance of intellect. By that same substitution, and not by the intrinsic merits of his own critique, he had for many eliminated the very possibility of any metaphysics.

Moreover, Maréchal argued (this time against the Neo-Thomists), only if that dynamism of intellect is explicitly (i.e. critically) examined could the philosophy of *esse* of Aquinas be grounded in Aquinas' acknowledged intellectualism. In short, a contemporary thinker must move beyond the medieval milieu

---

For a recent and extremely helpful introduction to the Maréchallian position (especially as related to the positions of Siewerth and van Balthasar), c.f. Hans Verweyen, *Ontologische Voraussetzungen des Glaubensaktes* (Patmos, 1969).

Moreover, *A Maréchal Reader* has been prepared by the authoritative Maréchal scholar, Joseph Donceel (New York, 1969). In fact, much of the present writer's interpretation of Maréchal owes its primary debt to the interpretative articles of Father Donceel over the years. Among other points, I believe, they show (indirectly) that Lonergan is not, strictly speaking, a Maréchallian. English readers may profitably study the articles on "transcendental Thomism" in *Continuum* since its inception, esp. Spring, 1964 and Summer, 1968, pp. 221–46.

For a distinct alternative to the Gilson-Maritain position one should, of course, recall the works of Leslie Dewart and his own comments on "transcendental Thomism" in *Continuum* (Autumn, 1968), 389–402. Rather than distract from present purposes to engage in that debate, we shall simply state that, whatever the virtues of Dewart's position, his rather "proof-text" interpretation of Rahner, Coreth and Lonergan is not a very fruitful hermeneutic exercise.

29

which historical and philosophical scholarship had exposed, beyond even the explicit words of St. Thomas to the mind at work through all those words. If he did, he might well discover—as Rousselot did—a dynamic intellectualism which could ground a critical philosophy of being. He might also find a mind that would be as willing to learn from Kant and Hegel as Aquinas once had been from Aristotle and the Neo-Platonists.

Such, very briefly, was the Catholic intellectual context in which Bernard Lonergan began his own study of Aquinas. It was clearly a context that no longer permitted any romantic recalls of an age that was dead. But it did permit, indeed demand, a careful hermeneutic entry into a long-ignored but intellectually exciting period which recent scholarship and thought had made available to anyone willing to undergo the labor of entering it. It allowed, moreover, for a context that was ripe with controversy and the intellectual stimulation such controversy affords. For it forced one into the fray of the three-pronged battle fought among the manualist followers of the great commentators, the "Christian philosophy" school of Gilson and Maritain and that final group, not so much a school as a movement, known as the "Maréchallians." And the influence and inspiration of the latter movement were to call forth the two men now generally recognized as having developed, in quite different contexts and in very different ways, the single most important theological movement in modern Catholic thought. For it is not insignificant that Bernard Lonergan and Karl Rahner both spent their early scholastic years trying to rediscover the mind and spirit of Aquinas at the most creative period of the Thomist revival.

The context of those years afforded Lonergan the opportunity to attempt "to reach the mind of Aquinas" first on a single question, then on a much wider front. That mind remained at the center of several controverted interpretations: whether on the single question (actual grace) which Lonergan chose to study for his doctoral dissertation or on the wider front of the correct interpretation of Aquinas' psychology, epistemology and metaphysics, all of which the later *Verbum* articles were to ex-

30

plore. By focussing on that first question he was able to move
beyond the Báñez-Molina dispute, which still dominated the
scene, into the world of authentic Thomist theological theory.
In the second he was able to work out a hermeneutic for
Aquinas' Trinitarian study of the human intellect's operations,
which pieced together those psychological facts which grounded
Aquinas' metaphysical statements and Trinitarian analogy. In
the negative moment of both studies, he advanced an attack on
the conceptualist interpretation of Aquinas and exposed the
genuine intellectualism at the heart of that theology. By accom-
plishing that, he freed the Catholic theological tradition from
Thomas' conceptualist successors and freed himself to advance
that intellectualism into the pressing needs of our later day. The
rest of this chapter, then, will present the principal advances of
his earliest work of Thomist interpretation: *Gratia Operans in
St. Thomas Aquinas.*

B. *GRATIA OPERANS:* THE MEDIEVAL
WORLD OF THEORY AS HORIZON

It is not in the immediate interest of this work to discuss the
now largely forgotten Báñez-Molina dispute on divine transcendence and human freedom. Suffice it to recall that this dispute of Renaissance Scholasticism split the Catholic theological
world for centuries between the Molinist (largely Jesuit) position, which emphasized human freedom along with the mysterious "scientia media" of God, and the Báñezian (largely Dominican) position, which emphasized divine transcendence along
with a "physical predetermination" of the human will. Both
sides, moreover, claimed Aquinas' position as their own. The
strategy of Lonergan in approaching the question of Aquinas'
actual position was as daring then as it now seems obvious.[6] He

6. One may note the firmness of Lonergan's resolve: "In the question treated in these passages it is notorious that for over three centuries, theologians have been studying St. Thomas' thought on grace

decided to ignore the sixteenth century controversy and, by taking advantage of the recent works of medieval scholarship by Landgraf, Lottin, and Grabmann, to investigate St. Thomas' own notion of grace and freedom as it developed throughout his works and as it could be crystalized in the single medieval problem on whether actual grace was operative or cooperative.

The results of his labor of interpretation are well known to Thomist experts: negatively, he rejected the claims of both Molinist and Báñezian to Aquinas' own position and, positively, he developed a whole series of central Thomist categories, which he used again and again throughout his own later works—the theorem of the supernatural, operations, habits, freedom, the law of psychological continuity, the fact of moral impotence and the transcendence of God.[7] But however important those two

---

with Molinists uniformly concluding that the medieval doctor would have been a Molinist and Báñezians with equal conviction arriving at the conclusion that he was a Báñezian. Unless a writer can assign a *method* [italics mine] that of itself attends to greater objectivity than those hitherto employed, his undertaking may well be regarded as superfluous" (unpublished thesis, p. 2). More fully, "A historical study cannot but be inductive. An inductive conclusion, though it may be certain when negative, can for the most part be no more than probable when positive" (*G.O.,* p. 3). Hence, Lonergan's firmness of rejection of the Molinist and Báñezian interpretations as contrasted with his lengthy argument for his own interpretation throughout the thesis. For a later development of the truth of such *probable* judgments, cf. *Insight,* pp. 299–304.

7. On the discovery of the theorem of the supernatural, cf. *G.O.* I, *Theological Studies* (1941), 301–06; on St. Thomas' theory of operations, *G.O.* III, *TS* 3 (1942); on the nature of habit, *G.O.* II, *TS* 3 (1942), 69–88; on freedom, *G.O.* IV, *TS* 3 (1942), 533–37; on the law of psychological continuity and on moral impotence, *G.O.* II, *TS* 3 (1942,) 69–87; on divine transcendence, *G.O.* V, *TS* 3 (1942), 537–53. For a systematic application of these notions, cf. *De Ente Supernaturali: Supplementum Schematicum* (Montreal, 1946); cf. also "Review: De Deo in operatione naturae vel voluntatis operanti," *Theological Studies* 7 (1946), 602–13. An historical study of Lonergan's own thematizations of the "God question" would be very desirable: from the theorem of divine transcendence of *Gratia Operans* through the *ipsum intelligere* of the *Verbum* articles through the "proof" for the existence of God in Chapter 19 of *Insight* to the more recent (and still developing) work on values, beliefs and religion in *Method in Theology.* Since the latter es-

achievements were for Lonergan, they are not the factors which deserve the principal emphasis in a study of Lonergan's own development. Rather, the key horizon expansion of those years was something both more personal and more immediately re-lated to Lonergan's own later development. The first is clear enough: his articulation and personal appropriation of the medieval problematic on the need for a scientific theology as it finds its final expression in Aquinas. The second is still more important for defining Lonergan's own life's work: the wider question of a method for all theology.

The Medieval Problematic: Theology as a Theoretic Enterprise

Lonergan's recovery of the particular theorems of Aquinas on grace led to his further articulation of the very heart of the medieval enterprise as a search for a scientific theology. Indeed, that search *is* the meaning of the medieval problematic. The word "problematic," moreover, does not refer to any obscure and esoteric question. It means, quite simply, nothing more than an attempt to order and locate precisely where the medieval is-sues lay. It demands that the medieval interpreter attempt to discover the types of questions raised by the medievals them-selves and now able to be thematized as such.

But before speaking directly of Lonergan's interpretation of the medieval search for theory, it would be well to remind our-selves of the more general context of the medieval period itself.

---

pecially is not available for quotation and critique (i.e. given its present tentative character) and since this book is intended principally to expose Lonergan's notion of theology as scientific method [and since the present writer has serious difficulties with Lonergan's thematizations], I have (I hope wisely) avoided the temptation of exposing Lonergan's specific conceptualities for God-language in this book and will instead use the occasion of a paper at the Lonergan Congress (Spring, 1970) to attempt to speak to them. All interested parties may, however, read the sources cited above for those specifications.

An indirect entry into that context might best be achieved by recalling the context which Lonergan himself, as a Catholic theologian, brought to bear on his interpretation of Aquinas. In the first place, then, there exists for a theologian in the Catholic tradition what might be called a dogmatic-theological context.[8] And just as every philosopher must attempt personally to appropriate the authentic moments in the history of philosophy, so too every Catholic theologian must attempt to make his tradition his own by careful study of at least its central achievements. In other words, before he may enter wholeheartedly into the contemporary problematic, the Catholic theologian is committed to appropriating the scriptural, conciliar and properly theological moments of the Catholic tradition. In Lonergan's own development, the chronology of those appropriations is of some importance. The full appropriation of the conciliar and patristic periods, for example, will come considerably later (in his works in Christology and the theology of the Trinity), the fuller movement into the scriptural context later still (with his methodological study of the role of positive theology in the wake of the biblical, liturgical and patristic revivals), and the full movement into the contemporary theological context only during his work in *Insight* and in theological method. At the period of the writing of *Gratia Operans,* therefore, his interest was in appropriating only one such moment in the Catholic dogmatico-theological context. That moment was the properly theological aspect of that context. It emerged when medieval reflection on Christian sources became a scientific enterprise. In short, it became theology.

But just as much as their contemporary interpreters, the medievals too had a context. In fact, they had the whole history of Christian contexts to consider in the new light of the categories made available by the entry of the Greco-Arabian culture into the Christian West. The general outlines of that context

8. Lonergan's most concise statement of this context may be found in his *De Methodo Theologiae.*

can now be sketched: Initially the Christian fact could express itself adequately in the kerygma, the evangelion, the didache. Or, to employ the categories developed in the last chapter, one might say that the initial Christian events and their initial movements were fundamentally in the worlds of community, of interiority and of transcendence. For the communities of the New Testament and the apostolic fathers were not concerned, nor need they have been, with the world of theory. Indeed, the Christian horizon only became dogmatic in the conciliar period and only started to become properly theological in patristic times. And the patristic theological achievements never entered wholeheartedly into the world of theory partially because the fathers were still too involved in purely symbolic and descriptive forms of expression and partially because they were more involved with individual questions and personal articulations than with any rigorously systematic attempt at theory. It is that latter enterprise which the Christian tradition owes to the medievals. For, assuming the scriptural, conciliar and patristic periods as their own context and opening themselves to the new horizon of a deepened religious conversion made possible by the gospel Christianity of the Mendicant movements and the new horizon of a genuine intellectual conversion made available to them above all in the newly discovered works of Aristotle, the medievals proceeded to move wholeheartedly into the world of theory. Nor, to be sure, was that movement Aquinas' alone. Behind Aquinas was the inquiring spirit of Anselm, the dialectical enterprise of Abelard, the techniques of the *lectio* and the *quaestio* determined especially by Gilbert de la Porrée as well as the earlier attempts at synthesis in the "solid but not very brilliant" *Sentences* of Peter Lombard and the Aristotelian enterprise of Aquinas' own mentor, Albert the Great.[9] Only because of those achievements could the later medieval attempts at more comprehensive synthesis in the *Summae* be dared. In other words, the entire medieval development represents a

9. See *G.O.* I, *TS* 2 (1941), 290–307; *De intellectu et methodo, passim,* and an unpublished essay, "The Medieval Problematic."

growing drive toward theory. They first proceeded from the positive base of the "authorities" (the scriptures, councils, fathers—especially Augustine), next signalized the real or apparent contradictions in those authorities (*Sic et Non* to *Sed contra est*), and then sought a solution by developing the technique of the *quaestio* and by employing the newly discovered Greek and Arabian rational and logical methods. Only after those achievements had been accomplished could the medievals seek what the Germans call a *Begrifflichkeit* (i.e. a related and structured set of cognate theorems, terms, operations and relations) in the earlier *Sentences* and the later *summae*. For by taking advantage of the large set of scientific techniques needed to construct the *Begrifflichkeit* of a *summa,* the medievals allowed the Greek discovery of *theoria* to be systematically brought to bear on the religious traditions of Christianity.

This is not to argue that the process was planned step by step. In fact, it might more accurately be described as the spontaneous development of a scientific method for theology. And it was precisely this method that constituted medieval theology. For behind all the most characteristic and indigenous products of the medieval period (the *quaestio,* the books of the sentences, the commentaries, the *summae*) was the same drive towards theory and the same increasingly systematic method of gaining one's theoretic aims. Lonergan's principal achievement in his earliest works was to thematize that medieval spontaneous movement towards theory through a careful study of one crucial question (actual grace as operative) as it was formulated and developed throughout the period and as it received its definitive medieval solution in the *Summa* of Aquinas. Principally operative in Lonergan's interpretation of Aquinas on grace, therefore, was Lonergan's own methodological interest in the question of how all knowledge is the realization of a scientific ideal. For that ideal remains immanent and operative in any scientific question as it slowly and methodically moves towards its goal. That ideal can be further determined as normative to all systematic theological discussion as the latter first desires, then guides and constantly corrects the discussion in its movement towards resolution.

It is true, of course, that this natural and spontaneous theological method was not reflected upon as such or thematized in the medieval period itself. That thematization awaited the twentieth-century historical work of a Grabmann, a Lottin, a Congar or the more thematically methodological interests of a Lonergan. First there must be the scientific performance. Only after that comes reflection upon and thematization of the performance. To complete the comparison one may return to the categories developed in chapter one. In their light one can say that the scientific theology of the medievals mediated the meaning of the Christian fact by means of the world of theory. Contemporary interpretation of the medievals, on the other hand, attempts to mediate both the Christian fact and the theoretical mediation of that fact by means of a properly methodological analysis of the believer's and the theoretician's operations. In short, contemporary developments demand an ever further movement into the world of interiority—whose exigencies were first expressed by Lonergan in his earliest methodological analysis of medieval theory.

Before moving more fully into that world of interiority via the *Verbum* articles and *Insight,* however, it would be well to dwell on the gains of *Gratia Operans.* In a general fashion, the conclusion of Lonergan's analysis of the implicit character of the scholastic method was that although methodical questions were raised and methodical discoveries made, still their properly methodological aspect was not explicitated. To clarify this conclusion one might draw an analogy between the medieval discussion of method and the patristic discussion of metaphysics. In either case the discussion was implicit. Explicitly the fathers and the medievals were doing something else: the fathers attempting to solve individual theological questions; the medievals attempting to develop a *Begrifflichkeit* that could handle all questions systematically. But implicitly the demands of the former forced metaphysical questions to the fore and the de-

37

mands of the latter impelled methodological questions and discoveries. For example, the key medieval distinction between nature and supernature implies an important methodical distinction between the horizon of a naturally known philosophy and the horizon of a supernaturally known theology. In relation to the objective pole of the medieval horizon (i.e. the worlds of meaning, the goals, fields, objects of medieval scientific theology) the distinction allows a legitimate differentiation between the fields of philosophy and theology. In relation to the subjective pole of the medieval horizon (i.e. the actual operations of the medieval theologian) the distinction makes the medieval separation and union of philosophical and properly theological concerns as inevitable as the fact that the theologian has a mind and uses it. As a second example, methodological *questions* were clearly raised in the medieval disputes. For the Aristotelian-Augustinian controversy forced the question as to whether the development of theology as a science could survive on Augustinian rhetorical and symbolic language or did not demand the properly technical and theoretical language available at that time in Aristotle.[10] Aquinas' response to this methodological dilemma is well-known: he appropriated the Aristotelian and Neo-Platonist categories, adopted them to the demands of his own metaphysics and of Christian interiority, and then proceeded to construct a fundamental theological *Begrifflichkeit*.

If Lonergan's interpretation of the medieval horizon of theory be correct, then, no Catholic theologian can any longer legitimately accept the conceptualism underlying the entire manual tradition. For Aquinas at least was not interested in a theological science exclusively concerned with the end products of intellectual inquiry (concepts). On the contrary, he embraced the theoretic attitude and scientific thrust peculiar to the medieval period and employed the method implicit in that period's achievements. In more contemporary terms, he operated scientifically: he started from data (i.e. the documented meaning-

10. On the Aristotelian-Augustinian conflict, see, for example, *Verbum*, p. 220; *De Methodo Theologiae*, pp. 15–16.

38

facts of the sources, especially as they were expressed in the *Sentences* and his own *Commentaries*); he next proceeded via a whole series of theoretic techniques (the *quaestio,* the structures of the *Summa,* logic, technical categories, etc.) to reach a strictly theological resolution of the problems set by the seeming contradictions of the original data. In short, he attempted and sometimes achieved not dogmatic certitude but that partial, analogous, incomplete but real theoretic understanding proper to the theologian. Nor is that more modest if more demanding enterprise without fruit:

There is a disinterestedness and an objectivity that comes only from aiming excessively high and far, that leaves one free to take each issue on its merits, to proceed by intrinsic analysis instead of piling up a debater's points, to seek no greater achievement that the inspiration of the moment warrants, to wait with serenity for the coherence of truth itself to bring to light the underlying harmony of the manifold whose parts successively engage one's attention. Spontaneously such thought moves towards synthesis, not so much by any single master stroke as by an unnumbered succession of the adaptations that spring continuously from intellectual vitality. . . . Such was the stamp of Aquinas.[11]

C. LONERGAN'S OWN DEVELOPMENT: THE EXIGENCE FOR THEORY AND METHOD

The basic theme of Lonergan's earliest work in Thomist hermeneutic, therefore, might best be summarized by recalling the quasi-slogan adopted by him as his own: *vetera novis augere et perficere.* One may further recall that he had adopted this adage partially to express his reluctance to enter into the demands of the *nova* until he was sure of the meaning of the *vetera*—more exactly, the precise meaning of the scientific nature of Aquinas' project. In Lonergan's opinion at that time, two basic methodological dangers lay in wait for anyone attempting to interpret

11. *G.O.* IV, 573–74.

Aquinas. In the first place, there was the danger of a purely positivist ideal of historical research.[12] That ideal (whatever its other advantages) could not hope to understand the medieval systematic exigence when its own scientific exigence was so weak and undemanding. In the second place, there was the more immediate danger of interpretation via the already existing Thomistic traditions. And whatever their other advantages, the underlying conceptualism[13] of those traditions could not hope to understand correctly (one is almost tempted to say "at all") the authentic intellectualism of Aquinas. In other words, the horizons of either the positivist historian or the conceptualist traditionalist tended not to reach up to and be transformed by the intellectualist and scientific horizon of the *"vetera"* of an Aquinas but to collapse those *vetera* into the narrow confines of either modern positivist ideals of interpretation or of Renaissance Scholasticism's more restricted exigencies.

As we have already insisted, the specific contents of that work on grace are not our major concern here. Rather, one may rec-

---

12. *Ibid.*, 3–4: for a later formulation of Lonergan's rejection of any "positivist" stance, cf. B. Lonergan, "Hermeneutics" (Notes for lectures, July 20, 1962, Toronto), on "the principle of the empty head" (p. 4); and *Insight: A Study of Human Understanding*, London and New York, 1957), esp. pp. 582–83; 585; 671–72. It is of some importance especially to the later chapters to note that an anti-positivist and anti-reductionist stance is shared by Thomists in general, by theoreticians in transcendental method, and by phenomologists (e.g. Husserl and Merleau-Ponty). In Lonergan's case, that stance is articulated in his earliest work (*G.O.*) and formulated anew and more critically throughout his later philosophical and theological career.

13. The term "conceptualism" for Lonergan refers to the mistaken exclusive concern for the end-products of intellectual inquiry (concepts) and the logical relationships between them as distinct from "intellectualism," i.e., in the case of Aquinas, the intellectualist will emphasize not the rarely treated concept but the perpetually recurring intellect. Note how Lonergan relates his own understanding of St. Thomas' intellectualism to some other classic Scholastic interpretations (*ibid.*, pp. 217–18); viz. P. Rousselot, *L'Intellectualisme de Saint Thomas;* J. Peghaire, *Intellectus et Ratio* (Ottawa and Paris, 1936); R. Hoenen, *Gregorianum* XIV (1933), 153–84; XIX (1938), 498–514; XX (1939), 19–54, 321–50. For the more comprehensive category of "extrinsicism," cf. *De Methodo Theologiae*, pp. 28–34.

ognize in *Gratia Operans* a more important project, viz. Lonergan's own search for a scientific method for theology, a project, to use more contemporary scientific language, for the scientific thrust and purely structural forms beneath and behind all particular scientific contents, a project, to use the later words of *Insight,* for the upper heuristic blade of scientific method.

In view of that project probably the most helpful commentary on Lonergan's methodology in his earliest period is the unfortunately never published introductory chapter to his *Gratia Operans* doctoral dissertation.[14] There one may find, isolated from the specific interpretation of Aquinas in the thesis itself, Lonergan's own understanding of the proper method for speculative theology. There, furthermore, certain later developments first reveal themselves: for example, the theological concern for analogies from the practices of theoretical physicists, the concern for understanding a position only by understanding it in its historical development, and the concern above all (if the reader will bear with some necessary repetition) for a strictly scientific and systematic approach to theology.

A brief summary, then, of his understanding of the nature of theological method would seem in order here. Basically, his analysis of Aquinas' theology freed Lonergan to argue for the possibility of moving beyond both purely positive historical research and merely traditional concerns in order to construct a "middle course" method for theology. To accept that latter course the speculative theologian must accept two basic tasks: first, a correct interpretation of the history of speculative theology in its long and arduous development; second, a personal systematization of that analogous, partial, incomplete but real understanding proper to all speculative theology (medieval or contemporary).

For the first task of interpretation, Lonergan suggests an interesting formulation: the interpreter should try to construct an

14. Since this section of his thesis has never been published, I have not given specific references to it in the pages that follow. It is available for study at Regis College, Toronto.

a priori scheme capable of synthesizing any possible set of historical data irrespective of place and time (just as the mathematician constructs a generic scheme capable of synthesizing any possible set of quantitative phenomena). That generic scheme is achieved, moreover, only by an analysis of the nature of speculative development in theology which is firmly grounded in a more general analysis of development in any human speculation. And this ambitious project is possible in Lonergan's view because the human mind *is* the human mind with certain inherent and invariant structures, norms and procedures (note the already sounded concern which will not find clear critical expression until *Insight* and his post-*Insight* work). If such an *a priori* generic scheme can be established, then it should be applied to the data of any given period in speculative theology's development in an inductive, *a posteriori* manner (i.e. be faithful to the data-facts as they are exposed by solid scholarship). In other words, a generic scheme based upon the nature of the development of understanding in any human mind will provide the interpreter with an upper blade of interpretative method capable of synthesizing any given set of data which, in their turn, are revealed by the inductive lower-blade procedures of the historico-critical method.

If that upper-blade heuristic method can be worked out and thematized, it will allow the theologian both to verify his interpretation of a particular speculative development (e.g. St. Thomas on actual grace) and, of equal importance, to self-appropriate that same speculative and systematic exigence. Most fundamental of all, it should make the theologian realize that (in Lonergan's words) "the content of speculative theology is the content of a pure form. It is not something by itself but the intelligible arrangement of something else. It is not systematic theology but the system in systematic theology."[15]

For the second task of personal systematization, Lonergan suggests that theologians can explicitate and order the four key

15. This important quotation is to be found in the unpublished section of the thesis, p. 12.

elements in methodical theological procedure, viz. theorems, terms, dialectical positions and technique.[16] In the light of his post-*Insight* work, this present list seems underdeveloped but can still bear study for its historical (and intrinsic) interest. The meaning of the first three "elements" is clear. *Theorems* refer to exact technical expressions of one's scientific understanding. They are not, therefore, to be confused with the "common notions" so prevalent in much of theology. For example, "going faster" is a common notion, "acceleration" a theorem; the term "supernatural" is a common notion in Peter Lombard, a theorem in Philip the Chancellor and Aquinas. *Terms* refer to that obvious transformation of words after scientific development. "Sacrament," for example, is an old word that became a term after receiving precise definition. "Actual grace" is a new term which does not occur ever in St. Thomas (he speaks of a "divine aid"). Terms become needed insofar as scientific development occurs. They become discarded or misused insofar as scientific exigencies are forgotten. *Dialectical positions* refer to the inability of any particular science to express its understanding at a certain stage of its development in other than seemingly contradictory theorems and terms. For example, in contemporary physics light is viewed as, from one point of view, waves and, from another, particles. In theology this dialectical aspect finds a classic expression in the scholastic insistence that *the* speculative understanding proper to theology is its recognition of the negative coherence of non-contradiction involved in each of the mysteries of the Christian faith. The fourth element, *technique,* is of primary methodological interest. In fact, the word is chosen to allow a latitude sufficient to embrace three central methodological procedures. First, the speculative theologian must be sure to consider the whole field of data or his thought will end unbalanced. Second, he must accomplish a philosophical analysis of the "natural" factors involved in his theological categories or his thought will be vague. Third, he must carefully order the questions that require solution or he will end with no

16. *Ibid.,* pp. 13–18.

better than the re-emergence of the initial problem in a more acute form. In short, *technique* provides the pure form analyzed above as the very meaning of speculative theology. By providing that form with some precision, *technique* methodologically determines the kind of contents (theorems and terms) to be sought.

Finally, Lonergan argues that the combination of the *a priori* generic scheme of interpretation and the thematization of the four central "elements" in all speculative development allow the theologian to determine with some accuracy the phases in the history of theological speculation. Indeed, one could legitimately interpret his own works of interpretation in Aquinas as revealing the possibilities of that hermeneutic method. In *Gratia Operans,* for example, the final chapter exposes Aquinas' resolution of the problem of actual grace as the achievement of a methodical correlation of the needed "elements" by means of the earlier gradual emergence of theorems, terms, dialectical positions and methodical techniques.[17] In conclusion, then, Lonergan's earliest work of interpretation revealed at once the theoretic dimensions of the medieval *vetera* and the methodological implications which that revelation might have for the as yet unconsidered *nova* of contemporary theology. Before those latter could be treated on their own, however, a still deeper penetration into the medieval *vetera* was required. That further penetration, expressed in the *Verbum* articles, might best be understood as Lonergan's hermeneutic attempt to move beyond and beneath the world of medieval theory in order to expose the world of interiority grounding it. The next chapter, then, will be devoted to analyzing that further task.

17. *G.O.* IV, *TS* 3 (1942), 554–78.

44

3. THE *VERBUM* ARTICLES:
THE RECOVERY OF THE WORLD
OF THOMIST INTERIORITY

A. GENERAL INTRODUCTION: THE WORLDS
OF SYMBOLIC AND THEORETIC INTERIORITIES

What Lonergan discovered in medieval theology, more specifically in Aquinas, was not some phenomenon isolated either from the specific cultural development of the West nor from the more general "laws" of development for a culture. On the contrary, medieval Scholasticism—for theology and through it for the entire Western intellectual tradition—represents the historical moment when Christianity in its Western cultural form moved conclusively from a world of community into the world of theory. At that particular time in its history, the Western Christian community came to the point where it had to understand itself to go on.

The theological achievements of the age previous to the Scholastic were fundamentally the achievements of a religious community whose self-consciousness found symbolic expression sufficient for its intellectual needs.[1] Its spirit had been one of

1. This interpretation is to be found in Lonergan's unpublished study of the medieval problematic. The qualification should be added that the conciliar and patristic periods (as distinct from the symbolism of the biblical) were also involved in *theoria* but on specific questions, not as a systematic enterprise as with the medievals. This interpretation of symbolic consciousness is more applicable to what might be called

often remarkable creativity, its products works of exceptional fertility and suggestiveness. Its symbolic spirit did not claim to be dominated by the detachment and disinterestedness native to the scientific mind. Rather, its "laws" were fundamentally those grounded in human religious affectivity and aggressivity; its spirit that of the attached, the committed, the artistic; its products a series of still powerful and dynamic images evoking the meaning of the Christian's life-to-God-and-to-the-world. Such symbolic consciousness was to the Christian community (as it is to every man) the first attempt of his consciousness of self, of world, of God to find its way back to its original unity and to express its discoveries along that arduous way. But because of the largely unrecognized influence of his own affectivity and aggressivity, the man of symbolic consciousness does not realize the essential ambiguity of his discovered unity. Above all, he does not recognize his self-consciousness as symbolic. He continues to judge the ultimate meaningfulness of all events and all truths by their direct relationship to himself. It is in this context that the medieval rediscovery of Greek *theoria* takes on its primary meaning. For *theoria* does not try to build a whole new world of symbols for man from the same affective source. Rather, it breaks clearly from *mythos* to *logos* and attempts to appraise critically and articulate rationally the sources of all such possible constructions. It attempts to realize the ideals of a purely rational mode of discourse by articulating its performance through the detached, disinterested, pure, abstract categories of science, of philosophy, of speculative theology. Yet only where a person has himself performed theoretically will he be sufficiently aware of the peculiar enrichment of abstraction to appreciate the demand of the medievals that one's religious experience also be made cognitively accessible.

But the lure of *theoria,* although at first denied, cannot for long be ignored by any sufficiently cultivated mind or culture. At first it may seem—as it did to the Augustinians of Aquinas'

---

the "negative" aspects (vis-à-vis theory) of symbolism. The more positive are emphasized in Lonergan's later work (and in Chapters 9 and 10 of this book).

46

day—"unreal," "strange," "pagan," even "repugnant" to one's religious sensibilities. But gradually he may come to realize that thinking is an experience too; that scientific thinking is not an impoverishment but an enrichment of all his experience; that systematic thinking promises to the "pure" among its practitioners the ability to order all their understanding in order to allow them to move more consciously and thereby more fully into that unity-in-diversity which their religious faith promises and their spirit seeks.

But the symbolic mind, not without reason, has always distrusted attempts at *theoria*. For symbolic consciousness offers the human spirit a richer, stranger world:[2] theoretic proof yields to reiteration or variation on the same theme; the principle of the excluded middle to a superdetermination which combines opposites; negation to positing and then overwhelming of what is posited; the single theme gives way to the simultaneous development of several themes. Further, the symbolic attitude is able to promise the human spirit a release for its affectivity and aggressivity, lacking to the theoretic attitude. The symbolic man really "knows" what it feels like to live at this time, at this place, with this experience. He knows how to create a whole series of artistic forms powerful enough to lead others as well to experience the same depths, the same joys, beauties, horrors of concrete human existence. And he knows that the symbols a man chooses or creates reveal not his "theories" on life but the more fundamental attitude or orientation which defines him. He knows who Dante or Joachim of Flora were. He can only be puzzled by the peculiar phenomenon of an Aquinas or a Newton.

But his puzzlement need not prove insoluble. Indeed, his very recognition that orientation is the key to the symbolic attitude may also provide him with the clue needed for the theoretic. For distracted as most of us are at first by our own unconscious acceptance of an extrinsicist account of theory, we fail to notice that the theoretic, like the symbolic, is not first a series of products but an attitude. That the theoretic attitude was first

2. Lonergan employs most of these contrasts from Suzanne Langer's well-known *Feeling and Form*.

fully revealed by the original Greek expulsion of *mythos* by *logos* is common enough knowledge. That its second manifestation came into the West with the scientific theology of the medievals is, to a world still attuned to Enlightenment propaganda, largely unrecognized. For at that period in Western intellectual history, a relatively small group of men, increasingly dissatisfied even with the brilliant images of as creative a mind as Augustine's, attempted and with Aquinas succeeded in bringing *theoria* to bear on religious truth. For Aquinas demanded in effect that the human mind be allowed the full range of its unrestricted desire to know; that it be allowed, even in the region of religious faith, to detach itself from the images needed for its period of intellectual gestation and simply to understand—in strictly scientific terms—on its abstractive terms, with its rigorous norms, with its theoretic demands; that it be further allowed to detach itself from its own act of understanding by finding that act's scientific self-expression in a concept, a theorem, eventually in a whole set of related and cognate theorems, a system.

But a possible objection to this interpretation must be faced. To many contemporaries it is fully credible to express the implications of the theoretic attitude for today's world—in the wake of the four hundred year history of the empirical sciences, the rise of the critical problem in philosophy and the already revolutionary results of the more recent human sciences. But can one really claim that such a genuinely theoretic attitude was the case with Aquinas? At first sight it seems unlikely. Not only is there the historical witness of the conceptualist interpretation of Aquinas of much of the "Thomistic" tradition to dissuade one, but there are also certain facts in Aquinas himself to make one wary. There is, first of all, the problem of the medieval context: The critical problem was not a thematic problem for Aquinas; the empirical sciences had not developed much beyond Aristotle's *Physics;* the human sciences were not clearly differentiated. There is, secondly, the fact that Aquinas' analysis of cognition (in his Trinitarian theology) is developed with metaphysical, not epistemological, categories.

The solution which Lonergan suggests in the *Verbum* articles to this hermeneutic dilemma is a critical return to the work of Aquinas on the analogy of intelligible emanations for the Trinity to see whether "there is to be pieced together from Thomist writings a sufficient number of indications and suggestions to form an adequate account of wisdom *in cognitional terms*"[3] (emphasis mine). Only such an account can hope to expose and thematize the grounding theoretic attitude of Aquinas. It might thereby mediate the metaphysical categories which thematized those cognitional facts for Aquinas and further mediate Thomist metaphysical expression to modern critical thought. For the Thomistic tradition itself, moreover, a cognitional approach might allow a more immediate entry into the intellectual self-possession of Aquinas and thereby free the contemporary Thomist to understand the specific theorems of Aquinas more accurately and, of equal importance, to develop new theorems at the level of contemporary discussion.

Nor may *Gratia Operans* alone be claimed to fulfill all these needs. For even though Lonergan's work there revealed both the development of a series of ever more adequate theorems on actual grace and the very meaning of the theoretic stance as a basic attitude, it is still necessary to try to ground that attitude critically by studying and explicitating the cognitional operations involved in it. In short, it was judged imperative to raise the modern critical problem in regard to the work of Aquinas himself. But this could be successfully undertaken only if one could develop a hermeneutic that could first expose the relevant psychological data and their epistemological implications before discussion of the involved metaphysical categories employed by Aquinas. As we shall see below, this approach was the one chosen by Lonergan for his investigation of the Thomist analogy of intelligible emanations.

A return, for the moment, to the technical metaphor "horizon" developed in chapter one may provide some final clarification of the problem of interpretation which the *Verbum* articles involve. A horizon, to repeat, is a maximum field of vision from

3. *Insight,* p. 407.

49

a determinate standpoint. It possesses both a subjective (operations) and an objective ("worlds") pole, each of which is conditioned by and conditions the other. The question which the *Verbum* articles raises might well be named "What was the intellectual horizon of Aquinas?" For although Lonergan's immediate concern there is with the limited objective of attaining a long-sought accuracy on Aquinas' use of the procession of the inner word in human knowing as an analogy for the Trinitarian processions, he quickly concluded that such objective-pole accuracy could only be adequately achieved after he had established some real grasp of the subjective pole—the actual performance of Aquinas' own intellect. For that reason the properly metaphysical discussions are postponed until the third article while the first two begin with an uncommon (for Thomists) search for the psychological facts of Aquinas: a search, in brief, for the subjective-pole (i.e. mind) of Aquinas in order that the objective metaphysical expression of that mind might later be determined with some precision.

Nor was such a hermeneutic effort unnecessary. Indeed, the history of the great Thomistic commentators alone affords ample evidence that exclusive concern with the objective pole of any great thinker's horizon can very rapidly result in an extrinsicism.[4] For example, if once the acts of understanding are overlooked and all one's interpretative energies are exhausted in setting the terms and relationships between the thinker's various concepts and theorems, a conceptualist tradition inevitably will arise. By the objective manipulation of the proper concepts, the conceptualist interpreter believes he can securely establish any thinker's system. His remaining energies are ordinarily spent defending his interpretation against others and de-

---

4. For a brief expression of Lonergan's interpretation of the dangers of such a tradition, cf. his Aquinas lecture, *The Subject* (Marquette, 1969). Cf. *Verbum*, pp. 72–73, 183–84, 186, 195, 219, and *Insight*, p. 372: "Five hundred years separate Hegel from Scotus . . . that notable interval of time was largely devoted to working out in a variety of manners the possibilities of the assumption that knowing consists in taking a look."

ducing yet further conclusions from his master's principles. But if concern for the intelligent generation of ideas is lost, it is not long before we are left without any real contact with the generative minds of our history. In the interim, we must try to satisfy ourselves with the ever-lesser syntheses of the various "schools." And if the particular problem in question is the very nature of cognitional operation (as in Trinitarian theology) then the loss may prove fatal.

Such, we suggest, is a primary source of the widespread dissatisfaction with Thomist Trinitarian theology. Such, moreover, seems to be the cause of the widespread lack of serious intellectual interest in Thomist cognitional theories. To the contemporary, post-critical mind the Thomists "objectify" the problem of cognition too rapidly. It is not so much that their resultant metaphysical explanations are unverified as that they seem unverifiable. Nor can the poverty of the manualist interpretation of Aquinas be solved simply by pointing out some metaphysical doctrines, however central, that have been overlooked. Rather, a more basic contemporary task is needed: a critical search, amidst the metaphysical expression of Aquinas' cognitional theories, for the psychological facts and epistemological implications (in a word, for the mind) which gave birth to that metaphysics. And then—but only then—for the metaphysics which brought that mind to self-expression.

To the non-Scholastic reader, at least, all this may seem to be belaboring the obvious. And the author is quite willing to agree that it is obvious. But a cautionary note must be added: the obviousness in question must not be allowed to remain a merely common sense obviousness but must rise to the level of explanatory clarity. With insight can come clarity and coherence and, if one will, obviousness. But scientific clarity only comes about as the result of an insight that has not rested content with that understanding—through images peculiar to descriptive thinking. It only arrives (as the *Verbum* articles and, more fully, *Insight* will argue at some length) from a scientific insight achieved in the purely intellectual pattern of experience that can pivot upon itself and elaborate its understanding into an explanatory concept or theorem. It is necessary, we think, to dwell on this point for a moment: for it is not the Thomistic schools alone that have been ridden with conceptualism. In fact, Lonergan's argument (as *Insight* will make clear) is with a much wider tradition. For him, the history of post-Scotist western thought has been permeated with the Scotist (and ultimately Platonic) conceptualist doctrine that knowledge is not identity (as for Aristotle and Aquinas) but confrontation. To express the problem in its simplest terms, knowledge is commonly considered by Western visual man as something rather like seeing. For what can be more obvious, it seems, than that understanding is somehow like seeing? It is taking a look: a confrontation between the knower "in his mind" and the reality "out there." Even metaphysical knowledge is somehow like that: it "intuits" more deeply, of course ("metaphysically"), but it still confronts.

But that knowledge cannot be so easily described can be shown by the simplest experiment: To see this page one has merely to open one's eyes; to cease seeing it, one merely closes them; but to understand it calls for a different kind of operation altogether. Opening or closing either real eyes or fictitious, intuitive, "spiritual" eyes does not help at all. One must make another, distinct effort: the effort to understand. One must catch the sequence of thoughts first singly and then as a sequence. Now one point may be clear. Now another. If one fails to understand the sequence, he must go over the same territory again and try to find out just where and why and how his effort to understand failed him. And only when he has achieved that identity of his knowing and the known (*not* confrontation of them) in his act of understanding may he move on to the further cognitional problems caused by the self-expression of that understanding in concepts. If he neglects that first key act or if—once the critical problem has become a real one to him —he fails to grasp its non-confrontational nature, then some kind of intellectual extrinsicism (usually conceptualism) cannot but eventually result. For if one systematically overlooks the

52

need for growth in one's understanding or in the author's in order to leap into the spurious joys of forming syntheses and comparing concepts, then one is well-prepared to misunderstand completely the question at issue here. If the question happens to be the very nature of cognitional activity (as in Aquinas' Trinitarian theology), then the resultant deeply "metaphysical" misunderstanding is disastrous. One is left, on the lowest level, comparing black marks on white paper. On a higher but still inadequate level, he is left comparing words, concepts, "meants." The meaning, however, is quite gone. And there will ordinarily emerge some later Romantic who, although himself quite innocent of cognitional theory, can understand enough to declare that the theological emperor has no clothes.

Perhaps the charge of conceptualism may ring true to many today for that pre-Kantian thought represented most clearly by Christian Wolff and the Scholasticism he influenced, but not for Kant and the post-Kantian period. But if Kant recognized the problem, it does not necessarily follow that he solved it. In fact, as the *Verbum* articles argue through their historical investigation of Aquinas' performance and as *Insight* will argue at length through its critical investigation of the structure of human intentionality itself, the Kantian attempt was ultimately a failure which produced its own series of ever lesser syntheses.[5] For the Kantian inability to retrieve the act of reflective consciousness and its self-expression in judgment as a distinct act and level of consciousness positing synthesis not simply synthesizing some more, helped to sidetrack the discussion of the critical problem into the immanentist maze of ever-more dazzling but ever-less successful "solutions." That maze still largely dominates the theological scene. But before speaking directly of it, it would be well to return to the perhaps less interesting but necessarily propaedeutic work of Lonergan's earliest struggle with the problem.

During the years which produced the *Verbum* articles, then, Lonergan, urged on both by the demands of the contemporary critical exigence and by his own previous discovery of the sys-

5. Cf. *Insight*, pp. 339–42: "Contrast with Kantian Analysis."

tematic exigence in the medieval world of theory, attempted to apply his findings to the data on Aquinas' analysis of the procession of the *verbum,* the inner word. The conclusions of that investigation were startling to Thomist and non-Thomist alike. They demanded an interpretation of Aquinas' intellectualism which challenged at a basic level the reigning conventional wisdoms of the day. For they leveled a charge that most of the reigning Thomistic and modern philosophical traditions were, in some basic sense, inauthentic.[6] The charge is serious but not made lightly. For if basic intellectual inauthenticity be defined as using one's mind yet speaking of it as if it were something else, then the charge rings true for any kind of extrinsicism (e.g. later Scholastic conceptualism) or even for any kind of non-judgmental immanentism (e.g. Kant).

B. THE CONTEXTS OF THE DISCUSSION

B₁ The Manualist Tradition

The basic shift in Lonergan's concerns from *Gratia Operans* to the *Verbum* articles, therefore, is best described as a shift from

6. Moreover, these concerns of the *Verbum* articles on the cognitional-epistemological question are treated later in a more personal and critical way (i.e. via *Insight*'s transcendental method and free of the hermeneutic difficulties of interpreting St. Thomas), which concerns shall be studied at length in the following chapters on *Insight* with cross-references given there to the Thomist interpretation of these psychological-epistemological-metaphysical realities in the *Verbum* articles. One may also refer, among other treatments of these questions, to the following articles: L. B. Geiger, *Bulletin Thomiste* VII (1952), 477–79; William A. Stewart, "Abstraction: Conscious or Unconscious?", *Spirit as Inquiry,* pp. 409–20; F. E. Crowe, "St. Thomas and the Isomorphism of Human Knowing and its Proper Object," *Sciences Ecclésiastiques,* 13 (1961), 167–90; [for a *Verbum* inspired (and, in this writer's judgment, authentic development of the *Verbum* interpretation)], cf. F. E. Crowe, "Complacency and Concern in the Thought of St. Thomas," *Theological Studies* 20 (1959), 1–39; 198–230; 343–95; for more negative responses, cf. Matthew O'Connell, *Modern Schoolman* XXIV (1947), 224–34; and L. Roy, *Sciences Ecclésiastiques* I (1948), 225–28; F. V., *Bulletin de la Théologie Ancienne et Médiévale* V (1948), 335.

an analysis of the medieval world of theory to one of the medieval world of Christian and intellectualist interiority. Still it remains necessary to study at least three of the further horizon-contexts involved before one can properly interpret the full nature of that shift: first, the horizon of the interpretation of the later manualist tradition of Aquinas' Trinitarian theology; second, the horizon of the Christian scriptural and dogmatic contexts assumed by Aquinas for his work; third, the horizon-context of Aquinas himself, best described in terms of his use of Aristotelian theory and Augustinian interiority.

B₂ The Medieval Tradition

If a concern with the world of interiority seems rather remote from the manuals' treatment of Trinitarian theology, the reasons for that remoteness are not difficult to locate. In the first place, there is the inability of the a-historical approach of the manualists really to enter into a horizon other than their own. Their general "proof-text" hermeneutic method should be sufficient demonstration of that difficulty. In the second place, there are the already discussed difficulties with the manualist horizon itself. The combination of the pedagogical approach of the thesis structure, the conceptualist scientific ideal and the general apologetic atmosphere preclude any real entry into the demands of cognitional and religious interiority. Nor is this impasse peculiar only to some of the minor figures in the manualist tradition. In fact, a clear expression of the difficulty may be found in the Trinitarian theology of as dominant a figure of early twentieth-century Scholasticism as Cardinal Billot. In his work on the Trinity one may find Billot arguing that the work of the imagination, not necessarily of intellect, provides all that is required "metaphysically" to understand Aquinas' analogy for the Trinity.[7] In effect, then, Billot has cancelled out the intellectualist insistence of Aquinas and substituted so purely "objective" a set of metaphysical categories that imagination can provide

7. *Verbum,* p. xiv, footnote 11.

55

all the "secondary" elements needed for the Thomist *psychological* analogy. In fact, it seems (as Lonergan remarks in another context) that truth for the manualists had become so objective that it could get along without minds.[8] So successful was its "objectivity" and so impeccable its metaphysics, that it could even do the psychological analogy for the Trinity without having to bother much about human psychology!

B₃ The Medieval Context

If the horizon-limitations of the manualist tradition were incapable of mediating Aquinas' psychological analogy, the task still remains of establishing the horizon-contexts of Aquinas himself before presuming to analyze his analogy. For no more than anyone else did Aquinas operate in an intellectual vacuum. Behind him, first of all, is the almost notoriously complex history of Christian reflection on the New Testament revelation of God as Father, Son and Spirit. Behind him, in short, is the entire scriptural-dogmatic-theological context assumed by the medievals as their own. They assumed, for example, the legitimacy of the shift from the "economic" Trinity of the Scriptures to the "ontological" *quoad se* speech of the early councils. They assumed the earlier struggles of the Eastern and Western fathers to find ever more adequate categories to express that central mystery of the Christian's faith. That is to say, they accepted as their tradition the results of the slowly unfolding dialectic of earlier Trinitarian thought: the conclusions of Nicaea, of Constantinople, of Ephesus, of Chalcedon; the variously successful attempts at clarification of a Tertullian, an Origen, an Athanasius, the Cappadocians. They accepted the gradual emergence of metaphysical categories like relation, procession, person as authentic developments. Above all, they accepted as their guide the Trinitarian theology worked out by the father of Western theology, St. Augustine, in his work *De Trinitate*. By accepting

8. *The Subject* (Marquette, 1968), p. 5.

the latter, they accepted the imperative of Augustine that Christians must move within themselves and listen to the language of spirit speaking to spirit if they would hope to find the most adequate human language for describing the mysterious nature of the Christian Trinitarian God.

But to understand correctly Aquinas' own transformation of the Augustinian imperative into an intellectualist analogy, it is further required that we tighten the present discussion by describing in greater detail the two central contextual factors that formed the horizon within which Aquinas' own work began. In terms of the categories used throughout this work, those factors may be called the world of Aristotelian theory and the world of Augustinian interiority.[9]

The world of Aristotelian theory which Aquinas studied and appropriated was a complex yet unified horizon achievement. Its foundation was a metaphysics, a general theory of being. But in a cumulative and descending fashion the metaphysics expanded to include a general theory of movement, a general theory of life and a general theory of sense and intellect. If Aquinas intended to employ Aristotelian theory for the psychological analogy, therefore, the psychological factors would be dependent upon the more fundamental metaphysics. The final result is not an unexpected one: the psychological analogy, while remaining psychological, receives the sea-change of a transformation into the language of metaphysics. From that point of view alone, then, the difficulties of interpreting Aquinas' analogy are considerable. A single example of the more general difficulty should suffice to indicate the horizon-shift needed for correct interpretation: the use of the word "object."[10] In the modern context "object" ordinarily refers to the "object" revealed by, grounded in or, more accurately, "constituted" by the intentional process. It is the "phenomenon" of Husserl, the "field" of any specialist, the objective-pole "worlds" of one's

9. Cf. the Preface to *Verbum,* pp. vii–xv, originally published in *Philippine Studies* 13 (1965), 576–86.
10. *Verbum,* pp. vii–ix.

horizon. Now it can be argued that such a notion was operative in the performance of Aquinas (see below). That it was the exact meaning of his Aristotelian thematization, however, cannot be maintained. For the fact is that Aquinas was using Aristotelian metaphysical language and following the Aristotelian mode of discovery of that language: the metaphysical essences are differentiated by potencies; potencies are revealed by acts; acts are specified by objects. Perhaps now the hermeneutic problem which Lonergan is trying to unravel becomes clear: the theoretic thematization of all objects (including the cognitional ones employed in the psychological analogy) will not, for Aquinas, find expression through an analysis of objects as constituted by intentional states but through an Aristotelian analysis of objects-acts-potencies-essences. Accordingly, the final language used to thematize those objects will not be phenomenological or epistemological or psychological but more properly metaphysical.

But a further question occurs: does not the fact of Aquinas' use of the Aristotelian theoretic approach redeem the "objective" interpretation of the manualists and eliminate at its root the interpretation of Lonergan? The ability to grasp that it does not is the ability to grasp the fuller implications of Aristotle's own position and the further and transforming factors involved in the position of Aquinas. In the first place (as Lonergan argues at length in the articles) Aristotle himself had too firm a grasp of the essential psychological and epistemological facts involved in human intentionality (insight into phantasm, question, act of understanding, concept, reflection) to admit of a purely conceptualist interpretation.[11] In the second place, Aquinas' position is not identical with Aristotle's. To anticipate somewhat, at least one key difference can be located. For just as the Gilson-Maritain hermeneutic showed how Aquinas was able to transform Aristotelian act into Thomist *esse* and thereby

11. "Aristotle's account of intelligence, of insight into phantasm, and of the fact that intellect knows itself, not by a *species* of itself, but by a *species* of its object, has too uncanny an accuracy to be possible without the greatest introspective skill" (Verbum, p. ix).

58

develop a philosophy of being,[12] so the Lonergan interpretation clarifies the psychological and epistemological side of that achievement. In a way to be studied below, Lonergan's analysis of the psychological analogy demonstrates how Aquinas was able to transform Aristotle's somewhat ambiguous position on judgment into the clear Thomist doctrine that judgment alone is the cognitional act by means of which the mind reaches the true and, therefore, the real. To use a later vocabulary, judgment is not further synthesis but the positing of synthesis.[13] But how this latter doctrine evolved can only be understood in the context of the further horizon-factor for Aquinas, viz. the world of Augustinian interiority.

It may be recalled from the discussion above that the Augustinian "movement within" in search of the speech of spirit to spirit for its Trinitarian analogy is not without its ambiguities. Besides the difficulties involved in the rhetorical language of Augustine and the largely polemical (anti-Arian) context of his *De Trinitate,* there is the deeper problematic of his interpretation of intellectual activity. Before examining that, however, one should first recall the Augustinian achievement. Augustine insists that his own deeper examination of the interior speech of spirit to spirit reveals the complex nature of human interior speech more accurately than does the then-reigning Stoic interpretation. In short, besides the speech of the Stoic *verbum prolatum* (the spoken work itself) and the *verbum insitum* (human rationality) there remains the purely Augustinian phenomenon of the *verbum intus prolatum,* i.e. the "inner word" of intellect's presence to self and self-expression in concept and judgment.[14] And precisely these inner-word phenomena of spirit's speech to spirit are the best analogies for a Christian's understanding of his Trinitarian God. On the basis of his own presence to self and his own inner-word expressions of that presence, an intelligent

12. Cf. esp. Etienne Gilson, *Being and Some Philosophers* (Toronto, 1952), and Jacques Maritain, *Existence and the Existent* (New York, 1945).
13. *Verbum,* pp. 48–66.
14. *Verbum,* p. x.

Christian may now both better understand and more adequately express his belief in the New Testament revelation of Father, Son and Spirit. He can do so by speaking of the speech of spirit to spirit in the Godhead Itself. In God, then, there is Infinite Understanding (Father) Who speaks an Infinite Word Who is Himself Divine (Son), and in mutual adoration, Father and Son speak an Infinite Word of Love Who is Himself Divine (Spirit). With Augustine the psychological analogy for the Trinity has begun.

And it is this rich horizon of Augustinian interiority which Aquinas accepts as his own when he begins his theological study of the psychological analogy for the Trinity. But once again he is not satisfied with simply repeating his master Augustine. Rather he moves past both the rhetorical and polemical contexts of Augustine's thought and then, without abandoning the insistence upon interiority, proceeds to transform the Augustinian analysis of the nature of intellectual operations. The central problem of that latter analysis was, of course, the famous Augustinian theory of illumination.[15] Now whatever be the correct full interpretation of that oft-analyzed Augustinian doctrine, at least some of its principal features are clear. That its background is fundamentally neo-Platonic seems certain. That it at least means that the mind possesses the possibility of certainty in its knowledge because it can somehow "see" the Eternal Ideas of God Himself through some higher kind of spiritual "illuminated" knowledge seems highly probable. But for an Aristotelian like Aquinas this transformed Neo-Platonism is unacceptable. Knowledge for the Aristotelian cannot be properly described in the terms of Platonist confrontation theory—not even the higher, more spiritual confrontation of Augustine. For human knowledge is at once a more human and a more secure phenomenon. It is not confrontation at all but identity. The root of true knowledge is, in fact, nothing more nor less than the identity of the knower and the known. To Aquinas, then, it is

15. Cf. *Verbum,* pp. 72–73.

possible for the human mind to serve as the analogy for the Trinity not because of what the human intellect has by way of spiritual sights and illuminating confrontations but rather by way of what the human mind *is*. It *is,* for Aquinas, a created participation of the divine mind. It reveals its character as such by its ability to know: its ability, in short, not to confront reality but to be identical with it through its power to understand its truth (i.e. its reality). To understand the fuller meaning of that Thomist transformation of both Aristotelian theory and Augustinian interiority into the higher synthesis of Thomist theoretic, intellectualist interiority demands a closer study of the *Verbum* articles themselves. To that task, then, we may now turn.

C. THE *VERBUM* ARTICLES: THE WORLD OF THOMIST INTERIORITY

Before one can properly understand the exact nature of the intellectualist analogy which Aquinas chooses to develop his Trinitarian theology, the complexities of a hermeneutic equal to understanding Aquinas on his own terms must first be forged. The contextual difficulties of that task have already been treated. The further complexities of Aquinas' own words and meanings are worked out through the slowly evolving strategy of the *Verbum* articles themselves. First, the pertinent psychological facts must be studied. Secondly, their metaphysical implications must be set into an explanatory framework. Thirdly, the psychological-metaphysical interplay behind Aquinas' central teaching on abstraction must be examined. After these preliminary steps have been taken, the general outlines of the Thomist Trinitarian synthesis may emerge: the intellectualist foundations will allow one to understand the meaning of Aquinas' insistence upon naming God *Ipsum Intelligere;* the structure and nature of that intellectualism will allow one to understand the exact meaning of the analogy of *intelligible* (not natural) emanation. Finally, the theological possibilities of an intellectualist and theoretic

61

attitude can be grasped after one has understood the concrete realization of those ideals in the classical context of Aquinas' entire Trinitarian theology. The principal results of that multifaceted analysis will be all that we can hope to discuss here.

For a beginning, let us try a simple approach to the crucial question: what is intellect for Aquinas and Aristotle? Initially, at least (as every listener to commencement addresses knows), it is that spirit of wonder and inquiry which Aristotle declared the beginning of all wisdom. The famous statement is deceptively simple. Perhaps a graphic contrast will help to provoke the necessary further questions: "When an animal has nothing to do, it goes to sleep; when a man has nothing to do, he may ask questions."[16] The point of the contrast is obvious enough: unlike dogs, no man (however stupid or however committed to skepticism) would wish to claim as his own the indeed singular achievement of never having wondered about anything in his life —or, for that matter, of never having understood a single object of his wonder. To enter into the region of Aquinas' discourse on *Verbum,* he need, initially at least, claim no more. He need not be able to find an exact definition for his understanding. He need not be able to analyze the exact nature and functioning of his understanding. All he needs for a starting hermeneutic is to cling to the personal certainties that sometimes he wonders and sometimes he understands. But such examples may not encourage him. Indeed, they may seem merely to locate experiences that are as unavoidable as they are unfruitful for further thought. But are they? Aristotle and Aquinas thought not. An example may help to clarify the issue: Show any man a wheel. Ask him if it's round. Record his annoyed reaction, "Of course it is; it's a wheel!" Then ask, Why? Ordinarily the further maieutic will merely further annoy him: "Look at it. Of course it's round. If you can't see that, you can't see anything." Now, it may be well to stop here a moment and notice the very commonplace but important psychological factors which both Aristotle and Aquinas and this simple illustration were attempting

16. *Insight,* p. 10.

62

to convey. The man has grasped—with seeming certainty—that the wheel is round. He may not be able to understand why he's correct. He certainly will not be able to tell you what a perfect circle is and why this wheel isn't one. But that it's round, not square, he is sure. For Aristotle and Aquinas the common human experience narrated here is the often overlooked psychological fact which, properly speaking, divides man from the other animals: the simple human ability not merely to stare at images but to understand something by and/or in them. This fact they called *insight into phantasm*.[17] One's recognition of its presence awakens one to three peculiarities of the human consciousness: first, that men wonder and question; second, that they sometimes achieve answers to their questions; third, that when men understand something they do so not as disembodied spirits but as incarnate consciousness—i.e. they use their senses, they learn to notice and form images (e.g. the wheel) by means of which they may grasp the intelligibility they seek.

Note further that the process throughout is a conscious one: the man wonders; he formulates questions; he sorts out the relevant data; he tries to remember other things which will help him to understand this single thing; he tries various images until the proper image arrives that helps him grasp the intelligibility behind the image—that helps him say "That's it! I understand this matter. It's clear to me. I can now go on to something else." He may not be able to go on from there to formulate an exact definition of his understanding but he will not retreat into animal gaping. Try as one will, one will not convince any man that never in his life has he understood anything. For, unlike any dog, even the world's most stupid man not only sees the wheel but understands (vaguely, perhaps, but really) that the word "round" somehow fits it. It is, as Americans so often like to say, a "fact."

Admittedly, to use the word "fact" already seems to involve one in the endless discussions of the "objectivity" of our knowledge. Actually it does not, for objectivity is not yet in question

17. *Verbum*, pp. 24–32.

here. The present question is simply this: is not the man's experience of understanding the "roundness" of the wheel as real (read, as intellectually conscious) to him as his former experience of simply seeing or touching the wheel was real (read, as empirically conscious to him). In short, both conscious experiences (seeing and understanding-through-image) are equally "facts" to him. They are more accurately named "cognitional facts." And, granted that this discovery is not a new revelation to man, still it bears surprising psychological, epistemological and metaphysical consequences. For what may come as something like a revelation (to the man of common sense at any rate) is the need to differentiate these two facts of his knowing explicitly so that he may follow its exclusively human, *intellectually* conscious aspects through their further intelligent and rational developments. To be willing to do that will free him to allow his criterion for the "real" to become not the sensible, not the imaginable but the intelligible. To refuse that differentiation will ultimately mean that the specific nature and power of his intelligent and rational consciousness will never be sufficiently freed from their original reliance on images to be able to explore the intelligibility of the universe of being with the freedom and the range it demands. In the present context, for example, that refusal will "free" him to misunderstand completely the nature of Aquinas' intellectualist approach to Trinitarian theology.

The first step, then, in Lonergan's hermeneutic for Aquinas has been taken. Its essential insistence was that in man there is not one but two facts of knowing: an animal knowing in which the real is what can be touched or seen or tasted or imagined; and a purely human knowing in which the real is also open to what is intelligible, what can be understood.[18] And if one does not clearly differentiate those two types of knowing in his own experience, he is in danger of retreating at critical moments to his animal knowing as the "really real" criterion for reality. Nor, unfortunately, is such a retreat peculiar to the man of com-

18. *Verbum,* p. 7.

64

mon sense. In Lonergan's judgment, it has afflicted entire philosophical positions as well. For, to the naturalist, the empiricist,
the naïve realist, the "real" is what he already has before he
understands. It is the comforting security of the "already-out-
there-now-real" world of what can be sensed, touched, seen,
smelt, tasted, imagined. The second fact in his knowing (his
understanding of the intelligible) forms no essential part of his
criterion for the real. The purely intelligible, unlike the imaginable, is too unlike that "real" world of immediacy which, even
before the age of reason, he already knew. For the empiricist,
for example, the intelligible reality reached by his properly human understanding is so unlike the first real world of his experience that it must be declared "merely subjective." For the Platonist, on the other hand, the intelligible reality reached by his
properly human knowing is so unlike the reality reached by his
senses that it must be grounded in some higher world—the
"real" world of the Platonic Ideas. Nor does the naïve realist
resolve these contradictions. For despite his metaphysical acceptance of the Aristotelian-Thomist program, his metaphysics
(if the subject is discussed at all) is grounded in a spiritual look
modeled not on the intelligently and rationally conscious nature
and threefold structure of a properly human knowing but on
the empirically conscious nature and lack of structure of a mere
sense knowledge. For Lonergan, at the core of the empiricist's
refusal to recognize the implications of the cognitional phenomenon of insight into phantasm and to differentiate the two
types of knowing already present in this elementary experience,
lies a perhaps unconscious refusal to leave the security of the
real world of the sensed and the imaginable and to enter into
the full demands of the world of intellect. At the core of the
Platonist flight into a world of pure intelligibility lies an inability
to make the legitimate differentiation between a human knowing
in which known and knower are identical (in the understanding
itself) and an animal kind of knowing (like the look of sight)
in which the looker confronts the looked-at object. At the heart
of the naïve realist's refusal to be critical about his knowledge

lies his inability to conceive of human knowing on other than a sense model, i.e. as a kind of "look" whose modality differs from animal knowing (from sensible to "spiritual") but whose nature (as confrontation, not identity) and whose structure (as singular not tripartite) remain the same.

As human, the human mind is essentially understanding. But that, as we have already argued, is not the whole story. As dependent on the images provided by the senses, no one act of human understanding can hope to understand everything about everything. Rather, the human intellect must constantly strive to understand the character of this particular person, the nature of this particular thing, the reality of this particular situation. In brief, its very dependence on the senses keeps human understanding from being a once and for all affair and forces it to reason-in-order-to-understand.[19] Even at its brightest moments, human knowledge makes its proverbial bloody entrance. It understands first one point, then another, then another until through an ever greater accumulation of insights it can intelligently handle increasingly more complex situations. Such, for example, would be the knowledge of a medicine man among some primitive tribe. He has no theorem from which he may deduce his solutions but that does not render him helpless. For after repeated failures he may eventually find some herb or some substance which when applied to this particular disease, in this particular way works. Why does it work? He has no idea—and usually no interest. But it works. It would not occur to him to realize that he is reasoning-in-order-to-understand, but, in his minimal way, he is all the same.

Yet, such relatively primitive reasoning is not the whole story of the human mind's progress. For besides the nurse who knows which medicine to prescribe but cannot scientifically tell you why it does the trick, there remains the man who does know why—the theoretician. Not the man who knows by accumulating cases that have worked, but the man who knows that the next case *will* work because it follows from a concept or theorem

19. *Verbum*, pp. 54–56, 65.

66

worked out by rigorously scientific understanding and repeatedly verified through carefully controlled experiments.

Moreover, it is precisely this difference between the understanding of the common sense man and the understanding of the theoretician which may help one understand the next key step in Lonergan's hermeneutic of Thomist cognitional analysis: the movement from insight to concept.[20] More exactly, the movement can be described as one of understanding the universal in the particular (insight into phantasm) to understanding the universal as common to many (concept). For human consciousness, as the history of western science alone makes clear, has potentialities beyond all common sense approaches. While sharing the intelligence of common sense, the scientific consciousness can still release itself more adequately from its original dependence on the image and pivot upon itself to free the idea to become an object-in-itself as concept, theorem, definition. By means of this delicate operation, the power of the theoretic approach is realized: it allows the universality of the pure intelligibility of the idea to become a permanent achievement and further allows the logical implications of that conceptual achievement to be resolved into a system, a science.

Once again an example may help to clarify this movement from insight to concept.[21] Let us return, then, to the example of the wheel. Animals, we recall, stare at wheels. Men also understand, in some way, that they are round or circular. That latter adjective is our present clue. The wheel is round. It is a circle. But what is a circle? Why, if it be a perfect circle, must it be round? A second look at the wheel may suggest an answer: it is a circle because the spokes are of the same length from the hub to the rim. Yet a very little reflection soon shows that this will not do: the spokes as material have different, not identical, thicknesses and widths; as such, they are related to the hub and the rim (neither of which is without the same material differences) differently. The rebuttal may be equally rapid: of course,

20. *Verbum,* pp. 11–16, 33–45.
21. *Insight,* pp. 7–13.

that's so; but that's only because there can never be a perfectly round *actual* circle. Exactly. But what does this prove? That the search for a definition of the circle as circle is illusory? Hardly. Rather does it not show that the search for universal definition cannot be carried out successfully if one confines oneself to the "reality" of the actual matter or its images (e.g. trying to "picture" a perfect circle to oneself)? But if man's sense knowing will not do, perhaps his properly human knowing will. For as intelligently conscious, he need not merely imagine but may also *suppose*. Suppose the spokes are just lines (i.e. with only length; no thickness, no width). Suppose the hub is just a point (i.e. a position without magnitude). Will he ever see such a phenomenon? No. Can he imagine one. No. (Those little lines he pictures still have width; that micro-point still has magnitude.) But can he conceive it? He can take his original insight into the phantasm (the relationship of spokes-hub-rim to the roundness of the wheel), eliminate the particularity of this wheel or any imagined wheels, conceive the necessary suppositions (line, point) and (after using essentially the same procedure for the "co-planar" problem) work out the definition of the circle which he learned years before ("a locus of co-planar points equidistant from the center"). The difference may now be that he not merely parrots the definition. He understands it. He understands it as a definition, as an exact expression of the universal intelligibility of his original insight. One has moved, in short, from insight to concept. And by that simple step one has taken the key step needed for one's understanding of what Aquinas meant by the strange word "intelligible emanation."

The concept, then, is the scientific response to Aristotle's and Aquinas' first question, *Quid sit?* What kind of thing is this? What is its intelligibility? What is its essence? Can we define that essence? Is the resultant definition clear, distinct, precise? Is it—in more contemporary language—not merely descriptive but explanatory? And that latter "procession" of the concept from its originating act of understanding is the meaning of the first intelligible procession which Aquinas uses for his later analogy. He intended to help his readers recall the power of their own intelligence to understand the intelligibility of a particular object and, by the conscious self-possession of that understanding, work out, suppose, conceive, formulate the concept, the theorem, the definition, the "meant" which expresses the original meaning exactly and which is further capable of universal application to all like particulars. Intelligent consciousness, then, does not follow causal laws imposed from without. Rather it itself, as intelligent, is the ground of the possibility (i.e. the intelligibility) of all intelligently grasped intelligible relationships. In a word, it is an intelligible emanation, not another example of natural causality. It is not like smoke as "caused by" fire nor like a memorized definition "caused by" the parroting operations of the memorizer, but it is the peculiarly human phenomenon represented by the intelligible emanation of the definition of the circle from its originating insight(s). That "inner word" emanation of concept from insight is not merely intelligible in the sense that the relationship can be understood. It is also actively intelligent: the concept is not merely produced by the insight, it is *because* of the insight.[22] Moreover, it is that very act of understanding which alone provides the long-sought link between the original image and the resultant concept. For behind and grounding its grasp of all its products lies the normative and constitutive demands of intellect itself. And nowhere else in nature is such constitutive (i.e. intelligent) intelligibility to be found.

Nor (*pace* the conceptualist interpretation of this process) can the movement from insight to concept be considered a quasi-automatic process. Throughout its unfolding the process is actively (i.e. consciously) intelligent. One must labor to understand. He must labor still further to conceptualize. And all his labors—if they are to be successful—must be directed by intelligence alone. At the present level of that intelligent activity, moreover, he must strive to avoid two temptations. On the one hand, he must not retreat back to image-thinking. On the other,

22. *Verbum,* pp. 33–34.

he must not attempt deductions from his theorems until he is scientifically sure that he possesses a theorem and not simply an insight. He must also be sure that his concept is the intelligent result of his insight. If he overlooks the need for insight, he may escape either into the "subjective" reality of his vivid images or the "objective" reality of a mere conceptualism. If he overlooks the need for definition, he may be tempted to rest in the full but ultimately unsatisfying flowering of all his bright ideas. If he moves forward to the level of concept as the product of an intelligible emanation, he is prepared to understand the scientific enterprise of the West and the classical analogy employed in Aquinas' Trinitarian theology.

Certain factors involved in the Thomist analysis of intellect have now been established: the originating drive of the human spirit is its spirit of wonder, its pure desire to know; the impelled inquirer formulates ever further questions about his every experience; such questions reach their first resolution in an insight into phantasm; this insight into the universal-in-the-particular further impels the scientific inquirer to want to be able to define that universal freed from the originating image as exactly and clearly as possible; he continues to reason-in-order-to-know; if successful, he achieves the intelligible emanation of a definition-concept-theorem from the original insight. That final resolution is his scientific solution to his final question on this level, is it clear?

But the human spirit's drive to know is not yet satisfied. For beyond its question "Is it clear?" lies the further question, yet to be resolved, "Is it true?" In more contemporary terms, one would say that beyond the mind's grasp of its understanding in clear and exact definition lies its demand for verification of even its best definitions. Beyond intelligent consciousness there is rational consciousness. In terms of our present interests, one can say that beyond the intelligible emanation of concept from insight there lies the second intelligible emanation of judgment from reflective understanding.[23]

23. *Verbum,* Chapter II, pp. 47–95.

70

It would be impossible, in fact, to overestimate the importance of judgment in the Thomist analysis of intellect. It is the key to the Thomist notion of objectivity. Understand it, and a critical realism may be structured. Overlook it, and an empiricism, an idealism, a dogmatism must result. Neglect it and there evolves a metaphysics that resembles a forgetfulness of being.

Like the definition, the judgment also proceeds from an act of understanding. But there the similarity ends. For definition proceeds from a direct act of understanding; judgment, a far more complex and supple process, from a reflective one.[24] That direct act of understanding, moreover, had for its object of inquiry the phantasm. The reflective act, on the other hand, demands a sweeping and critical review of the whole range of cognitional elements—the direct act itself; the dependability of the original image and sense experience; and, above all, the critical function of the constitutive force of intellect itself.[25] It is that latter element which makes the principal difference: direct understanding is content to allow the spirit of inquiry to perform so that the desired intelligibility may be achieved. Reflective understanding is not so easily satisfied. Its spirit of inquiry is one not simply of wonder but of critical wonder. Its exigence is to go beyond the knowing-as-identity which characterizes intelligent consciousness to that knowing-as-knowing-the-other which rational reflection requires. Its ultimate demand, moreover, is not merely to know the other as other in a series of particular judgments but rather to know any other as other because it first knows itself as intellectual light, as capable of intending and reaching the real-as-the-true and, consequently, as capable of making such second level distinctions as that between itself (as real subject) and the other (as real object of its intentionality).[26]

Furthermore, once the identity between knower and known

24. *Verbum,* p. 47.
25. This critical review is what Lonergan understands by Aquinas' *resolutio in principia; Verbum,* pp. 61–63.
26. Cf. the discussion of wisdom, *Verbum,* pp. 66–94.

has been grasped as present in every direct act of understanding, and the further exigence for critical verification of that identity has been allowed full play, the performative entry into the critical problem is not far away. For the conceptualist that problem will seem mere words. Trapped by his own oversight of the act of understanding grounding the concept, misled by his failure to investigate reasoning as primarily understanding-in-process rather than deduction, and satisfied by his own myth that knowledge is essentially a look, he cannot but treat any critical analysis of the reflective act of understanding in and through which one grasps the character of human intellect itself as, at best, a false question, at worst, a threat to the realism he asserts. And given that horizon, the reason for the failure of his mediation of Aquinas' Trinitarian analogy is not very hard to spot: since he fails to notice his own acts of understanding, it is not unexpected that he will overlook those of Aquinas as well.

It is to be hoped that sufficient attention has already been accorded the first intelligible emanation (insight-concept) to indicate how necessary it is for the second one (reflective insight-judgment) to avoid the same possible pitfall of extrinsicist interpretation. Once again one must differentiate carefully between the judgment and the reflective act of understanding whence it proceeds. The contribution of Lonergan himself, however, to the analysis of the nature of judgment is best left to his later, more contemporary and more sophisticated analysis in *Insight*. Yet at the present, at least one note of clarification of the strictly Aquinas-interpretation aspect of his work on judgment should be included here in order to eliminate any lingering temptations of extrinsicist interpretation. As those familiar with the complexities of the Thomist use of the medieval *compositio-divisio* terminology for judgment will be aware, the problem of the nature of judgment in Aquinas is initially (i.e. textually) not an easy one to resolve. Lonergan's own solution to the problem emphasizes, above all, a central distinction: judgment is not primarily synthesis but a *positing of synthesis*.[27] The point of

27. *Verbum,* pp. 48–59.

72

that distinction is a crucial one. For the ever-developing higher syntheses of the sciences (especially in the ever more exact unified field theories of the empirical sciences—from Newton to Einstein, for example; but even in the less rigorous but developing categories of the human sciences—the increasingly differentiated meaning of such terms as "romanticism," "classicism," "neo-classicism," for example) cannot be identified as an expression of some single act of direct understanding, but still they are *not* judgments. However complex they may be, they remain hypotheses. In the terms of our present discussion they remain acts of direct not reflective understanding. Their products are concepts and theorems, not judgments. For all syntheses are not posited, asserted, affirmed to be the case until the higher level of reflective and critical understanding has been operative. Nor is that level very easily achieved. Its full attainment, in fact, demands the properly critical level of thought called philosophy. Its partial attainment (in either common sense or science) demands the fulfillment of a whole set of complex cognitional conditions: the dependability of the original images; the fidelity to the intellectually patterned demands of intelligence and reason; the elimination of *a priori* desires, wishes, ideologies; the careful weighing of the evidence adduced; the critical weighing of intellect's own possibilities; the recognized sufficiency or insufficiency of the evidence for and against the hypothesis offered; the degree of probability the evidence affords and so on. It demands, in other words, not merely what the ancients called intelligence or science but what they named wisdom: the "wisdom" of a Caesar or Napoleon in military affairs, the conflicting "wisdoms" of an Einstein or a Bohr on the ultimate ideal of science, the *"esprit de finesse"* of a Pascal, the "illative sense" of a Newman, and above all the wisdom of the philosopher of the Western tradition—the man who has led the "examined life"; who has not allowed himself to collapse into the diversions of the "everyday"; the man who, either performatively or explicitly, has come to terms with the nature of his own intellect as intending the real to the extent that he will not allow the lesser criteria

73

of the sensed and the imaginable to serve as reality's criteria. For the authentic philosopher is satisfied with nothing less than the rigorous demands of the intelligible and the critically verified (the true) as his criteria for the "real" world. In short, the wise man, in the highest sense of that word, is a man not merely of understanding but of judgment.

It may be well to dwell for a moment on this judgmental aspect of wisdom. Wisdom, precisely as the habit of good judgment, is not first an ontological gift, nor is it ordinarily arrived at by reading one book or even a series of "great books." Primordially, philosophic wisdom is not something in books but in minds. And it is only by the philosophic intellect's slow, intelligent, self-correcting, critical search for its own nature and, through that, the nature of reality, that intellect, in its final moment, reaches up to and captures its own essence as an intending of the real and then structures and explicitates that discovery into the open, heuristic, explanatory framework called philosophy. In Aquinas' case, for example, this discovery is slow to evolve. All along the line, his basic question has been not what intellect does but what intellect is. Some of the results of that quest by now are clear: in its essence intellect for Aquinas is not primarily sensing nor imagining nor deducing but understanding (directly and reflectively). And since its starting point is the image and since its human intentionality (as human) is infinite in the questions it can raise[28] but not in the answers it can reach, human intellect (even in its highest philosophical acts of understanding) is never an understanding of everything about everything but remains always a reasoning-to-know everything that can be known. In the concrete, as we have seen above, such reasoning involves the dialectical interplay of question, sense, image, memory, insight, definition, critical reflection, grasp of evidence as sufficient and judgment. In the concrete case of Aquinas, moreover—as Lonergan's *Verbum* analysis argues—all those psychological factors are critically operative for structuring the world of Thomist intellectualism

28. *Verbum,* pp. 88–90.

74

which forms the basic horizon from which his Trinitarian theology may emerge.[29] But unless the interpreter can break clean from all extrinsicism, he can never understand the actual performance of Aquinas as he struggled to transform the worlds of Aristotelian theory and Augustinian interiority into the horizon of Thomist theoretic (in its metaphysical expression) and critical (in its actual performance) interiority.

Such then is the main outline of the horizon of Aquinas as it found expression in Lonergan's cognitional analysis. It is true, of course, that the analysis, focussed as it is on exposing the meaning of Aquinas' doctrine of intelligible emanations in the second and third levels of inquiry, does not have the fully critical, structural and methodical impact of his later work *Insight*. Yet it does, in this writer's judgment at least, offer a verifiable mode of entry into the tangled jungle of Thomist interpretation. How helpful such a psychological entry may prove for the further questions of the metaphysical expression and the scientific approach of Aquinas' Trinitarian theology, the remainder of this chapter will now briefly discuss.

(A) Metaphysics and Abstraction. The morass of terminological difficulties awaiting the unwary interpreter of Aquinas' Trinitarian theology is largely due to the difficulties involved with the metaphysical vocabulary employed to express the psychological analogy. On the basis of his former analysis of the underlying cognitional facts, Lonergan suggests a way out of the impasse. The already analyzed basic hermeneutic of his earlier articles betrays the nature of his argument: in the context of Aquinas' critical performance as it reaches to the level of philosophic wisdom, his metaphysics is best understood as isomorphic to that performance, i.e. it is its heuristic and explanatory expression. The two most important examples of that isomorphism, moreover, are the metaphysical expressions used for

29. *Verbum*, pp. 141–181; cf. also pp. 39–42, and William A. Stewart, S.J., "Abstraction: Conscious or Unconscious? The *Verbum* Articles," *Spirit as Inquiry*, pp. 409–19.

the two intelligible emanations themselves. Those familiar with the Aristotelian and Thomist metaphysical vocabulary will recall as a key distinction in Aquinas' Trinitarian theology the metaphysical distinction between agent object and terminal object. In the light of Lonergan's analysis of the significant cognitional facts, that metaphysical distinction is to be applied to each of the two cognitional levels within which an intelligible emanation occurs: First, on the level of intellectual apprehension, the *agent object* refers to the quiddity of a material thing, known in and through the phantasm illuminated by agent intellect; the *terminal object* refers to the inner word itself, the concept as *because of* the insight. Secondly, on the level of judgment, the *agent object* is the objective evidence provided by the senses and/or empirical consciousness as it has been understood and ordered conceptually and logically in a final, critical reduction to its first principles; the *terminal object* is the inner word of judgment itself as the reflective grasp of the true, in and through which the inquirer knows the final object of all his inquiry, the real.

A still more crucial and complex arena of interpretation is entered with Lonergan's discussion, in the fourth *Verbum* article, on the nature of abstraction for Aquinas. Lonergan's explicitation of this issue, moreover, was imperative: for the notion of abstraction is, for Thomists, both (in van Riet's words) "la notion centrale de réalisme Thomiste"[30] and the central issue of dispute between the conceptualist and intellectualist interpretations of Aquinas. Lonergan's solution to the complicated history of this dispute (centered around the discussion of the "three degrees of abstraction") is, once again, dependent upon his earlier analyses of the significant cognitional facts and their isomorphic metaphysical expression. In fact, for Lonergan the famous Thomist doctrine of the three degrees of abstraction (the third, or metaphysical, is more properly a

30. Cited in Stewart, p. 411n. One might also helpfully recall that van Riet's authoritative study of Thomistic epistemologies is extremely useful for background materials; cf. van Riet, *Thomistic Epistemology* (St. Louis, 1965).

separation) is actually an explanation (originally set forth in the intertwining complexities of Aquinas' psychological-metaphysical vocabulary) for the fundamental cognitional facts exposed earlier and now further differentiated in terms of the mind's power to abstract from the irrelevant and grasp the essential. In short, once the intellectualist interpretation of Aquinas has been understood, abstraction can be explained quite simply: it is the power of human consciousness to enrich the experience presented to the senses through its conscious grasp of the essential as known to be essential and its conscious elimination of the irrelevant as known to be irrelevant. That conscious enrichment develops, moreover, insofar as one makes ever further progress into the realm of pure theory. It reaches its apex when, after the initial purifications of empirical science and mathematics, one is able to realize the *separatio* defining that critical, purely explanatory knowledge named metaphysics. For the Thomist, at that level alone, the human mind understands all things from the point of view of their participation in being alone by means of its prior grasp of its own nature as a conscious, intelligent, reflective intention of all being. In essence, then, it is only after the interpreter has shifted his attention away from intellect's products to concentrate on intellect's intelligent and rational nature that he will be able to realize that Aquinas' theorem of abstraction leaves us "not a puzzle but a solution."[31] If one chooses to eliminate that attention to consciousness, the "metaphysical" profundities of the "puzzle" of abstraction will swiftly return. But if one focusses clearly and sharply on the conscious factors operative in Aquinas' theorem, then all false metaphysical problems tend to dissolve and the enrichment (not impoverishment) proper to all genuinely theoretic disciplines may quickly take hold.

(*B*) *The Intellectualist Mediation of the Thomist World of the Sacred: God and Theology as a Science.* The hold that the authentically theoretic exigence can have on a man or an entire

31. *Verbum*, p. 174.

culture cannot but give rise eventually to an intellectualist approach to the question of religion. In Aquinas' case, it need hardly be added, this clearly occurred. And if his former commitment to intelligence has made sense, then one should not complain about his daring attempt to be intelligent (not "rationalistic") in his speech on God and theology. Indeed, the very fact that Aquinas so clearly rejected the Platonic doctrine of knowledge by confrontation and fully accepted the Aristotelian theorem that knowledge is primarily and essentially act, perfection, identity forced him to reject the Platonic Subsistent Idea of Being and to accept the implications of Aristotle's approach to the Unmoved Mover only to transform that latter into his own doctrine of God as primarily *Ipsum Intelligere*.[32] And, still further impelled by his own belief in the Christian revelation of God as triune, he was able to distinguish far more sharply than Aristotle could between intelligence in act and its products of definition and judgment. Still more basically, he was able to transform the Augustinian theory of judgment, with its appeal to the mind's consultation of the eternal reasons, into his own theorem of intellect as itself a created participation in (not confrontation with) the Pure Intelligence Who is God.[33] In a double intellectualist movement, then, Aquinas speaks first of God as the pure act of understanding and thus as identity of being, understanding, thought and love and then (in his trinitarian theology) of God as that identity, yet as three: an inner Word proceeding from Understanding (the Father) who is *the* Word and an inner word who is the Spirit "because" of its intelligent-loving dependence on both Understanding and Word.[34] "Because," moreover, here means not any logical relationships between propositions but the real intelligible procession of the same identical intellectual substance. In short, as a philosopher Aquinas dared to work out the most far-reaching implications of his intellectualism to speak of God as primarily

32. *Verbum,* pp. 183–91.
33. *Verbum,* pp. 73–74.
34. *Verbum,* pp. 207–10.

Pure Understanding. As a theologian he dared to apply the still fuller implications of his intellectualist analysis of intelligible emanations by proposing the theological hypothesis that in God Himself there are the intelligible processions of Word from Understanding and Love from both where all three are identical with the same divine infinite substantial intelligence.

It was Aquinas' unashamed intellectualism, therefore, that allowed him to rise up to and resolve the principal questions of the medieval horizon: the need to distinguish clearly and systematically the spheres of the natural and the supernatural (and thus of philosophy and theology); the concomitant need to work out a natural knowledge of God and to place a scientific psychology at the disposal of the Christian's search for an analogy for the Trinity; and, finally, the need for theology to discover its own potentialities and limitations as a scientific endeavor. To express this multi-faceted achievement took Lonergan, as we have seen, fifteen years and two major works of interpretation. In *Gratia Operans* he first analysed how Aquinas developed his intellectualist theorem of operation and cooperation in order to resolve the complex set of questions involved in the medieval discussion of divine transcendence, grace and human freedom. For his prior intellectualism impelled Aquinas to formulate the conscious and intrinsically contingent nature of human freedom; the purely intelligible nature of all causal relationships; a theorem of transcendence proper to God alone as pure Self-understanding and Willing—a theorem, moreover, which was able to articulate how God, as Pure Intelligence, offers an *explanation* to all the data on the question of grace and not (as the later positions tended to suggest) as simply another datum to be explained; the concomitant intrinsically constitutive nature of divine causality; and, finally, the resultant fundamental differentiation between that transcendent causality proper to Pure Intelligence in Act and the human causality-in-time in potency and partial act. In the *Verbum* articles, moreover, Lonergan traced the implications for the critical exigence of Aquinas' intellectualism. For there, in the context of the yet more complex

79

data of medieval Trinitarian theology, Aquinas' intellectualist grasp of the potentialities and limitations of intellect freed him to ground man's desire for the beatific vision in his unrestricted desire to know and grounded man's affirmation of God as Pure-Intelligence-in-Act in man's own analogous "image-of-God" realization of the perfection-act-identity present in his own human understanding. Aquinas' intellectualism further enabled him to transform both the Aristotelian and the Augustinian horizons into an intellectualist scientific psychology which developed the originally Augustinian psychological analogy into the properly Thomist speech on intelligible processions in God.

In the light of that intellectualist interpretation of Aquinas' achievement, therefore, perhaps Lonergan's struggle with the conceptualist Thomistic tradition will be admitted to be justified.[35] For in Aquinas, as in Aristotle, science is principally understanding. Eliminate that concern with understanding and that high ideal very soon becomes merely that search for the security of the "certitude" of concepts that is so entrenched in most of post-Tridentine Catholic theology. But that theological cult of certitude cannot be attributed to Aquinas himself. It is, rather, a product of the fourteenth century which followed. It shares that century's concern with the end-products of scientific inquiry yet hesitates to accept its insecurity. Furthermore, the results of that post-medieval turn in Roman Catholic theology were nothing short of disastrous: for if one's exclusive concern is with the "certain," one will soon be left incapable of understanding either the genuine theological achievement of Aquinas or the still more complex needs of this later, post-Thomist age. Indeed, in retrospect, it seems as if "Denzinger theology's" chief competence was not to theologize at all (that could be left for "corollaries") but rather to spend its energies finding the right "theological note" for this degree of certainty. The struggles of Catholic thought to escape the confines of that ideal for theology are fairly recent history. The present author is perfectly willing to agree that the struggle is now past (except for

35. *Verbum*, pp. 211–13.

some rearguard action) and that the struggle at present is for a theology that can move fully into the problematic of our modern and not medieval age. But that present movement has only been made possible by the careful works of historical recovery of an earlier generation. And in that recovery of Catholic theology's biblical, liturgical, patristic, and medieval sources, the work of Lonergan in rediscovering and reformulating the scientific ideal and achievements of the age of Aquinas should be assigned a prominent place.[36] His aim had been to recover the *"vetera."* His achievement was to explicitate the medieval worlds of theory and interiority. The exigencies of the *"nova,"* therefore, could now be faced.

36. Perhaps a quotation of Lonergan's own claim would be useful to the reader here:

"It seems that intellectualism, if once it gains a foothold, never will be dislodged from the interpretation of Thomist trinitarian theory. If that is correct, I have reached my objective. Also, of course, if it is correct, many other things follow. To clarify the purpose of these articles, I hasten to add that I have not been concerned with them. From the viewpoint of history there are many questions beyond the bald fact that Aquinas adverted to understanding and made it central in his psychology. But these questions are further questions. They presuppose the bald fact and ask about its measure and degree, its emergence and development, its reinforcement and weakening from combination and conflict with other influences in Thomist sources and the medieval milieu. From the writings of Aquinas one can extend inquiry to other writers, prior, contemporary, subsequent, eventually to invite some historian of the stature of M. Gilson to describe the historical experiment of understanding understanding and thinking thought. My aim has not been to treat such further questions but to raise the issue of such treatment by settling a preliminary fact and indicating elementary landmarks" (*Verbum*, p. 219).

4. THE NEW CONTEXT: THE MODERN CONSCIOUSNESS OF THEORY AND INTERIORITY

To move our investigation from Lonergan's work in Aquinas to his *Insight* and post-*Insight* work is, quite literally, to move into a different world. More exactly, worlds. For the worlds of community, of theory and of interiority had developed in so many critical ways since the time of Aquinas that their meanings demanded radical rethinking and re-explicitation. And just as Lonergan's earlier work was his attempt to appropriate the horizon of Aquinas, so his later, more original and more important work (for which *Insight* is at once the entry and the most important published formulation to date) is Lonergan's own attempt at appropriation and explicitation of the gains of the post-medieval, i.e. modern, horizon.[1] To understand the full

1. The designation "modern" refers to the factors concerned with seventeenth-century empirical scientific revolution and the critical revolution in philosophy. The factors concerned with "historical" consciousness are more aptly labelled "contemporary" and dealt with in Chapters 9 and 10 of this book.

Those "contemporary" elements become clearly differentiated in Lonergan's later work (esp. *"Existenz* and *Aggiornamento," Collection,* pp. 240–252; or "Dimensions of Meaning," pp. 252–67). For both concerns as present in the *Insight* period, cf. *Insight* (empirical scientific method), pp. xxi–xxii, 125, 164, 179; as well as, of course, the first five chapters of the work; on the "critical" problem in philosophy, cf. esp. *Insight,* Introduction, pp. xvii–xxiii. The interest in the problematic of the human sciences is perhaps best revealed in *Insight,* Chapters 6 and 7 (pp. 173–242); and the Epilogue, pp. 742–48. For the latter interest, cf. also "Theology and Understanding," *Collection,* pp. 129–141.

intention and achievement of *Insight* demands, therefore, that one first grasp the meaning of Lonergan's earlier discovery of the authentic theoretic attitude in Aquinas and also understand the modern "horizon-context" as Lonergan understood it at the time of the writing of *Insight*.

It bears repetition, however, to recall that the single most important product of Lonergan's ten-year study of the thought of St. Thomas Aquinas was his recognition of what Henri Niel has called the authentic "theoretic attitude" of Aquinas.[2] In fact, the clearest expression of this insistence is Lonergan's own: "After spending years reaching up to the mind of Aquinas, I came to a twofold conclusion. On the one hand, that reaching had changed me profoundly. On the other hand, that change was the essential benefit. For not only did it make me capable of grasping what, in the light of my conclusions, the *vetera* really were, but also it opened challenging vistas on what the *nova* could be."[3]

What then were the key *nova* in Lonergan's judgment at the time of the writing of *Insight*? The answer, I believe, is clear: They were the scientific revolution and the critical movement in philosophy. Once again, these primarily contextual factors are of key importance for understanding the methodological gains of *Insight*. For now Lonergan's concern was not so much to defeat the extrinsicist interpretation of Aquinas or to regain the medieval scientific ideal for theology as it was to consider the key scientific developments in the Western intellectual tradition since Aquinas. Moreover, this problem of development cannot be overlooked by the theologian, for the contemporary scientific ideal is no longer purely Aristotelian nor is contemporary philosophy content with a performing critical spirit that does not thematize itself (or, more exactly, thematizes itself only in metaphysical and not epistemological categories[4]).

2. Cf. *Spirit as Inquiry,* H. Niel, p. 481.
3. *Insight,* p. 748.
4. For the continuity between Lonergan's "Thomist" and his *Insight* periods, cf. the important article "Isomorphism of Thomist and Scientific Thought," *Collection,* pp. 142–151.

A. THE SHIFT IN THE WORLD OF THEORY: ARISTOTELIAN TO MODERN SCIENCE

The first question, then, is that of the shift of scientific ideals from Aristotelian to modern.[5] For if the same theoretic drive is present in both ideals, one must still insist that the latter is both more expansive, more refined and, in certain key ways, different. The medieval ideal, in fact, remained *"cognitio certa per causas"* (with its attendant insistence upon universality, necessity, certainty and Aristotelian metaphysical causality). The contemporary ideal on the other hand is significantly different: it aims at "the complete explanation of all the data (i.e. including those in process) in terms of their mutual intelligible relationships" (with its attendant insistence upon development, probability, pluralism of methods and expansion of possible expressions of causality).

To discuss that differentiation more adequately, however, demands an explicitation of the more important differences between the Aristotelian and the contemporary scientific ideals. Furthermore, since the interest of this book is theological, theo-

---

It is to be noted that a footnote (p. 151) locates this article chronologically between the "historical" work of the *Verbum* articles and the "theoretical" work of the "forthcoming" *Insight*. Hence its interest to the present work for its transitional value. One might also refer to *"Insight:* Preface to a Discussion" (*Collection*, pp. 152–64) for the same concerns, although not as clearly stated (for chronological purposes) as the present essay. In the present writer's judgment, the most helpful analysis of the continuity from an ontological point of view between Lonergan's *Insight* work and traditional Thomism is his *De Constitutione Christi Ontologica et Psychologica* (Rome, Gregorian University, 1956), 150 pp. (*ad usum auditorum*); cf. esp. pp. 83–148).

5. Lonergan has treated these differences in several places; for the main *loci*, cf. esp. *De Intellectu et Methodo* (privately printed notes, 1962); "Dimensions of Meaning," *Collection*, pp. 252–67; "The New Context of Theology," *Theology of Renewal* (New York, 1968). Unless otherwise cited, the analysis given here is from those sources. Its fidelity to the concerns of *Insight* will be clarified in the treatment of *Insight* to follow.

logical examples will be used throughout the discussion of those differences. This is not to argue, of course, either that theology was the first science to develop this ideal or that the interest of *Insight* itself is principally theological. In fact, it clearly is not. Still the examples may help the theological readers of this work to realize the intrinsic importance of that horizon-shift of scientific ideals for theology. For, when all is said and done, the fact remains that every theoretician (including the theologian) must sooner or later try to explicitate the scientific ideal and method which structures all his work. And if that ideal be a classical one (as in Aquinas) or some conceptualist aberration of the classical ideal (as in the manuals) the resulting theology will be, in the first case, inadequate, in the second, thoroughly unacceptable for serious consideration by and in the contemporary theological problematic.

The first shift, then, can be described as the change from medieval concern[6] with the certainty of results to contemporary concern with probability. The contemporary scientist will not claim certainty for his conclusions. Rather, he is quite satisfied with a high degree of probability even for his most cherished achievements (e.g. the periodic table in chemistry). In theology such a shift is all-important. It was, in the first place, at the core of the widespread if often inarticulate dissatisfaction of the previous generation of Catholic theologians with any kind of "proof" theology. In the second place, it is behind the demand of so many theologians today that classical ideals and structures (especially the concern for "metaphysical" certainty) must yield to a transformation into a genuine, theoretic search for understanding, not certitude. For in theology too, as in any contemporary science, the age of certitude is over; and the age of

6. This statement, moreover, would demand considerable historical nuancing to be fully adequate. For present purposes, it would be best to consider the medieval concern for certainty as more faithful to their theory than their practice. For the "nuancing" in the highly complex medieval theological world, the present writer is preparing a work on the history of theological method for the *Catholic Theological Encyclopedia.*

85

truly probable understanding must begin in a full-fledged and unimpeded way.

The second differentiation is the correlative of the first: it insists that the scientist shift from Aristotle's concern with the changeless and the immobile to the contemporary scientist's interest in change, movement, development. An understanding of this shift provides a ready access into the gains represented by the development of calculus, of evolution-theory, of genetic psychology or of the dialectical interests of the various human sciences and philosophy. It also allows a more immediate entry into the emphasis on "heuristic method" and "moving viewpoint" in *Insight*. In theology, it allows one to understand the movement from a "dogmatic" theology innocent of any real historical sense to a contemporary theology in which the questions of development in doctrine, hermeneutic and history have become crucial areas of all theologians' concern.

Thirdly, Aristotelian necessity has yielded to the contemporary empirical, *de facto* intelligibility; in the latter case necessity has become, at best, a marginal notion. Such a shift of ideals was implicit, for example, in Galileo's success in formulating a mathematical expression of the actual empirical (not metaphysically necessary) intelligibility of a free fall. Moreover, that same shift is involved in *Insight*'s philosophic insistence that the critical problem is not "Am I necessarily a knower?" but rather "Am I *as a matter of fact* a knower?" In the theology of redemption another illustration of that same shift may be found: one will not find contemporary theologians posing the kind of "questions of necessity" exemplified by the classical redemption-theology of Anselm's *Cur Deus Homo?* Rather, one will find them attempting to find categories adequate for expressing the actual intelligibility of the historically factual death and resurrection of Jesus Christ.[7] In short, as the use of the empirical method upon biblical, liturgical, patristic, medieval, reformation and contemporary sources has continued to bear fruit, there has been a concomitant dwindling interest in all classical questions

7. In Lonergan's own case, cf. *De Verbo Incarnato*, pp. 502–43.

on the "necessity" of redemption along with a concomitant rising interest in finding "systematic" categories to explicitate the discoveries of positive theologians.

Fourthly, the contemporary scientist has moved away from exclusive concern with the universal to dominant interest in particular and concrete facts in the mutually intelligible relationships of their actual unfolding, development or decline. In contemporary empirical science, one need only recall the various theories on the origin of the universe, on the structure of the planetary system or on human evolution. In theology, this same movement is exemplified in such contemporary concerns as establishing the genetic-dialectic factors operative in the development of any doctrine or any theological theorem.[8]

Fifthly, there is the shift of interest from classical Scholasticism's discussion of formal objects to contemporary science's discussion of field. A formal object is the aspect under which (*ratio sub qua*) any theoretician considers and attains the object of his study. A field, on the other hand, can be defined as a region of the concrete universe which the particular science in question aims to master by the skilled use of those certain basic operations and methods peculiar to his specialty. In other words, the horizon-analysis method of the contemporary scientist demands a consideration of both objective (regions, worlds of being) and subjective (methods, operations) poles of the horizon of any particular science. In short, it demands a far more differentiated thematization of one's scientific method than the relatively unsophisticated Scholastic discussion of "formal objects" allows. In science, examples abound: group theory in mathematics, for example, or the whole range of methods which the theoretical physicist must master, or Harry Stack Sullivan's "field-theory" of interpersonal relationships in psychology. In philosophy, the difficulties associated with the highly disputed word "objectivity" will, I suggest, only bear fruit when philosophers study the field-analysis of their scientific colleagues more closely. In theology, moreover, the Scholastic discussions

8. E.g. *De Deo Trino*'s own attempt to do the same thing.

on the nature of the "formal object" of theology are too far removed from present scientific practice to actually resolve the
problems they pose. However, the concern with method, or
hermeneutic, or history reveals that theologians too have entered—somewhat hesitantly—into the discussion of "fields."

Sixthly, there is the contrast of the contemporary emphasis
on method with the classical emphasis on logic. For in classical
scientific method the process of inquiry can be described as
follows: there is an ascending order, as the inquirer moves
from particulars and then attempts to formulate his insights
into universal definitions, axioms and postulates; there is a second, descending order as the classical inquirer uses logic to
move from his principles, definitions, axioms and postulates to
his conclusions. In present scientific method, however, that
process is considerably more involved. Rather than being a
movement of ascent and descent, it may more accurately be
described as circular: one moves from carefully controlled data
through insight to hypothesis to verification via experiment and,
finally and secondarily, to logical deductions from the hypotheses. Often a further checking process uncovers unnoticed data,
or insights, or experiments so that the whole process must begin anew: from new data to fresh insight to more refined (or
different) hypotheses, to better methods of verification, to new
deductions etc. At each stage of the procedure the scientist
reaches an ever more probable rendering of the truth of the
region under study. In that wider context, then, logic continues
to function but not with the centrality accorded it by the classical mind. The importance of this methodological shift for theology, moreover, can scarcely be overestimated. Indeed, much of
what passed for theology in post-medieval Roman Catholicism
seems to have found in logic all the science it needed for its
"theological" method: one had, it seems, one's certain "Catholic" principles, definitions, axioms and postulates (Scripture,
councils, magisterial decrees, consent of the fathers, consensus
of theologians etc.); one next used logic to deduce equally certain conclusions from them; those conclusions were theology.

But especially since positive theology's manifold enrichment of the whole field of theological data, the built-in implausibility of so *simpliste* a "method" becomes obvious. For the "meaning" problem alone of the human data investigated by theology is so complex and manifold that no logic can hope to handle the hermeneutic difficulties of symbolic expression. On a yet more basic level, the theologian must constantly be criticizing the presuppositions of his own theological method and always open to as yet untried methods in the hope of approximating ever more closely to the scientific ideal he sets for himself. The development of Schillebeeckx, for example, from a fundamentally Thomist framework to the use of phenomenological categories and, more recently, to a deep involvement in the German discussion of hermeneutic represents but one of the more obvious examples of a widespread phenomenon.

Seventhly, the contemporary scientist realizes that it is no longer possible to determine the "essence" of any phenomenon as readily as the classical mind believed. In fact, the modern scientist has largely abandoned the classical search for essences (i.e. the one, ultimate, intrinsic ground of necessity, universality and per-se-ity) to face squarely the modern context of pluralism and perspectivism. A pluralistic stance recognizes that the reality under investigation may perhaps be too rich and manifold to be captured in a single essence uniquely formulated. For all complex realities, in fact, the contemporary pluralist tries not some single, "infallible" approach but rather a combination of different approaches. Perspectivism further recognizes that the significance of events may change as their history unfolds. As that significance changes, so too does the "reality," once thought captured forever in the essential definitions of the classicists. In science, this dual emphasis is most readily exemplified in the rise of the schools of sociology of knowledge. In Catholic theology the conflict of the majority and minority reports on the birth-control issue is ample evidence of the inability of the classicist to realize the shift at issue here. In more contemporary theological discussion, a similar pluralistic and perspectivistic stance

89

is realized in the works of such observers (and practitioners) of the involved theological scene as Peter Berger or Daniel Callahan. Whether such a stance must lead to the thoroughgoing "relativism" so feared by the classicist or is rather a transformation (*Aufhebung*), not elimination of the gains of classicism is, of course, another and deeper question to be resolved only on a later philosophical and theological level.

Eighthly and finally, where classical science was considered individualist and permanent in its achievements, modern science is ordinarily collectivist, collaborative and always open to further development. For even if it would be profitable for contemporary physicists to become more familiar with the history of their discipline (as Stanley Jaki has recently and laboriously insisted), still no physicist feels required to repeat every experiment presumed by his present work. Nor does this movement require him to believe that all his presuppositions are inviolable. If an error has occurred, sooner or later new data or new hypotheses or new experimentation by someone in the field will expose it. Similarly in theology, the age of the "schools" at last seems over as the age of a genuine and widespread attempt at an authentic collaboration among all theological practitioners has finally begun.

In summary, then, the eight differentiations described here cumulatively add up to a transformation of the Aristotelian scientific ideal assumed by Aquinas and all the lesser figures in classical theology into the contemporary scientific demand for a complete explanation of *all* the data in terms of their mutual intelligible relationships. The fuller theological implications of that shift will be discussed in the later chapter on method in theology. For the present, however, it is sufficient to note the change that such a shift involves for the world of theory of all scientific disciplines, including theology. The more detailed analysis of scientific method in *Insight* itself, moreover, will indicate more adequately the theoretic attitude of Lonergan himself. But for a correct understanding of that latter achievement, it is essential for the prospective reader to understand the contextual change in scientific ideals and thereby theoretic concerns which *Insight* and Lonergan's theology assume.

B. THE SHIFT IN THE WORLD OF INTERIORITY: KANT AND HEGEL

If Lonergan's study of contemporary mathematics and empirical scientific method forced him to re-examine and restructure the Aristotelian ideal of his own classical background, his study of the history of philosophy since Aquinas demanded that he also investigate the world of explicitly critical interiority present in post-Kantian philosophy and not explicit at the time of Aquinas.

Accordingly, parallel to the previous discussion on the shift in the scientific ideal in empirical science is the yet more intricate modern discussion of the very possibility and meaning of the philosophic ideal.[9] Even more urgently than the empirical

9. It is to be recalled that this discussion deals with the "modern" (i.e. Descartes, Hume, Kant, Hegel), not "contemporary" (e.g. Wittgenstein, Heidegger) period of discussion on the nature of philosophy. Moreover, this presentation makes no pretense to be fully faithful to the complexities of the Kantian or *a fortiori* the Hegelian position. Rather it follows Lonergan's own use of the Kantian-Hegelian concerns as revealed in *Insight* and especially in the unfortunately never-published introductory lectures to *Insight* given at Halifax in 1958. Unless otherwise cited, therefore, the chapter follows those sources.

Only the most basic influences and contexts have been indicated here. Indeed, besides the clear and careful context of empirical science, the Maréchallian movement and Thomism in general, one could indicate the influence of Newman on the Lonerganian enterprise. On the influence of Aquinas, the following *caveat* should be noted lest that influence be overemphasized:

"Finally, there is the question whether my prior allegiance to Thomism did not predetermine the results I reached. Now it is true that I spent a great deal of time in the study of St. Thomas and that I know I owe a great deal to him. I just add, however, that my interest in Aquinas came late. As a student in the philosophy course at Heythrop College in the twenties, I shared the common view that held the manuals in little esteem, though I read J. B. W. Joseph's *Introduction to Logic* with great care and went through the main parts of Newman's *Grammar of Assent* six times. In the early thirties I began to delight in Plato,

scientist, the philosopher must constantly ask himself, Just what is philosophy aiming at and how? For since the philosopher too seeks theoretic knowledge, there must be some implicit or explicit scientific ideal involved in all his philosophical operations and assumed by all the objects which those operations seek. In short, even more exigentially and more radically than the scientist, the philosopher must examine his horizon. Otherwise he may be building castles out of his own wishes—beautiful and impressive, no doubt, but ultimately groundless.

It was the genius of Immanual Kant to have forced this problem on the most radical level. Indeed, the greatness of his achievement is only enhanced by the fact that, at his time, the ideal of scientific philosophy seemed secure, certain and clear beyond all discussion. For the ideal of that time was the ideal of pure reason, classically represented in the work of Christian Wolff and the Scholasticism he influenced. Above all, that ideal involved the transference from pre-non-Euclidean mathematics to philosophy of a set of fundamental, analytic, universal, necessary propositions from which one could logically deduce equally universal and necessary conclusions. Or, to employ once more the horizon-language of this work, the philosophy of pure reason was composed of an objective pole which included all possible being and a subjective pole whose logical operations of possibility and necessity structured all of "pure reason's" objects.

Kant's first great critique was aimed directly at that ideal. And, whatever its other difficulties, Kant's critique finished once and for all the philosophical naïveté of the school of pure reason. For Kant was able to hit the nerve-center of that phi-

---

especially the early dialogues, and then went on to the early writings of Augustine. Only later in the decade when studying theology did I discover the point to the real distinction by concluding the *unicum esse* from the Incarnation and by relating Aquinas' notion of *esse* to Augustine's of *veritas*. Finally, it was in the forties that I began to study Aquinas on cognitional theory and as soon as the *Verbum* articles were completed (*Theological Studies,* 1946–49), I began to write *Insight."* Lonergan, *Proceedings of American Catholic Philosophical Association* (Washington, 1967), p. 257.

losophy's presuppositional difficulty: the mistaken analogy between mathematics and philosophy. In mathematics, for Kant
(writing in a pre-Riemannian age) pure reason is able to arrive
at its universal and necessary results because the mathematician
can construct mathematical concepts and categories by repre-
senting those space-time concepts in a pure *a priori* intuition.
However, the philosopher simply does not possess any similar
a priori intuition of being, the object of his inquiry. He cannot,
therefore, hope for any genuinely philosophical success by following the mathematical method of "pure reason." Instead he
must rather strive to articulate a more modest, because more
critical, enterprise: the construction of a transcendental method
based on a critical analysis of human consciousness. Kant, then,
called for a "Copernican revolution" in philosophy by insisting
that anyone claiming to do metaphysics must first critically defend the very "conditions of the possibility" of any such knowledge. Moreover, in the context of this very brief and too simple
discussion of Kant, it should be noted that although the negative conclusions of Kant's enterprise have received the principal
(in some cases, exclusive) attention of most "realist" commentators, that is not our primary concern here. Indeed, as will be
argued later, the Kantian "Copernican revolution" was something of a half-hearted affair whose own presuppositions and,
therefore, whose conclusions may well be challenged as in fact
they have been in subsequent German philosophy and in the
movement in the "realist" tradition associated with the name of
Maréchal. But, whatever the further and deeper complexities
and difficulties of the full Kantian position, for our present purposes it is sufficient to spell out as clearly as possible the positive results of his critical "revolution": the philosophic ideal of
"pure reason" was shattered and the possibility of all and every
objectivistic, pre-critical, classical approach to philosophy (including, therefore, *all* forms of "scholasticism") was called into
serious (i.e. critical) question.

And if, in Lonergan's view, Kant had initiated the critical
discussion by challenging a particular philosophic scientific

ideal, it was left to Hegel to intensify and widen that discussion incomparably by introducing a more general theorem (the dialectic) which demanded that *every* philosophic ideal be made explicit. It need hardly be added that the difficulties of Hegelian interpretation make even the Kantian seem relatively simple. But, as with Kant, our interest here lies with Lonergan's interpretation of Hegel, not with Hegel himself. If the latter were attempted, a book at least as long as the present one would be necessitated; but if the former contextual task were ignored, the prospective reader of *Insight* would be unable to appreciate how Lonergan's own interpretation of Kant and Hegel forced him into the critical (Kant) and dialectical (Hegel) enterprise of *Insight.*

For Lonergan, then, the Hegelian dialectic included a recognition of the need to explicitate all implicitly operative scientific and philosophic ideals. Moreover, the six central terms in Hegelian dialectic (implicit → explicit; abstract → alien; mediation → reconciliation) bespeak the presence of that recognition. In the first place, for Hegel, any attempt at scientific explicitation of an implicit ideal involves an ever-increasing abstraction of that ideal. But that involvement only serves to increase the problematic, for no abstraction can adequately express the whole of man's desire and capacity for the ideal. Consequently *any* such abstract explicitation (e.g. Scholastic theories of grace) is ultimately inadequate for expressing the actual concrete situation (i.e. the "grace-full" religious reality of the Christian).[10] In short, in every abstraction there always remains an opposition between the explicitation of the ideal and the desires of the subject in whom the ideal is implicit. That opposition is the Hegelian alienation (i.e. the alienation of the subject from an explicitated, abstract ideal which does not and cannot adequately represent his concrete situation). The Hegelian critique,

10. In the forthcoming *Method in Theology,* the chapter on religion explicitates this dialectical nature of theologies of grace in a manner complementary (religiously-existentially) to the theological-abstract discussion of Aquinas' theology of grace in *Gratia Operans.*

then, even more radically and clearly than the Kantian, expresses the existence of the critical problem of the philosopher's scientific ideal. For not only is the ideal of pure reason criticized (as it was by Kant) but the Hegelian argument pushes that criticism still further: any scientific or philosophic ideal will be an abstraction; it will ultimately be recognized as inadequate; that inadequacy will expose the reality of alienation which may give rise to another explicitation and yet another. Hegel's own solution to the problematic he exposed (viz. mediation-resolution via the dialectic) is well known, if variously interpreted. However, we may safely ignore discussion of that solution here as Hegelian hermeneutic is not really our present concern. Instead, we are interested in Lonergan's *Insight* view which insists above all that the Hegelian analysis reveals the radical, concrete difficulty of any theoretical enterprise, viz. that no one can take so much as a single step towards knowledge without invoking, implicitly or explicitly, some ideal of just what knowledge is.

With the preceding contexts in mind, therefore, it should be possible to enter more immediately into the problematic of *Insight* itself. For as the shift in scientific ideals has performatively indicated and as the critiques of Kant and Hegel have explicitly argued, any attempt at theory involves the use of some scientific ideal and all such ideals should be subject to critical investigation. That ideal need not be very explicit in its initial stages. Indeed, it usually only becomes so as the science itself develops. For example, the original Pythagorean mathematical ideal becomes ever more explicit as its products become ever more concrete (e.g. Archimedes) and differentiated (e.g. Galileo, Kepler) until seventeenth century scientists began to speak far more tellingly than Pythagoras ever had of the "mathematization of all nature." Moreover, that ideal received ever further concretization in particular laws (e.g. Archimedes' law for floating bodies, Galileo's for falling bodies, Kepler's for planetary movement) until such time as a more general displacement towards system (Newton) occurred. That latter development, too, is of major importance: for Newton is not

95

primarily interested in working out more particular laws as Galileo and Kepler were but rather in establishing a system (related sets of operations, definitions, postulates, axioms) on the basis of which all the particular laws of Galileo and Kepler and others might be deduced. The genius of the Newtonian system, furthermore, is best revealed by its success in correlating all particular laws and by the durability of its own success. Indeed, not until the rise of non-Euclidean geometries, of relativity theory, and of quantum physics did Newton's system collapse and become transformed into states and probabilities. But throughout these developing concretizations and differentiations in the history of the Pythagorean ideal, one should note the one primary factor of continuity: the constancy (amidst so much change) of the ideal itself. The mathematics available to the contemporary physicist are significantly different from that used by Pythagoras or Archimedes or Newton. The methods, measurements, experimentations are considerably more sophisticated. Still, the contemporary physicist attempts to understand nature through the use of mathematics as ardently as his predecessors did. Between his more complex and far more differentiated expression of his scientific ideal and the less sophisticated seventeenth-century "mathematization of nature" there exists, therefore, a similar mathematical ideal. And just as Kant attempted to defend the possibility of the Newtonian system against Hume's attack, so too Lonergan in *Insight*'s initial phase will be concerned to defend not any particular system but the scientific ideal itself through a critical examination of its actual performance in contemporary empirical scientific methods.[11]

But perhaps a more properly theological example would be more helpful to the readers of this work. For in theology too (as the previous analysis of Aquinas adequately demonstrates) a scientific ideal has been operative. We have already discussed the

11. It might be helpfully recalled that this insistence on the authenticity of the "scientific" ideal will bear important theological consequences. It will, for example, join Lonergan with the Whiteheadians and not with the Heideggerians on the question of scientific (objectifying) theological discourse.

eight key differences between the explicitation of the scholastic scientific ideal and the contemporary. We have also claimed that the explicit scientific ideal of the Scholastics is no longer equal to the problems, data and methods of contemporary theology for it is simply impossible to achieve "certain knowledge of things through their (metaphysical) causes" for the vast fields of human, historical data investigated by theologians of today. Yet this is not to argue that the scientific exigence initiated in medieval theology must now collapse and surrender to the lesser exigencies of more seductive, more "relevant" possibilities. For the simple truth of the matter is that, unless theology wishes to become "glossaliology," it is imperative for the theologians to realize that the present demands of theory are greater, not less, in every science and must be greater, not less, in theology as well. For example, the original scholastic ideal (as developed by Aquinas, among others) involved a double movement: a resolution of the reality under discussion into its causes and a composition from those causes. As we have already argued, a number of transformations of that ideal must be made. Yet, once made, cannot the basic analytic-synthetic structure of the entire enterprise be maintained—as it is, in fact, in Lonergan's own theologies of the Trinity and of Christ?[12] And more fundamentally still, must not the drive towards theory, the scientific exigence be firmly maintained in order, positively, to enrich one's religious understanding through the possibilities of *theoria* and, negatively, to keep religion from becoming a subject of interest only for the unsophisticated, the undifferentiated and the enthusiast?

In summary, this contextual discussion of *Insight* indicates merely the nature of the question which Lonergan is raising in that work. Indeed, as either the history of the scientific ideal in the West or the Kantian and Hegelian critiques of that ideal reveal, every search for knowledge is, at the very least, a heuristic search for an unknown. In every such heuristic, scientific en-

12. For the clearest expression of this factor, cf. *De Deo Trino*, II, pp. 36–54.

terprise, moreover, the ideal gradually becomes explicit through the actual performance of the particular science (e.g. Galileo–Newton–Einstein–Bohr; Anselm–Abelard–Aquinas). Furthermore, still further differentiations and explicitations of the ideal are to be anticipated. Is there, then, no way out of the alienation resultant upon all explicitation and abstraction? Or do the Hegelian and post-Hegelian (Marxist, existentialist etc.) philosophies exhaust the alternatives? Lonergan suggests that there is a way to see that they do not: there is the concrete possibility (in the words of the epilogue of *Insight*) of one's "appropriation of one's rational self-consciousness." The full meaning of that phrase must be left to our later discussion. For the present contextual discussion, the following articulation may suffice: that, although the scientific ideal anyone follows in seeking any unknown is either conceptually implicit or inadequately explicitated in the actual history of that science, still this fact does not make the ideal non-existent or the scientific exigence any less exigent. For behind any ideal there is the inquiring subject himself, as intelligent, as raising questions, as seeking and sometimes finding answers. In essence, then, it is possible in Lonergan's view to move into an investigation of those fundamental tendencies involved in all scientific inquiry and get hold of (i.e. "self-appropriate") not some hypothetically necessary structures of inquiry but rather certain cognitional matters of fact which are invariant in all inquiry and thereby independent of the Hegelian objectives. Lonergan's suggestion, therefore, is that the intelligent inquirer take what might be called a "step backwards"—past all explicitations of the scientific ideal (words, concepts, theorems, judgments, etc.) to the intelligent and rational subject himself as the source and ground of all explicitation: to the subject as questioning, as having insights, forming concepts, weighing evidence, reflecting, judging and deciding. His concern, to employ the more familiar Heideggerian vocabulary, must first be ontic before it becomes ontological. His concern, to use Lonergan's own vocabulary, must first be pre-conceptual, pre-predicative, pre-judicial, intentional.

Accordingly, the work *Insight* may most helpfully be described as a series of exercises in self-appropriation. It is a series of exercises designed to reach the factual, functionally operative tendencies expressed by the series of explicit theoretic ideals in science, philosophy and speculative theology. It is, to employ our earlier vocabulary again, basically an attempt to move behind the worlds of scientific theory to their grounding worlds of intelligent and rational interiority. In that real sense, then, the question that Lonergan is raising for his readers in *Insight* is a fundamental one. Indeed, in a real sense (as the earlier reviews of *Insight* witness), it is far more difficult to ask *Insight*'s question correctly than it is to answer it. For the question of the "discovery" of the self as intelligent and rational is too often thought to be somehow similar to, say, Columbus' "discovery" of America. The "self" is simply there—"out there"—and to "discover" it seems only to involve finding the right set of logical operations to sail one into the safe and waiting haven of the "metaphysical self." But the discovery involved in self-appropriation is not so simple an affair. Among other matters, it demands a prior critique of the subject's present performance. For, as we have argued above, no one starts the critical inquiry with a clean slate. Every man has been thinking for years and all his thinking (whether he knew it or not) included some operative ideal of what knowledge is. Hence, if he chooses to understand and judge that work, every prospective reader of *Insight* must be willing to work through the series of clarifying mathematical and scientific exercises in the early part of that work in order to be able to grasp the meaning of the at first strange-sounding "quasi-slogan" of *Insight:* "Thoroughly understand what it is to understand and not only will you understand the broad lines of all there is to be understood but also you will possess a fixed base, an invariant pattern, opening upon all further developments of understanding."[13]

The entire first section of *Insight,* therefore ("Insight as Activity") is Lonergan's own exposition and explicitation of the normative operations and structures of intelligent and rational

13. *Insight,* p. xxviii.

consciousness. The section, with its strategic unfolding of mathe-matical, scientific and common sense examples, often confounds and discourages prospective readers. Yet the point of the examples is neither to discourage nor to distract but to provoke: to provoke the reader's personal grasp of the clarity possible to human intelligence as that clarity is most graphically expressed in mathematics; to provoke the reader's own recognition of the heuristic nature of all human inquiry as it is most clearly re-vealed in the classical and statistical heuristic methods of contemporary empirical science; to provoke the reader's own understanding of the universality of the dual phenomena of understanding itself and of the flight from understanding as both those phenomena are revealed in the worlds of science and of common sense. In short, the first eight chapters are involved with understanding the act of understanding itself. In the next movement of the "moving viewpoint" of his work, Lonergan conducts the inquiry past the "Is it clear?"/"What is it?" ques-tions for all acts of direct understanding (and its expression in the concept) to the "Is it true?"/"Is it?" questions for reflective understanding (and its expression in judgment). The two chap-ters required to fulfill that task in turn give way to the central question of the entire book, self-affirmation (chapter eleven). For in that discussion towards which all "Insight as Activity" is directed and from which all "Insight as Knowledge" follows, the exact nature of the self-affirmation Lonergan seeks is explici-tated by him and, it is hoped, by the reader as well: the neither necessary nor hypothetical but factual experience, understand-ing and, above all, judgment of one's own intellectually pat-terned performance of experience, understanding and judgment. The technical formulation of that discovery (to be discussed below) as a "virtually unconditioned" affirmation, moreover, frees the dynamism of "Insight as Activity" to become the ex-planatory structure of "Insight as Knowledge." For the latter's formulation of such central philosophical notions as being, ob-jectivity, metaphysics, dialectic and transcendence are, for Lonergan, explanatory explicitations and developments of that prior discovery of one's intelligence and reasonableness as intelligent and reasonable. They cannot and are not intended to serve as logical conclusions from prior premises; they are rather the further explicitations required by the further relevant questions of the "moving viewpoint" of the intelligent and reasonable inquirer.

A more detailed investigation of *Insight*'s procedure, structure and conclusions will be the concern of the following chapters. At present, however, it would be well to recall the urgent need for a correct point of departure in one's investigation of *Insight*. And perhaps the clearest indication of that point of departure would be to return to the discussion of the ambiguity of the word "presence" described in our first chapter and now capable of more accurate description in the wider context of this chapter.[14] There is, then, a first, merely material presence as when I say that the desk on which I write is present in this room. I do not say (if I care to speak correctly) that the desk is present to the room or the room to the desk. For I cannot claim for either room or desk what not even the most ardent Teilhardian would claim for them. In short, I do not claim consciousness for them. At a second level, I can also speak of a dog's "presence" to me and I to him. But this second level of "presence" (technically expressed, a merely empirical presence) is also quite limited: it reveals an experienced but not necessarily intelligent consciousness. However, from the moment of such empirical consciousness on (i.e. from the dream-state on) a peculiar type of self-presence reveals itself: I could not be present to the dog nor the dog to me unless a prior, originating and grounding presence to self were first present. And precisely that peculiar act of presence-to-self as it structures itself through the empirical, intelligent, rational and existential levels of human self-consciousness is *alone* of interest for the kind of self-

14. For one of the clearest and shortest expressions of this, cf. "Cognitional Structure," *Collection*, pp. 221–39; also "Consciousness and the Trinity" (unpublished lecture delivered at North American College; Rome, Fall, 1963).

appropriation at issue here. For, in Lonergan's method of introspection, one is not trying to "move within" to capture some sudden, illuminating, confrontational and apparently spatial "look" at the self-being-conscious-to-the-self. In fact, even if such a fictitious introspective look were possible (and as the Augustinian-Thomist dispute outlined in chapter three argued, it is not) it would still be quite beside the point of Lonerganian self-appropriation. For what is important here is not the "looked-at" but the "looker," more accurately, the inquirer: the inquirer, moreover, as empirically conscious (awake), intelligently conscious (alert), rationally conscious (alive to the need for verification of even the brightest of his bright ideas) and existentially conscious (moral).

By way of conclusion to this contextual introduction to *Insight,* an often-voiced complaint should be raised and, as far as possible, answered. The complaint ordinarily takes a form somewhat like the following: if Lonergan's real aim is with the subject's presence-to-self, then why does he force his readers (especially his theological readers) to struggle through such a disconcerting number of examples drawn from those highly "objective" disciplines, mathematics and empirical science? The reply by now is, I trust, clear: because a close and careful absorption in the clearest and most rigorous objects of intelligent inquiry (viz. mathematics and science) will securely keep the introspecting subject from the temptation of seeking some kind of mysterious (if not magical) "look" at himself rather than engaging in the more difficult and seemingly more indirect method of bringing to the level of thematization the actual performance, structures and norms of his intelligent and rational self-consciousness. Nor can the theologian safely avoid this seemingly extrinsic enterprise. For he too, as a theoretician, seeks an unknown which he ever more adequately if never fully adequately seeks to make known. And unless he chooses to withdraw from the demands of his intentionally "examined," i.e. theoretic life by escaping into some personal religious vision innocent of its historical tradition and unencumbered by a contemporary scientific exigence, then he could do worse than take the necessary time out to study the nature of the scientific ideals employed in the history of his science (e.g. in Aquinas), the significance of the development from the Aristotelian to the contemporary scientific ideal, the critiques of Kant and Hegel on the possibility of science, philosophy and theology and the critique of *Insight* on the possibility of a self-affirmation which can provide a secure and personally verifiable guide to all methodical and scientific activity.

5. INSIGHT: ITS STRUCTURE AND ITS HORIZON DEVELOPMENT

After our prior examination of the context and intention of *Insight,* it would be well to express some of its more important contents.[1] Perhaps the best expression of its structure is Lonergan's own, viz. that the entire work is written from a moving viewpoint: each context is set up only to reveal by the very dynamism of the questions that it raises but cannot answer the need for a "higher viewpoint." Thus the entire movement of *Insight* itself is the development of context leading to context until all contexts lead to a deeper, structured and, at its final stage, self-affirmed recognition of the unrestricted desire to know as *the* moving viewpoint behind and grounding all explicit scientific, philosophic and theological ideals. With those basic procedural factors in mind, therefore, this chapter will merely attempt to expose some of the central features of the "moving viewpoint" of *Insight.* The chapter, moreover, is designed to facilitate entry into the already tightly constructed argument of *Insight* itself and not to supplant it.

1. The clearest expression of these concerns remains the Preface (pp. ix–xv) to the work. In this, as in all other cases not directly concerned with the problem of method but of indirect importance for the problem, the analysis presented here will adhere to the text of *Insight* but in a brief, i.e. non-expansive fashion. Other more directly methodical sections will receive more extended treatment. This is not to argue that the structure of *Insight* itself is such but that the interpretative point of view of this treatment (viz. the theological) requires such emphasis. The footnotes will indicate the sections treated, except where a quotation demands an exact reference.

A. THE HORIZON OF SCIENTIFIC METHOD
(CHAPTERS 1–5)

The first chapter ("Elements") intends to provide a ready entry into the phenomenon of insight by expressing some of its most basic characteristics. In the first place, there are what might be named the "universal" features of all insights revealed in the dramatic instance of Archimedes.[2] For in the perhaps apocryphal but surely graphic example of the shouting, naked, thrilled old man running from the baths in Syracuse to the mere pedestrian experiences of any of us "catching onto" some particular point, anyone can understand certain features of all insights: Insights come, often suddenly and unexpectedly, as a release to the tension of inquiry, insights pivot between the concrete (viz. the particular piece of metal in the waters of the path) and the abstract (viz. only those factors revelant to Archimedes question); insights pass, finally, into the habitual texture of one's mind.

The second principal movement of inquiry is equally universal: the drive to express the insight exactly, technically—as in Socrates' search for universal definitions, or as in Archimedes' formulation of his insight into the law for floating bodies, or as in the exact definition of the circle referred to in the *Verbum* discussion.[3] Such examples, in their turn, mediate an understanding of still further features of all insights and definitions: the need for an image to allow the insight (the cartwheel for the circle; the block of metal and the water for the Archimedean law); the need for a rigorous commitment to genuine inquiry (that wonder at the beginning of all science and philosophy); the need and ability to formulate the question correctly (e.g. "What is justice?" becomes not "What particular acts are those of a just man?" but "What definition may apply to all cases of

2. *Insight,* pp. 3–6.
3. *Ibid.,* pp. 7–13; cf. also David B. Burrell (ed.), *Verbum: Word and Idea in Aquinas* (Notre Dame, 1967), *passim,* esp. pp. 42–43, 37–38, 22–23, 24–25, 82–83.

justice and only to cases of justice?"); the need for a fully disciplined inquiry in order to arrive at exact formulations; the need, finally, to be sure that the concept is the self-expression of the insight itself and not merely of the image or words (e.g. the need to distinguish between parrotting words defined by another and *defining* on one's own).[4]

Thirdly, insights do not remain merely in isolation. They coalesce into sets of insights and sets of definitions, axioms, postulates. The very dynamism of inquiry, moreover, provokes ever further questions, some of which cannot be handled on the basis of the existing set of insights and theorems. In short, as one moves ever further into the inquiry, an exigence for an ever higher viewpoint begins to emerge.[5] For example, the exigence expressed in arithmetic's inability to handle negative numbers gives rise to the possibility (and eventually actuality) of algebra; the movement from Euclidean to non-Euclidean geometries; the movement from Aristotelian act to Thomist esse; the movement from the Jewish experience of God to the Christian; the movement, even in the political world, from an American age of innocence to an age of radical rethinking and restructuring of political options. One should further note that in the moving viewpoint each lower stage in its final functional moment serves as the image into which the human mind, impelled to further inquiry by the lower stage's inability to solve its ever further questions, reaches up to a higher insight which receives in turn a better definition—set of postulates, axioms, etc.[6] Nor is this process true only in the general dialectic of human development, for it is also true in as abstract a discipline as mathematics: "To each stage (in mathematics) there corresponds a symbolic image of doing arithmetic, doing algebra, doing calculus. In each successive image there is the potentiality of grasping by *insight* the need and possibility for a *higher set* of rules that will gov-

4. *Insight,* p. 9.
5. *Ibid.,* pp. 13–19.
6. *Ibid.,* p. 15.

106

ern the operations and by them elicit the numbers and symbols of the next stage."[7]

Fourthly, besides the direct insights discussed thus far there exists the peculiar and important type of insight called "inverse."[8] For all direct insights provide an act of understanding into an expected intelligibility while all inverse insights perform in just the reverse way: they allow an act of understanding that (on this question at least) there is *nothing to be understood*. But that an inverse insight is *not* an oversight cannot be overemphasized (especially in theological work). It does not flee from understanding and plead ignorance but rather (ordinarily in the context of a series of direct insights) it understands precisely where there is not intelligibility to be found on this question. In the history of science, moreover, the key horizon-shifts-movements often occur as inverse, not direct insights. For example, Newton's insight into the lack of intelligibility of motion classically understood freed science from its former improper questions on motion and impelled it to deal with the legitimate and fruitful questions of acceleration. In the history of theology, a similar inverse insight phenomenon has often occurred: for example, Aquinas developed a series of direct insights (e.g. on operation, instrumentality, law of psychological continuity, distinction of natural and supernatural orders) in order to allow the key inverse insight into the excess of intelligibility involved in the issue of freedom and providence, which inverse insight becomes precisely formulated as a theorem of divine transcendence.[9]

The final "element" of *Insight* to be considered here is Lonergan's peculiar notion of an "empirical residue,"[10] i.e. what is always left behind in all cases of genuine abstraction: the particular instances, the interference of different laws, the space-

7. *Ibid.,* p. 17.
8. *Ibid.,* pp. 19–25; for the theological discussion of this factor, cf. *De Deo Trino I* (Rome, 1964), pp. 274–75.
9. Cf. *Gratia Operans.*
10. *Insight,* pp. 25–32.

107

time continuum. In short, the empirical residue refers to that purely experiential reality which may be described as referring to real differences but only to differences that are purely "matter of fact" (e.g. particular times and particular places). Such differences, then, cannot yield an explanatory insight for they simply are not "insight-ful" realities. More technically, the empirical residue consists in positive empirical data that is to be denied any immanent intelligibility of its own but is ordinarily connected with some compensating higher intelligibility of great importance (hence its interest to science).[11] If Galileo in his law for falling bodies, for example, had foolishly tried to explain the particular time and particular place of his own performance as an intrinsic part of that law, then Galileo himself and every scientist since would have to have spent the rest of his life continuing ever new experiments for every new particular time and particular place. In other words, the two great corollaries of the scientific enterprise (viz. the possibility of scientific collaboration and of scientific generalization)[12] rest upon the human intellect's ability to abstract from the empirical residue. The further importance of this notion in the context of our present discussion is twofold. First, it immediately clarifies the distinction between the first and second levels of human cognition (experience and understanding) by locating the key differentiation involved: the presence of the abstracting, unifying-universalizing act of intelligence (insight) on the second level of *understanding* and the absence and indeed impossibility of insight on the first level of empirically residual data (*experience*). Second, the discussion of the empirical residue allows for the almost unobtrusive entry of the key notion of abstraction. There is, then, in all data an empirical residue from which intelligence always abstracts. Since abstraction is so often misunderstood as removing one from the "richness" of "concrete living" (itself an abstraction) rather than as an enrichment of that living by means of the specifically human activity of intelligence, it would be wise

11. *Ibid.*, p. 25.
12. *Ibid.*, pp. 27–28.

to signalize the real meaning of abstraction in Lonergan's own concise terms:

So far from being a mere impoverishment of the data of sense, abstraction in all its essential moments is enriching. Its first moment is an enriching anticipation of an intelligibility to be added to sensible presentations; there is something to be known by insight. Its second moment is the erection of heuristic structures and the attainment of insight to reveal in the data what is variously named as the significant, the relevant, the important, the essential, the idea, the form. Its third moment is the formulation of the intelligibility that insight has revealed. Only in this third moment does there appear the negative aspect of abstraction, namely, the omission of the insignificant, the irrelevant, the negligible, the incidental, the merely empirical residue. Moreover, this omission is neither absolute nor definitive. For the empirical residue possesses the universal property of being what intelligence abstracts from. Such a universal property provides the basis for a second set of heuristic procedures that take their stand on the simple premise that the non-systematic cannot be systematized.[13]

In summary, then, the first chapter ("Elements"), by means of a careful use of mathematical examples, is able to express some of the key features of human insights (experience–direct and inverse understanding–concept–higher viewpoint), and to define them with exactitude as "elements" of insight (insight, definition, higher viewpoint, inverse insight, empirical residue). In the second chapter, the "moving viewpoint" is again enlarged: for if the use of mathematics in the first chapter allowed one to examine the "elements" of insight in a necessarily somewhat static fashion, the use of empirical scientific method (by its very nature as "conspicuously and methodically" dynamic[14]) allows the reader to explicitate the intrinsic dynamism of all human inquiry. The movement this time, then, is not so much forward

13. *Ibid.,* pp. 30–31, cf. also *Verbum, passim,* esp. 156–57, 164–65, 179. For other, more strictly Thomist aspects of the problem of abstraction, cf. the index of *Verbum* under "abstraction," pp. 221–22.
14. *Ibid.,* pp. 88–89.

to yet higher viewpoints. It is, rather, a movement under and behind all scientific questions and methods in order to discover and explicitate the dynamism of all human questioning as fundamentally a *heuristic* enterprise.

But the problem peculiar to the scientist should not be misunderstood: he pins his faith not on any present system or set of axioms but rather on the scientific method itself. His problem is clear: how can he justify that method? If method be an ordering of means towards some end, how can the means be ordered to an end which is not yet known? The answer (as has already been indicated) is not too hard to find: it is the scientist's ability to develop heuristic methods which do not alter but specify the heuristic nature of intellect itself.[15] Galileo, for example, serves as a classic concretization of this heuristic feature of all human inquiry. In his very performance (if not in his explanation of that performance) his operations might be listed as follows: he named the unknown he sought (the mathematizable and empirically verifiable nature of a free fall); he worked out the properties needed to understand that nature (viz. distance and time); he next used these properties to direct, order and guide a series of experiments that eventually provided the correct mathematical explanation (d^2t);[16] he then formulated that explanation (the nature of a free fall was a constant acceleration) in a way that was independent of the primitive nature of his experiments (precisely as abstract and explanatory); that explanation, in fact, has survived not as a mere historical curiosity but has received constant if indirect verification from every later scientist's assumption of Galileo's formula. But the point of the example is not to praise Galileo but to indicate a more general human phenomenon. For the basic reason why Galileo was able to achieve his final formulation was not some peculiarity of his genius but rather his performative fidelity to the fundamental

15. *Ibid.,* p. 33.
16. Actually applicable in certain special cases; Galileo's formula probably was: distance traversed proportionate to time squared. The general formula d^2s/dt^2 demanded the later discovery of calculus.

heuristic nature of human intellect. Indeed, even in pre-scientific thought, all inquiry is heuristic.[17] It is true, of course, that the "unknown" non-scientifically anticipated is rather globally envisioned as the "nature of" a particular object. But that lack of contemporary scientific exactitude is due not to some lack of dynamic inquiry but rather to a pre-scientific (i.e. pre-Greek) inability to move beyond constructing descriptive classifications based on sensible similarity.[18] In recent theological discussion, for example, the significant differences between Greek and Hebrew (or Western and Eastern) thought patterns have too often led some rather free-wheeling speculators to suggest, in effect, that one is dealing with two altogether different types of human beings. But one is not. For however significant the differentiation made possible by the Greek breakthrough to logos, this does not rule out the possibility of genuine if descriptive inquiry in other cultures. On the other hand, it is true that the scientific differentiation of a methodical, consciously heuristic and abstractive inquiry (*theoria*) remains the Greek culture's legacy of enrichment to all human experience (including religious). For in all strictly theoretical work (including theoretical accounts of religious experience) there is a far more exact and exacting anticipation of the "unknown." In empirical science, for example, there is the heuristic anticipation of some unspecified correlation to be specified or some indeterminate function to be determined. Hence the scientific need for measurement, for reaching an insight into the tabulated measurements and for the conceptualization and definition of that insight through some general correlation or function which, once verified, may exactly define the limit upon which converge all subsequent appropriate measurements.[19] And the theologian who fails to understand

17. *Ibid.*, p. 44.
18. These are later developments: for description-explanation, cf. *Insight*, esp. pp. 277, 291–92, 295–96, 345, 415, 436, 504–05, 538–39, 546–47; for the distinction *"quoad nos-quoad se"* cf. *De Deo Trino* (Rome, 1964), esp. I, pp. 37–113; II, pp. 7–61; also *De Methodo Theologiae*, pp. 10–11.
19. *Insight*, p. 44.

THE ACHIEVEMENT OF BERNARD LONERGAN

this key differentiation between descriptive (*quoad nos*) and explanatory (*quoad se*) heuristic methods, simply cannot include within his horizon the theoretical enterprise called speculative theology. Moreover, he simply cannot understand the basically enriching character of the entry of the Hellenistic (or, for that matter, the Hegelian) horizon into the Christian community's heuristic understanding of its experience. Indeed, if the seemingly extrinsic cognitional factors considered here are overlooked, that oversight will deprive the theologian of the ability to understand the possibility, in fact, the legitimacy of the development of Christian thought from the *quoad nos* of the Scriptures to the *quoad se* of the conciliar, patristic, medieval, modern or contemporary periods. Finally, an inability to come to terms with the fundamentally heuristic character of all human inquiry may well foreclose the theologian's possibility of understanding the rise of the successive heuristic exigencies (systematic–critical–methodological) which have become differentiated throughout the long and arduous history of Christian theology.

To return, however, from the theological consequences of *Insight*'s present argument to the concerns more intrinsic to the work itself, one should briefly consider the further differentiation of scientific methods examined in the next step of the moving viewpoint of *Insight*, viz. the differentiation of classical and statistical heuristic structures.[20] Perhaps the easiest way to express that differentiation is to recall the already discussed distinction between direct and inverse insights. For in a directly parallel fashion to that distinction between insights, one can speak of two distinct heuristic anticipations of insights.

In the first place, all empirical method is a selection of the possible explanatory system (sets of insights, theorems, higher viewpoints) that fits the data of any specific region or field. Both the actual historical development of empirical science and the

20. The discussion of classical and statistical heuristic structures is, of course, central to this and the next three chapters of *Insight;* for an introduction to the distinction, however, cf. *ibid.,* pp. 46–49; for an important application of this distinction, cf. Philip McShane, "*Insight* and the Strategy of Biology," *Spirit as Inquiry,* esp. pp. 377–83.

intrinsic possibilities of all intellectual operation suggest that at best two empirical methods must serve to provide the necessary explicitation of the explanatory, heuristic operation of intellect in the domain-field-region proper to empirical science. Briefly, then, the classical empirical method (Newton-Einstein) represents the explicitation of an intelligent anticipation of the systematic and abstract upon which the concrete converges. On the other hand, the statistical empirical method (e.g. probability theory, quantum physics) is a more involved if less developed and much disputed method. It provides an intelligent anticipation of the systematic and abstract as it sets a boundary or norm from which the concrete cannot systematically diverge.[21]

B. THE HORIZON OF COMMON SENSE
(CHAPTERS 6–7)

These two basic scientific methods, therefore, allow the intelligent inquirer to move past all descriptive speech which seeks either some general "nature of" or "state of" a phenomenon, to exact explanatory language and method which seeks to determine either the unspecified function to be specified (classical) or the probability to be statistically determined (statistical) method. Since the interest of this work is theological, however, the three remaining chapters on empirical scientific method (its canons, its dual complementarity, and its specificity in the problem of space and time) will not receive explicitation here. For if, in fact, this brief and summary discussion of the key categories employed by *Insight* in its early chapters has communicated to the reader only the need for the strictly scientific differentiation in all study (i.e. including religious), then the theological repercussions of that insight will already have cast a

21. *Ibid.*, p. 103; the extensive treatment of *Insight* of these heuristic structures for the empirical sciences has been curtailed here as not directly concerned with the problematic of this book.

22. *Ibid.*, pp. 173–242, i.e. chapters 6 and 7.

sufficiently clarifying (and sometimes devastating) light on much of contemporary theological discussion.

However, this insistence upon a strictly scientific approach to the question of the nature, function and structure of intellect is not intended to depreciate any genuinely intelligent activity on the common sense level. In fact, as the two chapters on "common sense" rather amply indicate, Lonergan's exposition of the nature of scientific inquiry should not hinder but enhance an exposition of the nature of the intelligent use of common sense. For, as I trust I may be excused for repeating, the study of intellect in *Insight* is intended to be a study not merely of scientific but of all intelligent inquiry. And even if the example of mathematics and empirical science provide the clearest indication of insight's "elements" and its fundamentally heuristic nature, still the examples of "common sense" provide a further (if relatively undifferentiated) expression of those same factors.

In short, even if "insights" may best be examined in a scientific context, they are by no means restricted to one. On the contrary, they occur often and sometimes even effortlessly for any man who possesses what is ordinarily named "common sense." But although common sense uses the same intelligence as scientific reasoning, it would still be erroneous to assume that this common use did not allow for important methodological differences between the two.[23] In respect to the object of inquiry, for example, common sense is concerned wholly with the concrete and particular whereas science is concerned wholly with the real world as universal and abstract. Moreover, where common sense is concerned exclusively with the properties of concrete and particular objects, in terms of their relationship not to one another but to the inquirer (to his desires and his fears), science escapes this limitation to examine (in terms of a pure, detached, disinterested inquiry) the intelligible relationships of things among themselves. Yet behind such differences in the

23. *Ibid.*, pp. 173–81; one should further note Lonergan's definition of common sense: "Common sense, unlike the sciences, is a specialization of intelligence in the particular and concrete" (p. 175).

objective pole of these two horizons, lies the still more significant operational (subjective pole) differences. For although common sense may be characterized by an equally active intelligence, still its operations are spontaneous, not methodical, and its canons of operation relatively undifferentiated. Science, on the other hand, is consciously and differentiatedly methodical, for its methods consist in a precise use and explicitation of those characteristics of intelligence needed to reach the universal and the abstract.

However important these differences are, they do not provide an argument for simple separation. For there is the same human mind at work in both approaches, and there results consequently a functional complementarity between common sense and science. In Lonergan's words, "rational choice is not between science and common sense; it is a choice of both, of science to master the universal and of common sense to deal with the particular."[24] Still one must insist that common sense knowledge is not without its ambiguities. For its specifications of its object in terms of its relationship to us means, in effect, that there will result a constant change in the object for every change in the common sense subject.[25] And precisely because of that inherent, constantly changing nature of the common-sense horizon, Lonergan initiates his investigation of the subjective field of common sense by formulating his explanatory notion, the *patterns of experience*.[26] Indeed, some such explanatory notion is necessary in order to deal with the problem peculiar to common sense: for we may correctly describe common-sense operations as merely spontaneous, not methodical but not at the price of reducing that spontaneity to a series of disparate insights and sensations which lack any unifying factor. For there is such a unifying factor: it is the factor variously called conation, interest, attention, purpose, concern.[27] In the popular image of contemporary

24. *Ibid.,* p. 179.
25. *Ibid.,* p. 181.
26. *Ibid.,* pp. 181–82 (general notion of a pattern of experience).
27. *Ibid.,* p. 182.

literature, there exists not a series of atomic conscious moments, but a stream of consciousness. More exactly, there exist "streams." More exactly still, "patterns of experience." Technically expressed, then, any pattern of experience is a set of intelligible relations that link together sequences of sensations, memories, images, conations, emotions, and bodily movements.[28] Such a pattern, in the first place, is a purely biological one: i.e. the sequences converge upon activities like intussusception, reproduction or self-preservation.[29] On a second level, the subject can free himself from such purely biological domination to the self-authenticating joy of the experience for the sake of the experience itself. He may, in other words, find himself (in his play, in his acting, in his coming-to-be his unique self) an artist *malgré lui*. In short, he may discover ever more novel forms of work and action to verify and relate the acts and contents of what is named his *aesthetic* pattern of experience.[30] Yet once again (as in the earlier sections on science and mathematics), he may be impelled to move past even the richest products of his imagination in order to operate with the calm, detachment, disinterestedness, and purity proper to a third level, a purely intellectual pattern of experience.[31] He may then achieve the detached viewpoint of the authentic theoretical inquirer and study things in their relationships not to himself, not even his artistic self, but to one another.

Yet not even a Newton lives exclusively in the intellectual

28. *Ibid.*, p. 183.
29. *Ibid.*, pp. 182–84.
30. *Ibid.*, pp. 184–85.
31. *Ibid.*, pp. 185–86. This notion of an intellectual pattern of experience is extremely important for any interpreter of Lonergan's work. For the fact is that his consciously intellectualist stance demands that the interpreter himself be in the intellectual pattern of experience in order to understand Lonergan correctly (including on the other patterns of experience, all discussed from the point of view of the intellectual pattern). The problem, in short, is an interesting example of the applicability of Lonergan's own principles of interpretation (to be discussed below: for the present, cf. *Insight*, pp. 562–95.) to Lonergan's own work; cf. also F. E. Crowe, "The Exigent Mind: Bernard Lonergan's Intellectualism," *Spirit as Inquiry*, esp. pp. 317, 326–33.

pattern, nor a Picasso exclusively in the aesthetic. For all men live out most of their lives in some blend or mixture of all three patterns. By so living, each man achieves a style of life all his own—even if at its lowest level it be merely a new way of drifting. This self-actuating and at its highest level, purposeful style is called the *dramatic* pattern of experience.[32] That phrase, moreover, is meant to indicate the sometimes hard reality that each man must meet the exigencies of his own biological and psychic drives but must also strive to embrace or transform the concerns and purposes of his tradition, his culture, his epoch. Indeed, as the contemporary "third force" in psychology makes abundantly clear, most men have the resources and the need to consciously structure that self-actualization. Still, we must not become too sanguine: for a closer study of the dramatic pattern reveals not merely developmental possibilities but aberrant ones as well. For as either classical Freudian psychology or more contemporary existential psychoanalysis have documented, there exist in man other darker concerns, other and misleading interests. To employ the descriptive language of Freud, there exists the death instinct. Or, to employ the explanatory language of *Insight*'s analysis of common sense, the dramatic subject also has the possibility of bias, i.e. he may refuse insight,[33] refuse his own drive for intelligence and rationality and thereby consciously or unconsciously live out a life so filled with bias that it is unworthy of a man. Moreover, whether that bias be individual (e.g. the "operator"), group (e.g. the "bourgeoise"), dramatic (e.g. the sexually aberrant), general (e.g. "Don't waste our time with theory, we have work to do"), or more than likely, some painful combination of all four, the results are all too familiar to our post-Freudian age: scotosis, repression, inhibition, aberration, ennui, bigotry, violence. And not only is such a victimized human being unable to move to that level of detachment

32. Cf. *Insight,* pp. 187–89, for the general notion of the dramatic pattern.
33. *Ibid.,* p. 191 ("bias"); 191–92 ("scotosis"); 192–93 ("repression"); 193–94 ("inhibition").

and disinterestedness needed for all genuinely theoretical work, but imperceptibly at first and frighteningly at last even his "common sense" disappears. For gradually he becomes the prisoner of his own ideology, the sick believer of his own propaganda, the creature of a neurotic, mythic, deluded horizon within which he ultimately ends as both "sole actor and chief spectator."[34]

Yet alongside the analysis of the subjective pole of common sense operations (analyzed through the Lonergan's analysis of "pattern of experience" and the "biases"), there remains the need to analyze the objective pole of common sense inquiry. To that end, then, the seventh chapter of *Insight* ("Common Sense as Object") is devoted. The problematic by now should be clear: although it may seem, at first sight, that the objective pole discussion of common sense knowledge is a relatively simple thing (common sense-objects related to us; science-objects related to one another[35]), the realities of the situation are considerably more complex. For the subject (as the analysis on the patterns of experience reveals) is always open to change—in the direction of (at least) refinement of an already established horizon; often of development; sometimes, even, of conversion. Since this is so, his objective-pole worlds of meaning (those concrete and particular realities constituted by his various common sense patterns) will themselves continually change. For such common sense objects cannot achieve (indeed, do not intend) the stability proper to the abstracted objects of scientific thought. Common sense is not interested in the "realities" of abstract thought. In fact, it is not really interested in theoretical thought at all. It stands foursquare with the milkmaid against Thales, or with Dr. Johnson and his rock against the subtleties

34. *Ibid.,* pp. 194–203; this interesting development of Lonergan has possibly important implications for the science of psychology; cf. his references to the work of Stekel (pp. 202–03) and Freud (pp. 203–06); his later developments in his *Lectures on Existentialism,* pp. 3–6 (on Jaspers' use of psychological concepts) and to the "third" force in psychology in his forthcoming book *Method in Theology.*
35. Note that Lonergan's treatment of common sense is not a common sense treatment but "a pure theory of common sense"; *ibid.,* p. 267.

of a Berkeley. The knowledge that common sense seeks is not intended for the sake of pure contemplation for its concern (as with the proverbially pragmatic American), is not interested in the unrestricted desire to know but rather with the desire to make, to act, to perform, and, ultimately, to transform nature and, if possible, man himself.[36] And thus the "worlds" of the common sense man—his economies, his societies, his cultures —change as his intelligent use of common sense develops or retards. Moreover, just as the pre-conscious refusal of insight can result in a dramatic bias that may cause the individual's eventual collapse, so too a society, a culture, indeed an entire epoch may rule out the full, free, and normative sweep of intellectual inquiry only to collapse into a totalitarian or mythic or frivolous horizon. In short, a culture too may fall prey to the most devastating of all the biases[37]—a general bias that does not so much attack intellect as rule it out of court.

Is there not, then, a genuine need for theoretical reflection on the operations of common sense and the worlds of meaning they constitute? Surely the influence of a Marx or a Weber or Freud or a Dilthey is correct in insisting on the need for a scientific approach to human realities. And although the question of Lonergan's own understanding of the problematic of the human or behavioral sciences will receive greater emphasis in his post-*Insight* work, still even here he makes a suggestion of some importance. For, after his examination of the objective and subjective poles of the horizon of common sense, he argues for the necessity of some method that may handle the multifaceted, developmental (genetic) and aberrational (dialectical) possibilities of the common sense horizon. Such a method is called a dialectical one.[38] But this word does not here intend any elabo-

36. *Ibid.,* pp. 207–44.
37. Cf. the "biases" in the dialectic of community: "individual" (pp. 218–22); "group" (pp. 222–25); and especially, "general" (pp. 225–35) and its reversal through "cosmopolis" (pp. 234–42).
38. *Ibid.,* pp. 218–18, 244; this key concept is developed in a more refined and conceptualized way later in this chapter following its later development in *Insight* itself; cf. *ibid.,* pp. 373, 421–23.

rate, post-Hegel-like enterprise. Rather the present meaning of dialectic is the quite simple one referring to the concrete unfolding of linked but opposed principles of change, modified cumulatively by that unfolding. In the particular case at issue here, the opposed principles are sufficiently clear: the purely intellectual element in the field (insights and their patterned development) and the inertial effects and interference of misplaced human sensitivities and human nerves (refusals of insight and their pattern of decline). By the use of that dialectical tool, then, the reader of *Insight* has the occasion to explicitate and, if need be, criticize his own common sense horizon from the viewpoint of his fidelity to intelligence and reasonableness.

C. SUMMARY AND EXPANSION OF THE HORIZON: THINGS (CHAPTER 8)[39]

In summary, the discussion of the horizons of science and of common sense, involves the following central points: First, the elements proper to insight in the intrinsically heuristic nature of all inquiry, as well as the normative procedures (detachment, disinterestedness, unrestrictedness) of strictly explanatory inquiry were explored in the opening chapters' use of mathematics and empirical science. Secondly, an explanatory account of the relationship of the conscious and unconscious in any common sense subject or any aggregate of subjects (societies, cultures, etc.) was investigated in Lonergan's explanatory terms of the presence or refusal of insight and the presence or absence of an intelligent orientation. Thirdly, it is of major importance to recall that, no matter how useful some of *Insight*'s suggestions may prove to be for mathematics or empirical science or any of the human sciences (including theology), those results are not the central concern of *Insight* itself. Rather the entire study up to this point has continued to be an exposition of dynamic and self-structuring nature not of any particular intellectual product

39. *Insight,* pp. 245–71.

but of human intellect itself whose chief manifestation is the self-constitutive nature of human understanding and whose central orientation is the normatively intellectualist one proper to explanatory investigation.[40]

In that context, then, the chapters on common sense, following as they do upon the analysis of the nature of scientific insight, inquiry and conceptualization, provide at once a theory for the subjective pole of common sense (relating the preconscious and conscious in terms of insight or its refusal) and an ordered account of the dialectical development of the objective pole (development-insight vs. aberration-bias). Those chapters likewise provide a clear grasp of the universality of the issues expressed in the first five "scientific" chapters. For it is the unrestricted desire to know which grounds the common, indeed universal nature of both scientific and common sense understanding. It is the presence or absence of insight which provides the key to the development or decline of either scientific or common sense activity. And both methods must next meet a common problem: how does one properly ask and answer the further question of the concrete unity of whatever the reality is that survives the movement from common sense description to scientific explanation? In short, we must face the problem which Lonergan calls "things." If the inquirer into cognitional operations does not, then besides the inauthentic refusal of a legitimate and pressing question, certain disastrous repercussions are sure to follow: the loss of the possibility of intelligently defending the continuity of scientific thought, for example, or the loss of a cognitional foundation for one's philosophical defense of the notion of change and continuity, for another.

On the basis of the previous analysis of the distinction between commonsense and scientific inquiry, therefore, Lonergan is able to elaborate a concomitant distinction between "things" and "bodies."[41] The distinction (perhaps his best known one) is easy enough to grasp if the previous chapters have been un-

40. *Ibid.*, pp. 242–44.
41. *Ibid.*, pp. 247–48.

derstood. A "thing" is the intelligible unity grasped in data as individual (i.e. as understood and expressed within the purely intellectual pattern of experience),[42] a "body," on the other hand, is a sensibly or at best imaginatively charged instance of the unity perceived by the naïve realist. "Body," in brief, is the felt unity of any object of animal extroversion.[43] It is, in Lonergan's oft-used phrase, an "already-out-there-now-real."[44] It is the "real unity" of the real rock kicked by a Dr. Johnson, of the real bone desired by a dog, of the real "church" imagined by aspiring archaists. The argument, however, is not to deny the "reality" of either Dr. Johnson's rock or of the well at the feet of Thales. It is simply meant to express the very different criteria for the "real" by a scientist on the one hand, a man of common sense on the other. For the man of common sense the "real" is, quite frankly, what is "out there"—to be kicked, perhaps, or stumbled over, or imagined but always out there with that security peculiar to the biologically extroverted pattern of experience. For the scientist, on the other hand, the "real" is the intelligently grasped, i.e. in terms of mutual intelligible (congugate) relations, and the rationally verified. The "things" discussed by science (e.g. Eddington's theoretical explanation of the table in terms of its physico-chemical properties) and the "bodies" described by men of common sense (e.g. the "real" seen, felt, imaginable table upon which I am now writing) are both "real," but the criteria for their realities are quite distinct.

Moreover, in the development of the objectification of the known (objective pole)—whose fruits are not the real concern of this study but may at least be indicated here—the discovery and articulation of the notion of the "thing" allows Lonergan to make certain assertions. First, it allows him to defend the continuity of the scientific movement from descriptive "bodies" to explanatory "things." Secondly, it allows him to defend the

42. *Ibid.*, pp. 253–54.
43. *Ibid.*, pp. 250–52.
44. This now famous phrase of Lonergan's has a very exact technical meaning and is not meant rhetorically; cf. the meaning of each term, *ibid.*, p. 251.

122

reality and underlying continuity of the phenomenon of change. Thirdly, it impels him to join that notion to the "world view" of emergent probability articulated in earlier chapters in order to argue for the probability of the eventual emergence of intelligent consciousness.[45] Or, more to our present concern, it argues for the recognition of intelligent consciousness as not merely a "higher viewpoint" to the lower physical, chemical, biological and sensitive conjugates but also (by the very breakthrough of free intelligence and not mere intelligibility) it recognizes the emergence of intelligent and rational consciousness as itself the source of ever higher viewpoints (societies, cultures, sciences, religions, etc.).[46]

D. FURTHER HORIZON EXPANSION OF THE "MOVING VIEWPOINT": THE NATURE OF REFLECTIVE CONSCIOUSNESS AND OF JUDGMENT (CHAPTERS 9–10)

Therefore, in the analysis of the heuristic structure of intellect, all the questions raised (scientific and common sense) might be characterized (in Aristotle's terms) as *quid sit?* What is it? questions. The inquirer seeks, in short, to know "the nature of" or the "state of" the object under inquiry. Is it clear? Is it distinct? Is it coherent with the insights and theorems already known? In the earlier part of *Insight* Lonergan has (to use Husserl's language) "bracketed" the question of the actual existence of the objects under study. But the other kind of second-level questions—*An sit?* Is it true?—can only be bracketed temporarily for the very exigence of the pure desire to know demands that the intelligent inquirer asks of even the brightest of his bright ideas, of even the most coherent and logically satisfying

45. *Ibid.*, pp. 259–62.
46. *Ibid.*, pp. 265–67. Note the importance of this distinction for the later, more properly contemporary discussion of the *Geisteswissenschaften* problematic.

of his best theorems, the inevitable question—is it true? And that question elevates the level of questioning to a new and differentiated level: the level not merely of intelligence but, in Lonergan's phrase, of reflection.[47] Furthermore, such reflective questions demand for their self-expression, not the concepts and theorems proper to the level of intelligent consciousness but the judgment-expression proper to the level of reflective consciousness.[48] The next two chapters of *Insight* attempt to articulate the nature of that level. In Lonergan's view, just as the analysis of the insights of direct understanding yields an explanatory account of the method and results of the sciences and of common sense, so too an analysis of critical inquiry and its self expression in judgment may provide the cognitional factors needed to answer the further questions set by the Kantian problematic.[49]

For, to recall a central and often overlooked factor in Lonergan's argument, the analysis of the dynamism of human questioning reveals three differentiated, functionally interdependent and indeed self-structuring levels of inquiry. The questions for intelligence (what? why? how often?) provoke insights and concepts on the level of understanding. But the questions for reflection (is it so? is it verified? is it true?) provoke the further and quite district type of reflective insights and judgments. Moreover, the emphasis Lonergan gives to this level as the *only* level upon which the critical problem may be properly raised and answered can scarcely be exaggerated.[50] For it is on this

47. *Ibid.*, pp. 269–70. Note also the transitional note on method (p. 270): ". . . just as an account of insight is an account of method and so an account of what method cannot but yield at the term of inquiry, so also an account of critical reflection and the possibility of judgment will reveal unavoidable judgments."

48. *Ibid.*, p. 271.

49. This latter principle will be demonstrated most clearly in the chapter to follow (Chapter 9: "Self-Affirmation of the Knower") as the "breakthrough" to a critical metaphysics; cf. also *Verbum*, esp. pp. 66–67, 82–83, 140, 193; 47–48, 65–66, 140, 194; as well as David B. Burrell, "Analogy and Judgment," *Spirit as Inquiry*, pp. 434–47.

50. *Insight*, p. 272.

third level alone that there emerge the notions of truth and falsity, of certitude and probability, of yes or no. On this third level alone there arises the personal commitment that makes one responsible for one's judgments: for on this third level there appear the utterances that express one's affirmations or denials, one's assents or dissents, one's agreements or disagreements.

As a propaedeutic to the discussion of this level, therefore, it may prove helpful to provide a schema for the three, self-structuring and functionally interrelated levels of the cognitional process.[51]

1st Level: Data: Perceptual Images–Free Images–Utterances as expression

2nd Level: Questions for Intelligence: Insights–Formulations (concepts or image-symbols as expression)

3rd Level: Questions for Reflection: Reflective Insights–Judgments (truth as expression)

In short, the questions for intelligence presuppose something to be understood—the first level of data. Then intelligence questions and, after sufficient labor, grasps in its given or imagined presentations an intelligible form that is emergent in the presentations themselves. Conceptualization next formulates this insight. Finally, the question for reflection asks whether or not the understanding and formulation are correct. Judgment answers that they are or are not.

Two factors, above all, should be signalized in the entire process: the role of the question[52] and the meaning of the three levels.[53] In regard to the first factor (the role of the question) note that it is not a conceptualization. Rather the question rep-

51. *Ibid.*, p. 274.

52. This clarification owes more to Lonergan's later articulation in "Metaphysics as Horizon," *Collection*, pp. 202–21, esp. pp. 204–06.

53. This clarification is to be found in *Insight* itself, but may also be found, in more summary and clear fashion, in the article "Cognitional Structure," *Collection*, pp. 221–40.

resents the pure activity of inquiring intelligence striving to achieve the transition from the first to the second level and the pure activity of critical intelligence in moving from the second to the third level. (When a dog has nothing to do, he falls asleep; when a man has nothing to do he, sometimes at least, asks questions.) This interest in the nature of the questioning process itself, therefore, is critical, for it is the pure activity of questioning that most adequately reveals the dynamism of intelligence and rationality. For every authentic question involves a heuristic anticipation of an unknown (the questionable) that is in some way already known (as questioned). The schema, then, does not represent any easy recipe or series of automatic steps to judgment. Rather it represents an explicitation of the actual questioning and answering activity of the intelligent and rational inquirer as he moves forward to ever further questions. For it is that questioning activity itself which provides the "upper blade" of all intelligent (especially methodical) inquiry.[54]

The second factor (the meaning of the three levels) also bears expanded treatment: For, at the heart of Lonergan's analysis, is an insistence upon the qualitative difference of each level which does not allow any level to be reduced to the one below it. The qualitative distinction between insight and experience or between reflective insight and direct allows for the direct inclusion of the category "ever higher viewpoint" into the moving viewpoint which is intellect. Hence Lonergan argues that each level "presupposes and complements" the next through the self-structuring dynamism of intelligent and rational consciousness.[55] Finally, the core of Lonergan's attack upon all

54. It is imperative to recall this critical structure for a proper understanding of Lonergan's most important contribution to theological method (the notion of "functional specialization"), to be treated in Chapter 10 of this book.

55. It is important to emphasize this: for precisely his analysis of judgment as differentiated frees Lonergan from the charge of Kantianism (cf. *Insight*, pp. 339–42) or relativism (*Ibid.*, pp. 342–47). A single German word, *"Aufhebung,"* expresses this central factor more succinctly. The origin of the phrase is, of course, Hegel's. For Lonergan's

reductionism (either the obvious positivistic type or the idealistic reduction of the level of reflective consciousness to the level of intelligent consciousness) lies in his carefully explicitated treatment of the nature, structure and norms for all human cognitional activity.

But, if the third level is distinct in a way not realized by either the Kantian or Hegelian critiques, then it is necessary for Lonergan to specify that difference as exactly as possible. For the question recurs: what is it that reflective consciousness grasps in a way parallel to but distinct from the grasp of the unity or system of ideal frequency of direct understanding? Is it not, as Newman suggests at great and laborious lengths in his *A Grammar of Assent*,[56] that the evidence, as best we can determine it, *is* sufficient for stating 'this is (probably or certainty) true.[57] But the question can recur again: how much evidence is sufficient? Granted that the process of reflection is a far more involved and delicate operation than the process of understanding, still an appeal to Pascal's *esprit de finesse* on Newman's *illative sense* or Thomist reflection as reduction to first principles may pinpoint the act but it does not adequately explicitate it. In short, the Thomist *reductio* uses language too immediately metaphysical and the Newmanian or Pascalian positions language too intrinsically descriptive to be of any lasting value for raising and answering the critical problem. For what is needed

---

distinction from the Hegelian *Aufhebungen,* cf. *Insight,* p. 374: "As his *Aufhebung* both rejects and retains, so also in their own fashion do our higher viewpoints. As he repeatedly proceeds from an *an sich,* through *für sich,* to *an und für sich,* so our whole argument is a movement from the objects of mathematical, scientific and common-sense understanding, through the acts of understanding themselves, to an understanding of understanding." For Lonergan's negative critique of Hegel, cf. *Insight,* pp. 372–74. It is to be noted that Lonergan regularly uses the two English words "presuppose" and "complement" rather than the single German word *Aufhebung,* e.g., in this context, pp. 274–76.

56. *Ibid.,* p. 279. It might be noted that here the oft-noted influence of Newman's analysis in the *Grammar of Assent* seems especially prominent. For that influence, cf. F. E. Crowe, "The Exigent Mind," *Spirit as Inquiry,* p. 320.

57. For this important distinction, cf. *Insight,* pp. 297–304.

(in the categories of *Insight*) is an explicit movement from the metaphysical language of the Thomist position or the descriptive language of the pre-Kantian Newmanian position to a critically explanatory thematization. In his own attempt at such explicitation, Lonergan develops what many commentators consider his most important and original technical innovation, viz. judgment as a virtually unconditioned.

Accordingly, in the short section, "The General Form of Reflective Insight,"[58] lies much of the strength of the entire argument of *Insight*. In Lonergan's terms, the grasp of the sufficiency of evidence for a prospective judgment is a grasp of that judgment as a virtually unconditioned. The meaning of each phrase is critical. "Virtually," first of all, refers to the fact that there are conditions for the judgment but such that the conditions are fulfilled. In short, the inquirer is not dealing with a "formally" unconditioned (i.e. a judgment which has no conditions at all), but with a "virtually unconditioned," which involves three principal elements:

(1) a conditioned,

(2) a link between the conditions and the conditioned, and,

(3) the fulfillment of the conditions.[59]

Hence, any prospective judgment (e.g. Am I understanding this argument?) will be a virtually unconditioned (and thereby a grasp of the evidence as sufficient) if:

(1) it is conditioned—but the very fact of the actuality of *question for reflection* (Am I understanding?) shows that it is conditioned. For the posing of the question itself indicates a conscious recognition of the need for evidence that will insure a *reasonable* pronouncement.[60]

(2) the conditions are known and (3) they are fulfilled (e.g. Am I alert at present? Have I understood the context and meaning of the question? Am I detached, disinterested, pure in my inquiry? Am I asking the question in the intellectual pattern

58. *Ibid.*, pp. 280–81.
59. *Ibid.*
60. *Ibid.*

of experience? Do I realize the meaning of the word "virtually"? Am I seeking a matter of fact judgment or an absolutely necessary one? etc.) In short, do I realize that the very meaning of reflective insight is the power of my own rationality to make precisely that move?[61] The reflective experience (which may provide the link) is common enough to any inquirer as it merely refers to the actual everyday performance of any man whether while driving (e.g. Is that other car far enough ahead to avoid crashing?) or conversing (Why are you voting for X?) or verifying scientific theories (How and how far does the Michelson-Morley experiment verify relativity theory?) or philosophy (Why do you reject Ontologism?) Indeed, Lonergan's explicitation of this universal reflective process as the movement of a prospective judgment from a conditioned to a virtually unconditioned by means of a grasp of the (usually) myriad conditions of the conditioned and their fulfillment is meant to be not some *deus ex machina* (illumination, intuition, vision) to save the epistemological day, but rather a relatively simple explanation (explicitation) of the matter-of-fact (*not absolutely* necessary) behavior of all rational activity. In other words, if the critical inquirer grasps that the question for reflection actually constitutes the conditions, then he may further grasp that behind, within and grounding the "link" (the fulfillment of the known myriad conditions of every case for reflection) is *the condition* of all rational behavior: that rational and structured exigence immanent and operative in all cognitional process—an exigence which always demands a sufficiency of evidence and is satisfied with nothing less. It is, then, the immanent cognitional structure itself, set into operation by the reflective question and finding fulfillment only in a reflective act of understanding, which allows, indeed impels the critical inquirer to make the judgment *it is* (or *it probably is*) or it is *not* (or it probably is *not*). Consequently, adequate reflection upon reflective consciousness demands an explicitation of that matter-of-fact process, i.e. it demands the questioning and mediation of the rational norms,

61. *Ibid.,* p. 281.

structures, and grounds of all reflective activity. Such an attempt is Lonergan's own when he argues that the best explanatory explicitation of the nature of rational activity is his explanation of every judgment as a virtually unconditioned. Hence, that technical innovation rises or falls upon its ability to communicate the actual performance of reflective thought. For that reason, then, one may turn to certain types of judgment[62] to see if each may be said to fulfill the conditions needed for reaching the virtually unconditioned judgment that Lonergan's analysis of judgment as a virtually unconditioned is true. In every case, moreover, the basic link operative will continue to be the subject's own consciousness of the nature of his rationality. For no more than anyone can stare at "$e = mc^2$" and understand it, as Einstein understood it, can anyone stare at (or use) "judgment is a virtually unconditioned" (or as is more likely, "Lonergan says that judgment is a virtually unconditioned"), without going through the personal labor of critically appropriating that statement. Indeed, as Newman reminds us, in philosophy, egotism alone is true modesty. Indeed, Lonergan's notion of judgment as a "virtually unconditioned" is not to be understood as some clever attempt to save the day for realism but is rather a more modest and more reasonable enterprise: it strives to bring to thermatic self-expression what rationality actually is.

Five types of judgments may now serve to clarify this crucial matter.

First, in formal inference the *link* is provided by the hypothetical premise, if the antecedent, then the consequent (If A, then B). The fulfillment is the minor premise itself (but B).

Secondly, in judgments of fact (e.g. Is it snowing out?) the link is the correct insight or set of insights (e.g. I remember what rain is like as distinct from snow, hail, etc.). The fulfillment is the present and/or remembered data (e.g. step out, one

62. To cite them: "concrete judgments of fact" (pp. 381–83); "insights into concrete situations" (pp. 283–87); "common sense judgments" (pp. 289–99); "probable judgments" (pp. 299–304); "analytical propositions and principles" (pp. 304–09); "mathematical judgments" (pp. 309–15).

becomes wet from what is ordinarily called rain, not snow).

Thirdly, in judgments on the correctness of insights the *link* is that the insight is correct if there are no further, pertinent questions (e.g. Am I sure I know what snow is? Is this an illusion? Is it natural snow or is it man-made? etc.). The fulfillment lies *not* in deduction but, quite reasonably, in the self-correcting process of learning itself reaching its limit in familiarity and mastery (in short, *the* link is human rationality itself).

Fourthly, in generalizations (e.g. All correct analysis of judgment must make the distinction between the second and third level of the cognitional process) and analogies (e.g. Lonergan's position on judgment is analogous to that of Peirce) the link is the cognitional law that similars are similarly understood and the fulfillment lies in a grasp of such similarity (i.e. an understanding of Lonergan and Peirce in their general and specific positions on judgment).[63] That grasp realizes that further, pertinent questions are answered not only in the correctly understood particular case but in the generalized or analogous one as well. It is worth noting here that the key theological task of analogy-construction cannot be resolved by any *deus ex machina* theory of analogy (logical or otherwise) but only by the grounding of metaphysical (e.g. nature, person) and cognitional analogies (e.g. intelligible emanations) by carefully determined and rationally controlled cognitional fact.

Fifthly, in *probable* judgments (so important for all the sciences, including theology), the link remains the same: insights are correct when there are no further pertinent questions. The fulfillment, however, is quite different—for the reflective grasp here is that, although the self-correcting process of learning has not yet reached its limit, still it is headed towards it in a critically approximate fashion which allows one to affirm it as truly probable (e.g. Einstein's relativity theorem is more truly probable an explanation of the phenomenon of gravitation than Newton's system, or, Moltmann's interpretation of the Chris-

63. Cf. David B. Burrell, "C. S. Peirce: Pragmatism as a Theory of Judgment," *International Philosophical Quarterly* 5 (1965), 521–40.

tian's relationship to this culture is more truly probable than Barth's).

In summary, the analysis of the level of reflection and judgment demands that the inquirer enter into the critical level of intelligent and reasonable interiority. It also demands that he attempt to thematize that critical performance. Lonergan's own thematization is that judgment is a virtually unconditioned in the precise meaning he gives to those terms. The reader may verify or reject that thematization by his own analysis of his own experience of any (or preferably all) of the kinds of judgment mentioned above. He may analyze the legitimacy of the entire enterprise, moreover, by studying the next and central factor in *Insight*'s argument, viz. the self-affirmation (judgment) of the knower as knower.

6. INSIGHT AS ENTRY
TO BASIC HORIZON

A. BREAKTHROUGH TO BASIC HORIZON:
SELF-AFFIRMATION OF THE KNOWER

The eleventh chapter of *Insight* can accurately be named its central and most important section. To it all that has been discussed thus far leads. From it, all follows. To express the matter more technically, this chapter explicitates critically and explanatorily all the cognitional elements that "Insight as Activity" uncovered, but now in terms of the reader's own self-affirmation. By means of that self-affirmation, moreover, the chapter provides the essential breakthrough needed to allow the "envelopment and confinement" of the metaphysical position which will follow. In terms of the dominant interest of this work, it explicitates the basic method (intelligent and rational activity itself) which penetrates and underlies all the particularized methods of the various sciences (empirical and human, and, in a distinct but related way, philosophical). As shall be discussed in a later chapter, moreover, Lonergan's notion of self-affirmation provides the propaedeutic necessary for any understanding of the full range and usefulness of his later theological method.

The most expeditious point of departure for the discussion will be a continuation of our earlier discussion on the nature of judgment. Indeed, the issue here is the fact of a singularly important particular judgment, viz. "I am a knower." Such a judgment—and no other—is the meaning of Lonergan's at first mysterious term "self-affirmation."[1] To understand that phrase more accurately is to recall the definitions made available by our previous discussion. By "self," for example, is meant a concrete unity-identity-whole ("thing" not "body"). By "self-affirmation" is meant that the self both affirms (reflects and judges) and is affirmed (reflects and judges upon his reflection and judgment). By "self-affirmation of the knower" is meant that the self as affirmed is characterized by the cognitional activities outlined and explicitated in "Insight as Activity"—sensing, perceiving, imagining, inquiring, understanding, formulating, reflecting, grasping the virtually unconditioned and affirming. In other words, there is no attempt to re-instate the "universal and necessary judgments" of a Scholasticism influenced by Christian Wolff[2] and already devastated by Kant's critique. For the judgment at issue here is *not* "I am absolutely and necessarily a knower" but "As a matter of fact, I am a knower and by knowing I mean no more than my performance of the proper cognitional acts."[3]

In the first place, "self-affirmation" is an affirmation. As such, it must fulfill the criteria for the virtually unconditioned nature of all true judgments.[4]

(1) The *conditioned* is the statement "I am a knower": it is constituted as a conditioned by the reflective question raised, "Am I a knower?"

(2) The *link* between that conditioned and its conditions may be spelled out as follows: I am a knower if I am a concrete and intelligible unity–identity–whole characterized by acts of sensing, perceiving, imagining, inquiring, understanding, formulating, reflecting, grasping the unconditioned and judging. The

1. *Ibid.*, p. 319.
2. For a helpful study of this influential thinker. cf. John V. Burns, *Dynamism in the Cosmology of Christian Wolff: A Study in Pre-Critical Rationalism* (New York, 1965).
3. *Insight,* p. 319.
4. *Ibid.*, pp. 319–20. The explicit enumeration is my own for purposes of clarity.

link, therefore, is simply a statement of meaning—for the "elements" it lists are precisely those acts already investigated and verified in "Insight as Activity."

(3) The fulfillment of the conditions is the problematic factor involved. And that fulfillment can only be accorded by the nature of consciousness itself.[5] Nor is this to explain the obscure through the mysterious. For the development of the entire first section of *Insight* was, in effect, that the nature of conscious activity is neither as obscure ("intuitions") nor as mysterious ("spiritual looks") as many analysts have suggested. Precisely on this crucial question, in fact, the fruits of our earlier study begin to come to light. In fact, it should not be difficult for anyone who has already understood the central and constitutive role of insight (direct and reflexive) uncovered in the earlier section to realize here that reflection on consciousness (*pace*, positivists and naïve realists) is not exhausted by the kind of introspection that pretends an "inward look" of the subject at himself. On the contrary, such an essentially simpliste and/or erroneous confrontation theory solution is impossible.[6] For human knowing possesses two characteristics which render that interpretation not merely obsolete but erroneous. In the first place, knowing includes not one undifferentiated level, but three differentiated ones, the higher of which presupposes and com-

5. This analysis of consciousness (*ibid.*, pp. 320–28) is, of course, at the center of Lonergan's critique. For an earlier formulation, cf. *Verbum* (Notre Dame, 1967), esp. pp. 34, 74–75, 77–79, 86–87, 141, 190; for an analysis of Lonergan's notion of abstraction as conscious (in the *Verbum* articles) in contrast to other scholastic positions, cf. William A. Stewart, "Abstraction: Conscious or Unconscious?" *Spirit as Inquiry*, pp. 409–420; for an analysis of Lonergan's notion of consciousness in contrast to other Anglo-American positions, cf. James G. Hart, "Theories of Consciousness: Lonergan and some Contemporaries" (unpublished M.A. thesis, Catholic University of America, January, 1965); for some of the more important theological applications of the theory by Lonergan, cf. *De Constitutione Christi; De Deo Trino* II: *pars systematica; De Verbo Incarnato* (Romae, Pontificis Universitas Gregoriana, 1961), pp. 264–312; in briefer form cf. "Christ as Subject: A Reply," *Collection* (New York, 1968), pp. 164–98; "Consciousness and the Trinity" (unpublished lecture, Rome, 1963).

6. *Insight*, p. 320.

THE ACHIEVEMENT OF BERNARD LONERGAN

plements the earlier and lower one. Judging, therefore, cannot
be reduced to thinking nor thinking to experiencing. Nor are
any analogies (spiritual "looks," etc.) which obscure those distinctions of any real aid in serious analysis for they suggest an
analogy to sense knowledge which cannot bear the burden of
the far more complex (as structured and, in fact, self-structuring)
nature of human knowledge. In the second place, understanding
and judging (the two levels proper to human knowledge) are
characterized not by some mysterious, super-refined sense experience confronting the object known but only by *insight* itself.
For as the multiple mathematical, scientific and common sense
examples employed in *Insight* make clear, insight is nothing
other than the awareness immanent in all cognitional activity
uniting, not confronting knower and known. In brief, knowing
is a structured dynamism whose peculiarity is its intelligent and
rational consciousness of and in its acts. To affirm that peculiarity of human consciousness is to affirm the peculiarity of the
awareness immanent and operative in all cognitional activity.[7]
In a word, it is to affirm the peculiarity and centrality of insight
(direct and reflexive). On the simplest level, it is to affirm the
peculiarly human awareness not present in unconscious acts
(e.g. the growth of one's beard) and present in conscious ones
(e.g. shaving one's beard, thinking about shaving one's beard,
reflecting on why one chooses to shave one's beard, deciding to
do so).

It is possible, however, to further differentiate the levels of
consciousness. For the awareness immanent in all cognitional
acts is present in three clearly distinct acts of the cognitional
process (experience, understanding, judging). There are, therefore, three levels to consciousness itself: empirical consciousness
(proper to the acts of sensing, perceiving, imagining); intelligent (proper to inquiry, insight and formulation); and rational
(proper to reflection, grasp of the unconditioned and judgment[8]). The second and third levels are those proper to in-

7. *Ibid.,* pp. 320–31.
8. *Ibid.,* pp. 322–24.

tellect. For it is intelligent consciousness that grounds inquiry's demands for intelligibility in insight's grasp of that intelligibility and the concept's expression of it. It is rational consciousness that grounds critical reflection's demands for sufficient evidence, as well as the difficult but possible grasp of a virtually unconditioned as a rationally conscious compulsion which we cannot but assent to.[9] Grounding all such activities, finally, is that spirit of wonder, that intellectual alertness, attention, concern which *is* the unrestricted desire to know and which understands and affirms itself as such in the critical judgment proper to the reflective man: "I am a knower."

But to speak of three levels of consciousness is not to deny a unity pervading all of them.[10] But what is that unity? To grasp its nature will provide one with the final fulfillment of the conditions for the self-affirmation towards which the entire argument has been aimed.[11] That unity is, in fact, easy enough to locate even if difficult to explicitate: it is the single conscious agent involved in the several cognitional acts.[12] For the agent alone, precisely as possessing an unrestricted desire to know, *is* the identity present throughout the diversity and multiplicity of the process. And although that unity can be mediated through the type of cognitional analysis represented by *Insight,* it still remains a mediation of an immediate *given.* Just as through the judgmental process of scientific checking and verification we can revert to the *sensibly* given, so here through the judgmental process of self-affirmation, one can revert to the *consciously* given. Nor are those givens unavailable: Rather the careful, deliberate and painstaking analysis of "Insight as Activity" here bears its full fruit: for the givens of consciousness (its structure, its norms, its heuristic and dynamic nature) themselves fulfill the conditions necessary for the affirmation "I am a knower."

That the judgment of self-appropriation, finally, cannot be an

9. *Ibid.,* pp. 323–24.
10. *Ibid.,* pp. 324–28.
11. *Ibid.,* pp. 324–25.
12. *Ibid.,* p. 326.

automatic nor a deductive one should by now be obvious. It is (to state it in its starkest terms) a personal achievement or it is nothing. Lonergan's *Insight,* then, is merely an attempt to make that achievement possible and to explicitate it explanatorily. But the analysis succeeds or fails in accordance with the reader of *Insight*'s ability to travel the whole route (aided perhaps but not supplanted by the brief analysis of *Insight* given above). "Above all, self-appropriation must not be vicarious."

Since the issue is so central to understanding Lonergan's achievement, it would be well to rephrase in summary fashion some of the principal factors to be kept in mind when pursuing the often elusive argument of *Insight.* Once again, the centrality of the *question* must be affirmed. Yet note that the question on this level is not just a question for inquiry but one for reflection. (Am I a knower? not, What is knowing?) By the very exigencies of that question's demands, the "authentic inquirer" is forced to be dissatisfied with even his most brilliant hypotheses. He is forced, for example, to consider all "Insight as Activity" as merely a brilliant theory unless he raises the further question which he alone can answer for himself, viz. Is it true? Can I— and do I—personally verify it to be the case? And when he asks *that* question, a somewhat paradoxical situation is revealed: the very positing of the question exposes the presence of an intelligently and rationally conscious inquirer.[13]

That question, moreover, is not just any question. For if I ask it at all adequately, I already know[14] (in a rudimentary fashion at least) what it means. For example, I know, even if I could not explicitate it adequately, that there is an *I,* i.e. a conscious unity pervading all my conscious acts. I also know that the demands set into force by that question are real to me whether or not the diverse conscious acts which have been characterized as constituting knowledge are recognized as mine.[15] Mine, not

13. *Ibid.,* p. 330. The emphasis on the role of the question is my own but faithful to Lonergan's interpretation, cf. "Metaphysics as Horizon," *Collection,* pp. 202–21.

14. *Insight,* p. 328.

15. *Ibid.,* Chapter 5: "Self-Affirmation."

as Lonerganian definitions I can learn to parrot, but, on the first level, as personal conscious experiences, and, on a second level, as experiences thematized through my own self-affirmation. For I too sense, perceive, inquire, imagine, understand, conceive, reflect, grasp the unconditioned and assent to it. In fact, after personally verifying those experiences and raising that question, I find that I cannot avoid the judgment "I am a knower" except at the unwelcome price of self-deception.[16] If I were as intelligent as David Hume, perhaps I might, indeed, be able to think up an explanation of my conscious experience that would deny its intelligent and rational nature. But if I were as intelligent as Hume, my own keen, probing, demanding intelligent and rational performance would provide me with all the evidence I would need to know that—at least in the case of David Hume—the Humean analysis is nonsense.

Does consciousness supply the fulfilment for the other conditions? Do I see, or am I blind? Do I hear, or am I deaf? Do I try to understand or is the distinction between intelligence and stupidity no more applicable to me than to a stone? Have I any experience of insight, or is the story of Archimedes as strange to me as the account of Plotinus' vision of the One? Do I conceive, think, consider, suppose, define, formulate, or is my talking like the talking parrot? I reflect, for I ask whether I am a knower. Do I grasp the unconditioned, if not in other instances, then in this one? If I grasped the unconditioned, would I not be under the rational compulsion of affirming that I am a knower and so, either affirm it, or else find some loop-hole, some weakness, some incoherence, in this account of the genesis of self-affirmation? As each has to ask these questions of himself, so too he has to answer them for himself. But the fact of the asking and the possibility of the answering are themselves the sufficient reason for the affirmative answer.[17]

Such self-affirmation, therefore, is a factual judgment which anyone capable of asking the question authentically can find his

16. *Ibid.*, pp. 329–32.
17. *Ibid.*, p. 328.

way to affirming. Yet it is something more as well. That contingent affirmation, precisely as fact, reveals and explicitates to the self-affirming knower the natural spontaneities and natural inevitabilities which constitute that fact.[18] For no more than any man can I avoid experience—or be satisfied with it alone. I do not really need the splendid example of Socrates or the dictum of Aristotlian "wonder" to experience, even as a child, the wonder, the inquiry, the unrestricted desire to know that, more and more, can become a sophisticated yet ever more demanding exigence for one's entire adult life. For the wisest of men are simple men. Not with the simplicity of childishness but with the childlike simplicity of a disciplined wonder which has never died. They have not given into the temptation of the many and allowed their education to begin in wonder only to end in routine. Rather they have disciplined that wonder by means of the theoretic enterprise first discovered by the Greeks and the critical enterprise carefully articulated by their European successors. For no truly honest man is ever finally satisfied with even his best "probes." Rather he demands of them nothing less than a grasp of the unconditioned before he will assent to them. The authentic inquirer, in short, will question everything but he will not question the possibility of questioning itself.[19] For, in the last resort, he knows that his power of questioning does not rise Venus-like from the mind of Zeus but emerges as a personal fact of his own experience.[20] Indeed, it emerges as a demanding, often exhausting fact forcing him ever further into the actual performance of knowing whose exigencies he cannot ignore and

18. Note *conditionally* necessary, thus avoiding the trap of the Wolffian ideal; cf. *ibid.,* p. 331.

19. *Ibid.,* p. 330.

20. This is not the place to prove this point, but in the present writer's judgment, precisely the shift of the scientific and philosophical ideal (from absolute to conditional necessity) differentiates Lonergan's critique from the similar enterprises of such diverse figures as Hegel, Husserl or Hartshorne, all of whom seem to this author to assume the scientific and philosophical ideal of *absolute* necessity. Once again, therefore, Lonergan's analysis of judgment as a virtually unconditioned is crucial to his entire critique.

whose reality he can only deny at the price of stupidity. At heart, man is this drive to know[21] and he can call it into question only by calling into question his own hold on reality.[22] He may, if he wishes, content himself with a personal worldview built upon some curious mixture of animal faith and neurotic or ideological fervor. What he may not do is expect others to swallow his madness. For they may prefer the more demanding, if less emotionally charged, world of intelligent and rational meaning exposed to them by their own natures as wanting to know and, sometimes at least, actually knowing.

Basic Horizon as Explanatory[23]

There is one final aspect of Lonergan's doctrine of "self-affirmation" which should not be overlooked. For if, as was argued in "Insight as Activity," the very meaning of scientific method is its ability to move past a descriptive (thing-to-us) analysis to an explanatory (thing-to-thing) one, the question naturally arises: is Lonergan's analysis of self-affirmation descriptive or explanatory? Nor is this question without important consequences. For if self-affirmation is merely descriptive, it may provide inspiration for other cognitional theorists (as, for example, Newman's analysis did for Lonergan) but it would not provide any definitive, critically explanatory breakthrough (as, for example, Polanyi's quite similar analysis has not). Perhaps it is not expecting too much on the part of the reader to realize—even on the basis of this brief analysis of *Insight*—that Lonergan's notion of "self-affirmation" is not descriptive but explanatory. It is not, granted, the same type of explanation as that employed in empirical science but that does not remove its explanatory nature.[24] For the difference between the affirmation of self as

21. *Insight*, p. 331.
22. "Cognitional Structure," *Collection*, p. 230–31.
23. *Insight*, pp. 332–35.
24. *Ibid.*, p. 334.

knower and the affirmation, for example, of relativity theory begins with a difference of data, not of method. In empirical science the data (given) is empirical even if, or through ever more refined instruments, it is often at some reach from immediate contact with the senses ("the naked eye"). In self-affirmation, on the contrary, the data (given) is consciousness itself. And yet the explanatory procedure in each case remains essentially the same. Indeed, at the level of the self-affirmation of *Insight* the subject may reflect upon the nature of the structured path of consciousness which he has just traveled. He may then, perhaps for the first time, notice that in "Insight as Activity" the initial procedure of description gradually yielded to definition by relation[25] (viz. experience, understanding, judgment and their expressed correlates all of which, note, are related to one another by their relationship to the central act of insight itself). But such definition-by-relation-of-things-not-to-me-but-among-themselves is exactly what explanation as distinct from description means. Moreover, the difference in the data under examination determines another important corollary. In short, it occasions the impossibility of fundamental revisions.[26] Nor is the reason for such an impossibility as dogmatic as it may seem at first sight. For revision appeals to data. It asserts that previous theory does not satisfactorily account for all the data. When the data under investigation is, for example, the ever-expanding, ever more carefully measurable data of sense, revision becomes as necessary theoretically as it has been constant historically. But when the data is the very consciousness providing the necessary presuppositions for any and all inquiry (including this one on the possibility or impossibility of revision) then radical revision is not really a possibility—unless, of course, the nature of consciousness itself changes. But the immediate possibilities of an "angelic" consciousness are at best remote. Consequently, if Lonergan's "self-affirmation" principle adequately explicitates the nature of consciousness in its dynamism, structures and norms, it is not open to radical revision.

25. *Ibid.*
26. *Ibid.*, pp. 335–36.

For the prospective reviser cannot appeal (this side of the "beatific vision" at least) to some new data of consciousness to deny the present and only consciousness he humanly possesses. He cannot appeal to new "behaviorist" insights to deny his insights into such techniques as behavior determination, nor to some new Humean conceptualization to deny conceptualization, nor to some new-found and rationally articulated idealism to deny his present reflective experiences.[27]

The conclusion to this exposition of Lonergan's meaning of "self-affirmation," therefore, may be stated rather bluntly: self-affirmation is a fact and its explicitation, if exact and complete, is explanatory. In essence, self-affirmation means nothing more nor less than the conscious subject's reflectively conscious grasp of *the* method grounding all human methods (common sense and scientific, philosophical and theological) viz. the pure, detached, unrestricted desire to know which is the authentic spirit of human inquiry.

Perhaps, then, the basic horizon category of chapter one, "intellectual conversion" can now be more properly understood. For intellectual conversion, in its earliest stages, means to turn from what seems to what is. As incidental, it means a turning away from a particular error to a particular truth. As radical or basic, it means nothing less than the self-affirmation of *Insight* for it makes explicit, explanatory and normative the pure desire to know itself as the ground of all intelligent and rational activity, as that peculiar activity which defines a human being as human. The notion of "intellectual conversion" is not intended to be a new doctrine or technique but rather a means of criticizing and/or developing all intelligent and rational notions and techniques by means of one's conscious and methodical grasp of reason in its basic norms, structures and procedures. It is,

27. *Ibid.*, p. 336. This is not to deny, of course, the possibility of minor revisions in Lonergan's analysis: "Nor do I mean that once explanation is reached, there remains no possibility of the minor revisions that leave basic lines intact but attain a greater exactitude and a greater fullness of detail" (p. 335). For a concrete example of such greater exactitude (on the question of instrument), cf. Patrick Heelan, *Quantum Mechanics: A Study of the Physical Philosophy of Werner Heisenberg.*

moreover, invulnerable in the most basic sense: to object to it is to appeal to some form of obscurantism or, at the limit, to stupidity. It may function logically to steel the authentic inquirer against all temptations to obscurantism and silliness. It may function psychologically to pull him away from the dominance of any lesser exigence, whether brutal or philistine, pragmatic, romantic or merely utilitarian. Indeed, if he is willing to allow intelligence and reasonableness to become the central commitment of his life, it may allow him to endure the demands of a radical openness to whatever may be intelligently conceived and reasonably affirmed. It can, in short, break the hold of any purely relative horizon or any impeding bias and free him for the demands of attempting to appropriate openly and actually the basic horizon possibilities of the intelligent and reasonable man.

B. BASIC HORIZON: ENCIRCLEMENT AND CONFINEMENT: BEING, OBJECTIVITY, METAPHYSICS

B₁ The Notion of Being

To employ the military metaphor of Lonergan himself,[28] self-affirmation provides the essential "breakthrough" needed, for not only does it ground all scientific methods in *the* heuristic method which is the actual performance of intellect but it also makes possible a fresh, indeed a critical approach to the question of a properly philosophic method. And if self-affirmation provides the essential "breakthrough," the first "encirclement" (to continue the metaphor) of the philosophic question is made by a study of the notion of being.

Being, Lonergan asserts, is the objective of the pure desire to know.[29] That definition makes sense to the reader in direct pro-

28. *Insight*, p. 484.
29. *Insight*, p. 348. For its uniqueness in the Scholastic tradition, cf. Jean Langlois, "The Notion of Being According to Lonergan," *Spirit as Inquiry*, pp. 425–34.

144

portion to his grasp of the notion of self-affirmation. For the pure desire to know is nothing other than man's very spirit of intelligent inquiry and critical reflection.[30] It is pure insofar as it alone gives full and unbiased rein to man's highest possibilities of intelligence and knowledge. It is a desire to know insofar as it will never rest content with any issue until it reaches a virtually unconditioned, i.e. an intelligently grasped and rationally affirmed *known*. Being, consequently, may be further designated as all that is known and all that remains to be known. As such it is unrestricted in its intention (from the horizon of the "known known" to the heuristically affirmed "known unknown" to a radical openness to an "unknown unknown"). Essentially, then, the desire to know is properly named neither an idea nor a concept of being but rather a notion of being.[31] If the pure desire to know were an idea of being it would understand all that is insofar as it is and all that is not insofar as it is not. And if it were a concept of being it could bring such complete understanding to a self-expression. Yet not even the most committed rationalist would claim as much for this "clear and distinct idea" of being. Why, then, Lonergan asks, should one call being an idea or a concept for man? Why not be more accurate and refer being to the cognitional fact that does refer one immediately to being: not an idea, not a concept but the heuristic intention of the drive to know as itself the heuristic notion of the being implied in all inquiry and all reflection. What this unusual use of the word "notion" signifies for Lonergan can be further examined by the use of the technique of "clarification through contrast." In fact, one may cite three factors which at first sight may seem like notions but actually are not in the precise meaning Lonergan gives to that term.[32] A foetal eye, for example, is orientated towards seeing. But it does not see and, precisely as unconscious, has no "notion" of seeing. A "notion" arises, then, only

30. For the remainder of this summary paragraph, cf. *ibid.,* pp. 348–50.
31. *Ibid.,* pp. 354–56.
32. *Ibid.,* for the specific examples.

insofar as present understanding discerns future function in present structure. Hunger, as a second instance, may seem to be a notion: for it is clearly orientated towards eating. It is, further, an empirically conscious desire for food. Yet, precisely as only empirically and not intelligently conscious, it too cannot be called a notion in Lonergan's strict sense. As a third instance, a plan or clearly outlined purpose is orientated toward some end or action. But the cognitional elements guiding that action are already known. They are prior to the action and constituted, therefore, not by the intelligent activity itself but by the careful planning which preceded it. A strictly deductive approach to the question of being (or theology), for example, is not strictly speaking a notion of being. Instead, whatever material elements are involved in it are present in the presuppositions of the formulations of "being" or "God" from which the entire enterprise follows.

The pure desire to know, on the other hand, is conscious. It is conscious intelligently and rationally.[33] It does not claim to know being itself but it does claim to head towards being intelligently, rationally, i.e. heuristically. For its intelligent inquiry demands an intelligible, and achieves in every insight a partial fulfillment of the complete intelligibility it seeks. Its critical reflection further demands a groundedness to all its insights. It reaches that final ground partially again but really in and through every virtually unconditioned. And, more basically still, the very desire to understand and to know heads carefully, structurally, slowly but successfully towards nothing other than its unrestricted objective, the as yet unknown real totality about which all its questions are asked and towards which all its answers are partial fulfillments.[34]

33. This has been, of course, the very meaning of the argument of *"Insight as Activity."*
34. It is to be noted that the criterion, although explicitly critical, is also explicitly (as critically) realistic. The discussion, in short, is neither for all *possible* being nor for *absolute* necessity but for what *is*; cf. the discussions, *ibid.,* "The Core of Meaning," pp. 357–59; "A Puzzling Notion," pp. 359–64; and for a clarification-through-contrast with classical and modern theories of the notion of being, cf. pp. 364–74. In

Nor should such a notion seem alien to the careful reader of *Insight*. For are not the heuristic methods of the scientist and the spontaneous strivings of common sense both illustrations of a more basic human phenomenon? In fact, at the core of scientific method, as we have already seen, is the use of heuristic notions: name the unknown, work out its properties and relations and thereby anticipate the type of act through which the unknown will eventually become known. In other words, the power of questioning what grounds and unifies all particular human inquiry is not just an empty drive, nor merely an empirically conscious one, nor an already known one, but is rather an intelligent and reasonable drive which performatively heads toward the to-be-known and actually (if only partially) reaches that known in every increment of human knowledge. In self-affirmation, moreover, the intelligent subject may bring that power to expression by recognizing and affirming his heuristic nature as an unrestricted intention and as an unconditioned result. Intellect is, in short, an intelligent and reasonable anticipation of being—of all that is known or remains to be known; of all that is *true* and, in that fundamental sense, of all that is real:

We should learn that questioning why is not only about being but also is itself being, . . . being in its openness to being, being that is realizing itself through inquiry to knowing that, through knowing, it may come to living. This being of the questioning questioner is the latent metaphysics from which explicit metaphysics is derived; and in explicit metaphysics it is the primary analogate through which other being as being is understood.[35]

It should now be possible to realize, more clearly perhaps than previously, the centrality of Lonergan's self-affirmation. For "self-affirmation" is not meant to be some salvific "meta-

---

short, the absolute in question for Lonergan and achieved by his critical method is this virtually unconditioned absolute of *fact. Ibid.,* pp. 329–31.

35. "Metaphysics as Horizon," *Collection,* p. 206.

physical" move to save the day for realism. It is at once a more modest and a more rational achievement: the ability to bring to self-expression what intellect is. If the knower has affirmed himself as knower and not only as in some prior state of "existential" consciousness, he can recognize and affirm that the pure desire to know driving him past experience to inquiry and understanding, reflection and judgment, is, in fact, the real cause of the affirmation itself and of the self that is affirmed. He may further realize that the desire to understand and know all that is, the concrete universe, the totality of true judgments, everything about everything—is, in fact, nothing other than a notion of being.[36] Only if he chooses to retreat to some prior level of inquiry for which the real is the "out there" will the affirmation that the real is the true upset him. But that retreat is solved not at this stage of the discussion but only at the previous one wherein intelligence and rationality were allowed full range to reveal their power and their possibilities.

B_2 The Notion of Objectivity

In the continuing envelopment of the fundamental features of the basic horizon whose entry point is the radical intellectual conversion of self-affirmation, the next logical question is the traditionally thorny one of objectivity. On its simplest level, that question might be expressed as follows: does that desire to know reach the objectively real? But if the question of objectivity is unavoidable, indeed inevitable, so too are the temptations to answer it in a less than adequate fashion. Just as self-affirmation, if not grasped as an appropriation of one's rational self-consciousness, can seem to have already been reached in some prior "existential" state where desires are high, passions keen

36. For the later expansion of this idea, cf. *Insight,* pp. 644–46. It is to be emphasized that the distinction is grounded in Lonergan's earlier distinction between "notion," "idea" and "concept" which, in other positions, are almost synonymous but carefully distinct in Lonergan, cf. above on "heuristic notion," "idea" and "concept."

and the resultant reality of the "self" scarcely deniable. And just as "being" can either be the objective of the pure desire to know if self-affirmation has occurred or some already-out-there-now-real objective of some less demanding exigence if it has not, so too the Lonerganian notion of objectivity[37] can either be explained in the context of self-affirmation or misapprehended in the context of its absence. If the latter be the case, moreover, some essentially *simpliste* solution readily follows: for the naïve realist,[38] for example, our minds "obviously" reach-intuit-"see" the "real"; for the idealist, our minds are brilliant machines capable of ever-more fertile categories and symbols but, alas, not capable of reaching the "really real." For the critical realist, however, intellect (precisely as a dynamic structure conscious empirically, intelligently and rationally) has already been affirmed as a more complex and structured reality than either the naïve realist or the idealist suspects.

The criterion for objectivity, therefore, will have to be nothing less than the dynamic, structured and self-affirmed criterion of "human knowing" itself. That dynamism, moreover, will reveal the intrinsic objectivity of all intellectual activity as grounded in its very "intentionality," i.e. in its far-reaching and never fully satisfied drive past all experience through inquiry to understanding and formulation, to reflection and judgment. To state this factor in more familiar vocabulary, the intrinsic relation of human knowing to reality is not *pensée pensée* but *pensée pensante,* not *intentio intenta* but *intentio intendens,* not *noema* but *noesis.*[39] Or, to employ Lonergan's own vocabulary, the intrinsic relation of human knowing to reality is the intelligently and rationally conscious drive of all genuine intellectual activity as it moves beyond data to intelligibility, beyond intelligibility to

37. *Ibid.,* pp. 375–77.
38. For the most succinct expression of this tripartite comparison, cf. Lonergan's contrast of Gilson, Kant and Coreth in "Metaphysics as Horizon," *Collection,* pp. 206–12.
39. For a defense, therefore, of the "correspondence" theory of truth, cf. Lonergan's reply to Leslie Dewart, "The Dehellenization of Dogma," *Theological Studies* 28 (1967), 339–41.

truth and through and in truth to being as real; beyond every known truth and being to all the truth and being still to be known.[40] And as it moves beyond, it does not leave behind. On the contrary, it groups all its past and present experiences, all its acts of understanding and, above all, all its judgments into a patterned critical subject-object context (a horizon) from within which the subject presently operates. It is this critical-contextual aspect of objectivity (of exceptional importance for the theologian) which Lonergan calls the "principal" notion[41] of objectivity insofar as it allows the critical subject a principal framework-horizon by means of which he may qualify or change all his later achievements as distinct subjects or objects.

If the dynamic and cumulative aspects of intellectual inquiry allow some understanding of the intrinsic and principal notions of objectivity, so too does the structural reality of all inquiry afford a better understanding of certain other important aspects of the complex phenomenon of objectivity. For the dynamism of intellect is also a structured, in fact, self-structuring process. There is an experiential component in human knowing that resides in the pure givenness of the relevant data (experience).[42] There is a normative component which resides in the inquirer's fidelity to the detached, disinterested, unrestricted norms of intelligent and rational inquiry.[43] There is an absolute component reached only after reflective understanding combines the experiential and normative factors in a virtually unconditioned.[44] If self-affirmation allows the knower to know himself precisely as knower, and in accordance with that discovery to realize the drive to know as itself a notion of being, then, the being thus reached (i.e. as intelligently grasped and rationally affirmed) can be further designated as the real—the objectively real. But it is imperative to note that the criteria of objectivity involved here yields

40. For explicitation of this question (in reference to Godel's theorem), cf. *Insight,* pp. xxv–vi.
41. *Insight,* p. 375–77.
42. Hence "experiential objectivity," *ibid.,* pp. 381–83.
43. Hence "normative objectivity," *ibid.,* pp. 380–81.
44. Hence "absolute objectivity" (i.e. *de facto* absolute *via* the judgment as a virtually unconditioned), *ibid.,* pp. 377–80.

neither to the simple experience of the "reality" of our child-hood experience nor to any classical empiricism nor to the coherence of the "reality" of idealism nor to the absolutely necessary "reality" of the rationalist. Instead the Lonergan notion of objectivity is only structured in accordance with the notions of intentionality and being already determined. In short, objectivity is not a simple process but finds its intrinsic justification in the intentionality of all intellectual activity and its structural nature from the dynamic structure of intentionality itself as it moves from experience (experiential objectivity) through understanding (normative objectivity) to reflection and judgment (absolute objectivity) to a patterned set of judgments (principal objectivity) from within which still further questions emerge as the drive to know heads more and more towards being, i.e. towards the objectivity real.[45]

B_3 Confinement of Basic Horizon: Position vs. Counter-Position

In the light of the key issues just raised (knowledge, being and objectivity) it should now be possible to present what Lonergan calls his "chief tool" for explanatory metaphysical method. This discussion should serve as a summary of the issues treated up to now, a study of the interrelationships of those issues and a "confinement" of them to a metaphysical method. That confinement is essentially achieved through the employment of Lonergan's much-discussed notion of the dialectic between position and counter-position.[46] Essentially, this notion is similar to the critical tool for metaphysics that Coreth calls the "dialectic of

45. *Ibid.,* pp. 383–84.
46. The designations "position" and "counter-position" are Lonergan's own: cf. *ibid.,* esp. 387–90, 488–89, 495–96, 499–500, 513–14, 537–38, 624–25, 680–83, 690–91, 738–39. Cf. "Metaphysics as Horizon," *Collection,* p. 204, the reference to Coreth: "The proper tool in this mediation of the immediate is the rejection of the counter-position. Explicit judgments can contradict the latent metaphysics that they presuppose; but one has only to bring this contradiction to light, for the explicit judgment to be evident nonsense, and for its opposite to be established."

performance and concept." In short, both Lonergan and Coreth locate the essential philosophical dialectic not in the clash of system vs. system but rather in the dialectic of the performance behind any system and the system itself (Coreth) or in the dialectic of the position (i.e. all accurate formulations of the nature of knowledge, being and objectivity) and the counter-position (i.e. all inaccurate formulations of those key issues). The "position," therefore, is grounded in and thematizes the intelligently and rationally conscious performance of the inquirer and is thereby able to judge any inadequate thematization of that performance.

For Lonergan, then, every philosophical position will be a basic "position"[47] if: first, the notion of "reality" in the system is the concrete universe of being as intelligently grasped and reasonably affirmed; second, if the subject's notion of *knowledge* is grounded in an affirmation of his intelligent and rational consciousness; third, if his notion of *objectivity* is constructed upon an intelligent inquiry and critical reflection as a heuristic and structured performance.

On the other hand, every basic counter-position will depart from one or more of these positions. Its notion of the "real" may be merely a subdivision of the "already-out-there-now-real." Its notion of the subject's knowledge of himself as subject does not demand rational self-affirmation but is content with some prior existential state. Its notion of objectivity is conceived, in the final analysis, not on the basis of the nature of intellect but on the basis of the senses. It becomes the property, therefore, not of the intelligent and rational desire to know but of some vital anticipation, extroversion or satisfaction.

The possibility of articulating and defending Lonergan's basic position, of course, is completely dependent upon the reader's agreement with and appropriation of the entire argument of *Insight*. No more than his previous notions (e.g. judgment as a "virtually unconditioned") may his notion of the "dialectic of position vs. counter-position" be used as a *deus ex machina* to

47. *Ibid.*, on position and counter-position.

save the philosophical (or theological) day for troubled "realists." For the fact is that their troubles may run more deeply than they suspect. Indeed, unlike most "realistic" positions, the "critical realism" of Lonergan-Coreth-Rahner *et al.* is not meant to provide a *via media* between the "extremes" of empiricism and idealism. It attempts and defends a far more radical task: the need to establish critically a realistic position for which idealism is but a half-way house in the route from empiricism. Its break with that kind of scholasticism incisively labeled by William James "common sense with a college education" is complete. Accordingly, it does not aid any honest "dialogue" to shade over that difference with banner-waving about yet another entry into the *philosophia perennis*. That there is such a *philosophia perennis* (i.e. "basic position") Lonergan agrees. But that it can be arrived at by anything less than a critical *performance* (e.g. his interpretation of Aristotle and Aquinas) and, in the present situation, a critical thematization of that performance via introspective psychology is the precise point at issue here. A realism less exigent in its demands may, in fact, be nothing more than yet another thematization of the "really real" world grounded in some mixture of human error and animal faith. For, in his first awakening to wonder, every man does not perform through the carefully differentiated states and stages of consciousness articulated in "Insight as Activity" but operates rather in an essentially undifferentiated (i.e. polymorphic) horizon.[48] In a second stage-of-horizon-development, that original polymorphism attempts to overcome itself by moving into some kind of systematization (symbolic or scientific) of its performance. At this stage, however, precisely because the root-problem (viz. the horizon of polymorphic consciousness) has yet to be clearly differentiated into its invariant structures, nature and norms, the results are usually a dialectical disarray of positions and counter-positions. In a third stage, finally, the

48. *Ibid.*, p. 390; the phrase "undifferentiated" is more familiar to Lonergan's post-*Insight* work after his employment of Piaget; cf. *De Methodo Theologiae*, pp. 2–3.

latent metaphysics immanent and operative in every inquirer may finally succeed in conceiving itself, in working out its implications and techniques and in affirming them. In short, there may develop the genuine possibility of an explicit metaphysics.

But the metaphysics in question here must not be defined as a cover-word for one's vague feeling for life, nor as some personal or traditional *Weltanschauung,* nor only as a process of linguistic clarification. Rather, for Lonergan at least, it is to be defined as a heuristically structured anticipation of all that is to be known. To be more exact, it is the integral heuristic structure of proportionate being.[49] It is a true department of human knowledge whose scientific function is to underlie,[50] penetrate, transform and unite all other departments explanatorily and whose possibility is in direct proportion to the "metaphysician's" grasp of the basic-horizon "positions" on the questions of knowledge, being, and objectivity.

It would be well, however, to pause for a moment in the general argument and explain each of the terms in Lonergan's technical definition of metaphysics as the integral heuristic structure of proportionate being.[51] "Proportionate" is the first word to need clarification: it signifies that, at this stage of the "moving viewpoint" of *Insight,* there is no authentic metaphysical speech about transcendent being. For the metaphysics in question here must be fully proportionate to the horizon of man as he actually is—i.e. not merely to his understanding and affirmation (where the transcendent may or may not enter) but also to his specifically human (i.e. incarnate) experience. Hence proportionate being means whatever is to be known by human experience, intelligent grasp and reasonable affirmation. The second phrase requiring clarification is "integral heuristic structure."[52] Essentially, it is an expansion of the already defined key concept, heuristic notion. In other words, a heuristic struc-

49. *Insight,* p. 392.
50. For an expansion of how metaphysics "underlies," "penetrates," "transforms" and "unites" all other departments of knowledge, cf. *ibid.,* p. 390.
51. *Ibid.,* p. 392.
52. *Ibid.,*

ture is an ordered set of heuristic notions. An integral heuristic structure is the ordered set of all heuristic notions. The latter alone, in Lonergan's view, may be named "metaphysics":

This heuristic structure [metaphysics] is immanent and operative in all human knowing, but initially it is latent and the polymorphism of human consciousness makes it problematic as well. None the less, it can be conceived, affirmed, and implemented, and from that "implementation" there follow a transformation and an integration of the sciences and the myriad instances of common sense. But knowing is knowing being. So the integral heuristic structure of proportionate being, as determined by the sciences and common sense, is knowledge of the organizing structure of proportionate being. As has been said, such a metaphysics is progressive, nuanced, factual, formally dependent on cognitional theory and materially dependent on the sciences and on common sense, stable, and in its outlook, explanatory.[53]

B₄ Methodical Entry into Basic Horizon

Metaphysical Method: From the Polymorphism of Latent Metaphysics to the Isomorphism of Explicit Metaphysics

If one factor remains clear beyond all discussion in any interpretation of Lonergan's understanding of metaphysics, then, it is his insistence that metaphysical method must be critical, or it is nothing. This has already become obvious in the study of *Insight*. Later it will become yet more obvious in an analysis of the contrast and interrelation of empirically scientific and philosophic methods. For the present, however, it would be well to pause and emphasize this crucial point in a more directly methodical way. One may note, then, two central facts: first, *Insight* itself has attempted to differentiate the materials of insight, affirm them as a personal attainment and thematize that attainment as a metaphysics. In short, it has thematized the upper blade of all intelligent procedure, of all method, viz.

53. *Ibid.*, pp. 395–96.

human knowing itself. By that attempt it could not avoid the historically vexed question of method in metaphysics. For it is metaphysics, traditionally known as the science of being, which treats explicitly of that intellectual conversion (implicit in classical thought, explicit in post-critical philosophy) and that allows being to be treated scientifically. Secondly, *Insight* is written from a moving viewpoint whose ever further movement from lower context to higher viewpoint is designed to stimulate, differentiate, affirm and articulate the structure and dynamism of intellect itself. In other words, all that has occurred up to this point in *Insight*'s moving viewpoint may be summarized by recalling the previous material under the new rubric of the movement from latent to problematic to explicit metaphysics. For *Insight* in its search for the basic method of all human activity —the dynamic structure of intellect—must itself employ that same method. Indeed, if method is a set of directives that serve to guide a process towards a result, and the result desired is an explicit metaphysics of proportionate being, then the general movement of *Insight* can now be seen as a strictly methodical search for an explicit metaphysics as the first explanatory formulation of a basic horizon.

And yet, because of the very nature of that explicit metaphysics, the only successful entry into *Insight*'s search for method could be its process from a latent through a problematic to an explicit metaphysics. For metaphysics must start with people as they are—unable to renounce their experience of their intelligent inquiry or their critical reflection (latent) and unable as well to clearly grasp and thematize these exigencies before they have recognized the original, polymorphic state of their own consciousness (problematic) and until they have differentiated the various patterns of their experience, notably the strictly intellectual pattern (explicit)—"Insight as Activity." Thus, only at the level of the "breakthrough" of the self-affirming subject is the subject ready to issue the directives needed to effect an explicit metaphysics. He can, first of all, reorientate his common sense and his scientific knowledge in the light of his own self-affirmation of the notions of being and objectivity. He now knows how and when common sense may be trusted and when it may not for he knows that the very polymorphism of his own consciousness can generate a dramatic, an individual, a group and a general bias whose aberrant exigencies do not allow for the authentic development of intellect. He also knows that science is not necessarily to be trusted in its extra-scientific opinions on the nature of knowledge, of being or of objectivity. Moreover, and herein lies his second major task—he can realize the isomorphism[54] that obtains between the structure of the known and the structure of his knowing. For if his knowing is clearly and *critically* affirmed as consisting of a related set of acts, the known cannot be other than the related set of contents of those acts. Thus the pattern of relations between the acts is similar in form to the pattern of relations between the contents of the acts. This movement into explicit metaphysics, moreover, has provided one of the most interesting results of *Insight:* the possibility of verifying the traditional metaphysical categories (potency, form and act) as the structural contents isomorphic to the cognitional acts, experience, understanding and judgment. Briefly then, a critical study of human knowing reveals for Lonergan the possibility of explicitating the latent and the problematic metaphysics of the human mind (trapped, as it were, in its own polymorphism) into an explicit metaphysics within which the self-affirming knower may grasp the fundamental isomorphism between his knowing and the known and thereby (1) verify his metaphysical statements by grounding them in cognitional fact; (2) reorientate his common sense and scientific knowledge on the basis of his metaphysical; (3) integrate all his proportionate knowledge in terms of a verifiable metaphysics which allows not a closed system, but rather an open, heuristic structure (potency-form-act) within which all proportionate being (human experience, understanding, judgment)

54. On isomorphism, cf. *ibid.,* p. 399–400. Since the interest of this work is on the method of philosophy as distinct from the contents, this otherwise central Lonerganian concept is left undeveloped in its content.

may be explained; (4) lead to a clear recognition of the peculiar nature of metaphysical method as distinct from empirical scientific method; (5) lead to the possibility of *critically* investigating the history of various metaphysical positions in terms of the methods which are their core; (6) lead to a *methodical* undoing of several disputed questions in traditional metaphysics as well as a *methodical* development of several key traditional metaphysical notions (e.g. potency, form and act, as central and conjugate; explanatory genera and species) and, above all, to a clarification and verification of certain important metaphysical notions (e.g. distinctions and relations); (7) break from all obscurantism thoroughly enough to allow an authentic intellectual opening to the further questions of ethics and transcendence; and (8) provide a heuristically open and verifiable metaphysics whose critical example and whose fundamental features a basic theological method will later transform and employ.

Clarification Through Contrast: Scientific Method and Philosophic Method[55]

Although metaphysics is strictly speaking a science its method bears distinct and important differences from the methods em-

55. Since it is not to the immediate purpose of this book to add the series of clarifications-through-contrast with other methods, we have included in this section only a presentation of Lonergan's interesting and important analysis of the key differences between empirical scientific method and metaphysical scientific method since that analysis provides an excellent summary of the methodological points made thusfar. The other clarifications are: Deductive methods (*ibid.*, pp. 402–08); universal doubt as method (pp. 408–11); empiricism (pp. 411–18); common-sense eclecticism (pp. 416–21); Hegelian dialectic (pp. 421–23). It should be mentioned again at this point that there is an urgent need for serious study of Lonergan's theory vis-à-vis other major positions. As far as the present author is aware, there are doctoral dissertations in preparation at present on a critical comparison of Lonergan with Kant, Husserl, Maréchal, Gadamer, Rahner, Heidegger and Newman at the following universities: Louvain, Basel, Münster, Fordham and Chicago. Since none of these is completed at present, the author of this work has been reluctant to employ their already fruitful results (made previously available) in this crucial interpretive area.

ployed by the empirical sciences. The basic differences is that empirical scientific method is prior to that work and independent of particular scientific results, whereas philosophic method is coincident with philosophic work and so stands or falls with the particular results of one's fundamental philosophy. In order to be scientific, in other words, philosophic method cannot accept the easier criterion of the empirical sciences but *must* become critical for it stands to philosophic conclusions as the genesis to the attainment of a single all-inclusive view. Empirically scientific method, on the other hand, stands to scientific conclusions as a genetic universal to generated particulars. As critical, moreover, philosophy must be a personal attainment or it is nothing. For unlike the empirical scientist (who can rely on the experiments of the past unless new data upset those conclusions or new questions occur), the philosopher cannot rely on the "experiments" of past philosophers or the "consensus" of living ones. He either appropriates his own rational consciousness or he does not. If he does, philosophy as a science becomes a real—indeed an urgent—exigence for him. If he does not, he must attempt to develop a method (ranging from a common-sense eclecticism to Hegelian dialectic) which will on the terms of Lonergan's analysis of philosophic methods inefficaciously ground his philosophical enterprise.

Moreover, the confinement imposed upon all metaphysical positions by their employment of the scientific tool of rejecting all counter-positions (on knowledge, objectivity and being) in favor of the position established on these issues provides the conditions for the possibility of a critical metaphysics. For that latter metaphysics alone can, for Lonergan, secure and thematize the invariant (as isomorphic) structure of all proportionate being as explained or as to be explained. Metaphysics, therefore (precisely as explanatory), can anticipate the invariant structure of the universe as explained through and in the various sciences. This unitive function (which moves, secondarily and mediately, to the universe as described through common sense) unites with metaphysic's transforming function to impose on both the sciences and common sense a critical upper blade. And once

159

that critical foundation is securely laid and the position is allowed full development, the inquirer may move methodically to erect the integral heuristic structure of proportionate being—in what *Insight* describes as the four key "moments" of all metaphysical inquiry:

    (1) First moment: dialectical criticism (position, counterposition) can criticize and transform all commonsense and scientific views

    (2) Second moment: cognitional theory brings to light the four methods of all scientfic inquiry and reveals the possibility of their integration within a proportionate metaphysics. At this point it would be well to study these four methods more exactly. This is especially urgent here because only the first pair (classical and statistical) have been explained so far since the second pair (genetic and dialectic), although operative even in the empirical sciences, could not be explained until a critical position had been established. On the assumption, then, of the breakthrough, envelopment and confinement established in the earlier section it becomes exigent for Lonergan both to explain classical and statistical methods and to recognize the need for genetic and dialectic method. To understand that explanation, we should recall the following cognitional facts:[56] (a) that understanding leads to the formulation of systems; (b) that systems will either remain constant over time or change in time; (c) that there are two kinds of understanding: the direct act that leads to the formulations of systems and the inverse act that recognizes that on this question at least there is no intelligibility to be understood or systematized.

Hence: (a) will lead to the recognition of *classical method*

56. For an excellent summary of this section on these methods, cf. *ibid.*, pp. 483–87, esp. p. 485. Earlier footnotes have indicated the principal locations in *Insight* where each of the four methods is discussed at length (as does the excellent Index of *Insight* under each of these titles). The present section merely intends to summarize those results.

(heuristic anticipation of constant system);

(b) will lead to the recognition of the need for a *genetic* method (heuristic anticipation of an intelligibly related sequence of systems)

(c) will lead to a two-fold recognition correlative to (a) and (b), i.e. an understanding of the peculiarity of inverse insight as grounding a lack of system leads to an acknowledgment of *statistical* method (heuristic anticipation that data will not conform to system) and of dialectical method i.e., the heuristic anticipation that the relations between successive stages of changing systems will sometimes not be directly intelligible either because of the entry of a counter-position on knowledge, reality, or objectivity in the sciences, or of the presence of some bias in common sense procedures.

These four methods, taken collectively, are for Lonergan exhaustive of the four lower-blade methods employed by the upper blade of human knowing to explain any given set of data. For data must either conform or not conform to system. And systems must either be related intelligibly (positions develop) or unintelligibly (counter-positions err).

(3) Third moment: metaphysical understanding unites (1) and (2) in a unifying (2) and transforming (1) manner in order to obtain the integral heuristic structure of this universe

(4) Fourth moment: an understanding of the isomorphism of knowing and the known leads to the possibility of realizing the fundamental metaphysical elements of the integral heuristic structure of being as explanatory. For the pattern of relations immanent in the invariant dynamic structure of cognitional acts (experience, understanding, judgment) will also be found in the contents of the heuristically anticipated acts and will continue to be so found whenever anticipation gives way to actual content (potency, form, act).[57]

57. This understanding is expanded in *Insight* into the important content chapter (15) called "Elements of Metaphysics" (pp. 431–87)

Interesting as such content questions are in themselves, however, they are not really the principal interest of this work. For even though Lonergan's understanding of potency-form-act will prove extremely helpful for his resolution of many theological problems (e.g. on the ontological questions in *De Verbo Incarnato*[58]) and his verifiable metaphysics of distinction, relations and unity will prove invaluable for clarifying Trinitarian speculative problems,[59] still the "elements" of his metaphysics are not, in the present writer's judgment, his chief philosophical achievement. Rather his very notion of a *critical* metaphysics as the *only scientific* one freed him to transform that tool (in the light of the further exigencies of intellect, of faith, and of theology) into a *critical* theological method as well. For no less than metaphysics, theology cannot content itself either with its former classical understanding of itself as a science (in the light of the contemporary transformation of the very notion of science) nor with a purely empirical scientific understanding of itself (in the light of the critical revolution in philosophy). But it is time to conclude this at once too brief and too lengthy chapter. Indeed, the most helpful summary is Lonergan's own:

But it may not be amiss to locate once more our position in the history of philosophy. There exists a necessary isomorphism between our knowing and its proportionate known. But that parallel is missed by Spinoza's deductivist "ordo idearum est ordo rerum."

---

on potency, form, act (pp. 431–44); central and conjugate forms (pp. 434–37); explanatory genera and species (pp. 437–42); potency and limitation (pp. 442–44); potency and finality (pp. 444–51); and the notion of development along with expansion and explicitation of the notion of genetic method (pp. 451–71). The following chapter further expands that content character with analyses of distinctions (pp. 488–90); relations (pp. 490–97); the meaning of metaphysical elements (pp. 497–509); and the unity of proportionate being (pp. 509–20). In the interests of brevity and of continuity with the more methodical interests of this book, these elements will not be discussed although, needless to say, they play the central role in Lonergan's actual *explicitation* of his metaphysics.

58. *De Verbo Incarnato,* pp. 213–68.
59. *De Deo Trino,* esp. pp. 15–52; 291–315.

The correct locus of the parallel is to be found in the dynamic structure of our knowing. Inquiry and understanding presuppose and complement experience; reflection and judgment presuppose and complement understanding. But what holds for the activities, also holds for their contents. What is known inasmuch as one is understanding, presupposes and complements what is known by experiencing; and what is known inasmuch as one is affirming, presupposes and complements what is known by understanding. Finally, the contents of cognitional acts either refer to the known or are identical with the known, and so the dynamic structure of knowing is also the structure of proportionate being. This was grasped by Artistotle and more fully by Aquinas and, while the present account of the matter does differ in details from their position, the difference lies in the fact that modern science has made it possible to distinguish very sharply between preliminary description and scientific explanation.[60]

60. *Insight*, pp. 486–7.

7. EXPANSION OF BASIC HORIZON: MORAL, RELIGIOUS AND CHRISTIAN CONVERSION IN *INSIGHT*

A. MORAL CONVERSION

The present work's limitations of both space and interest prevent an analysis of many of the important notions developed in the concluding chapters of *Insight*.[1] This analysis, therefore,

1. Viz. the interesting and important concerns of Chapter 17 ("Metaphysics as Dialectic"), which concerns are, in an important sense, superseded by Lonergan's post-*Insight* analysis of the many dimensions of meaning. In fact, two *caveats* should be recalled by any reader of that chapter. (a) Note that for Lonergan, myth bears an essentially negative meaning (*Insight,* pp. 536–46), but mystery a fundamentally positive sense (*ibid.,* pp. 546–49). And both terms are dialectically related by Lonergan to the "meaning of meaning" via critical reflection on the direct and reflective consciousness already established in *Insight*. Hence these terms as Lonergan uses them are given a quite explicit meaning which cannot be confused with the often different meanings given the terms by other authors. For a later expansion of this study of meaning, cf. "Dimensions of Meaning," *Collection,* pp. 252–67, for an abbreviated form; and for a more expanded and critical study, cf. Chapter 6 ("Meaning") of Lonergan's forthcoming *Method in Theology.* (b) The contrast of this Lonerganian analysis to the analyses of phenomenologists on the relationship of the scientific world and the *Lebenswelt* should be emphasized, lest misinterpretations of both positions occur; cf. esp. "Lectures on Existentialism" (1957). Also, even in the general movement of thought called "transcendental method," the analysis of Lonergan on meaning and metaphysics is not directly related to the analysis of incarnate consciousness of those more influenced by phenomenology. For the most obvious example, cf. K. Rahner, *Spirit in the World* and

will content itself with an examination of only major developments in that work's moving viewpoint. The approach of Lonergan to the key questions of ethics, of God, and of Christian belief will be articulated not so much for an analysis of these questions in themselves but as further expansions of the basic horizon of *Insight*.

The eighteenth chapter of *Insight*, entitled "The Possibility of Ethics," reveals certain important developments in Lonergan's analysis of the horizon-expansion of the authentic inquirer. In the first place, it allows for a systematic and explanatory recognition of the possibility of an ethical stance that is not superimposed or counterpoised to one's basic metaphysics but rather presupposes and complements it. In essence, then, ethics allows for the movement to a yet higher viewpoint: a viewpoint which any serious analysis of the problematic of the human sciences (including theology) must include. On the structural level, the movement is from the level of knowing to that of deciding and doing.[2] And the determining factor in the drive to that higher ethical viewpoint is again the dynamism of the human spirit itself. For the rational consciousness which self-affirmation confirms cannot (in the name of its own fidelity to rational consistency) remain content with its confinement to the field of knowing. Rather it must extend its domain into the field of doing-acting-making.[3] Nor is that plea for consistency between one's knowing and one's doing satisfied with any vague Emersonian "hobgoblin" consistency. Instead it demands an honest, complete consistency of an inquirer who possesses a willingness whose universality and unrestrictedness is equal to, because grounded in, the unrestricted desire to know itself.

From that dynamism there may follow an ethical stance

Hearers of the Word; for the consequent analysis of the notion of mystery (in a philosophical-theological context), cf. Karl Rahner, *Theological Investigations*, IV (Baltimore and Dublin, 1966), pp. 36–77.

2. *Ibid.*, p. 594.

3. *Ibid.*, pp. 602–04. For an examination of Lonergan's ethical viewpoint, cf. Donald Johnson, "Lonergan and the Redoing of Ethics," *Continuum*, 5 (Summer, 1967), pp. 211–20.

whose method completes and parallels the method of proportionate being in certain important ways. First, just as the dynamic structure of our knowing grounds a metaphysics, so too that structure's prolongation into human doing grounds an ethics.[4] Secondly, the isomorphism obtaining between metaphysical elements and cognitional facts finds its parallel in the isomorphic structure of the ethical object of proportionate good[5] (a compound of objects of desire, intelligible order and values). Ethics articulates the rationally self-conscious subject's attainment of that good through his authentic development from the manifold of experience to an ordering of his experiences by intelligence and, finally, to a rational choice of the good as true good. Thirdly, the metaphysical dialectic of position vs. counterposition finds its ethical counterpart in the dialectic of ethical systems emerging insofar as one's rational values are true or false,[6] one's intelligent principles ordered or disordered, and one's desires unnecessarily frustrated or allowed full range into the detachment and disinterestedness of rational self-consciousness. Moreover, just as the various philosophical counterpositions invite their own reversal by their inconsistency with intelligence and reason so too, all ethical counter-positions either bring about their own reversal or cause their carrier's self-destruction.[7]

Fidelity to those further demands for consistency between one's knowing and one's doing reveal, then, a fourth and distinct level of human consciousness—the level of decision, of rational *self*-consciousness or, to use a more contemporary vocabulary, of existential consciousness. In short, that fidelity expresses the need to add a genuine moral conversion to the intellectual conversion already achieved.

But in order to clarify the crucial Lonerganian development

4. *Insight*, p. 604.
5. *Ibid.*, pp. 605–07. This analysis is later developed (in a post-*Insight* context where the further dimensions of meaning are explicitated) into the schema for the concrete human good; cf. taped lectures at Regis College, Toronto (Summer, 1962) on "Method in Theology."
6. *Insight*, p. 607.
7. *Ibid.*, p. 604.

166

(to receive still greater emphasis in his post-*Insight* work) one should relate that fourth level to the three levels already examined. The first three levels are sufficiently clear: we are empirically conscious inasmuch as we are on the level of pure experience. We are intelligently conscious inasmuch as we inquire, understand and conceptualize. We are rationally conscious inasmuch as we reflect, grasp a virtually unconditioned, and judge. Finally, we are rationally self-conscious[8] inasmuch as (after we have critically scrutinized the motives and the object of our acts) we decide to act in conformity to our intelligence and reason. Our deliberation only ends in fact if and when a personal decision intervenes. For decision (as the act of the willing) consents or refuses, as judgment affirms or desires. In its fundamental nature, therefore, decision is a fourth and distinctive level of human consciousness. It is the final enlargement and transformation of consciousness insofar as the empirically, intelligently and rationally conscious subject both demands that his action conform to his knowledge and that *he* accept the rigors of that demand by rational decision and good action. Indeed, the horizon of man's consciousness expands from judgment's rationally conscious acknowledgment of actuality to decision's rationally self-conscious[9] bestowal of actuality —in fact, of that peculiarly human actuality (meaning) whose meaning-reality the human sciences (including theology[10]) attempt to explore.

Yet there is a further corollary to be added to Lonergan's discussion of ethics: viz. that the contingent necessity of rational consciousness has yielded place to the pure contingency of ra-

8. It is to be noted that at every stage of his development, Lonergan is fond of quoting the scholastic maxim: *"Verum et falsum sunt in mente: bonum et malum (sunt) in rebus,"* as an insistence upon the concrete.

9. In his post-*Insight* work, this level will be designated "existential consciousness"; for a brief example of this, cf. *"Existenz* and *Aggiornamento," Collection,* p. 242.

10. Thus, Lonergan's emphasis in his later work on the category of "conversion." For an abbreviated expansion of that interest for theology, cf. "The New Context of Theology," *Theology of Renewal,* L. K. Shook (ed.), I, pp. 340–47.

167

tional self-consciousness. For although we cannot possibly grasp a virtually unconditioned and not judge (if one is rational), anyone can recall any number of instances when he has reflectively grasped the right thing to do and has not done it (in spite of the fact that he is rational). In short, at the fourth level of consciousness man realizes with sometimes Nietzschean clarity, that he is, in essence, free.

In this context, then, freedom (precisely as an actuation of one's rational self-consciousness) involves a special kind of contingence.[11] Its real contingence arises not from the horizon of that empirical residue grounding all materiality nor from the non-systematic residues of his successive physical, chemical, biological and psychic levels but only from the horizon of the order of spirit.[12] Or (if one considers that word's history too mystery-laden) freedom emerges from the ordered horizon of intelligence, reason and decision. For not only is every particular object of a free choice a free possibility for the subject but, at a far more basic level, the subject need not choose at all to extend his rational consciousness into the horizon of a genuinely good life. In the phrase familiar to students of all cultures, knowledge is not necessarily virtue. For even if each man is essentially free inasmuch as he possesses, more exactly, *is* a dynamism towards freedom, he cannot claim that he is always effectively free.[13] One's effective freedom, in fact, can be seriously limited by external circumstance or by the limitations of one's sensitivity, one's intelligence and one's willingness. There always exists a gap between the proximate effective freedom one actually possesses (as measured by the insights, judgments, and decisions already achieved) and the remote and hypothetical effective freedom one might possess if certain conditions (e.g. time to reflect) were fulfilled. Such an existential gap is aptly named man's moral impotence[14] for it affects the very functioning of

11. *Ibid.,* pp. 615–19 contrast with the discussion of "The Significance of Statistical Residues" (pp. 607–08), and "The Underlying Sensitive Flow" (pp. 608–09).
12. *Ibid.,* p. 618.
13. *Ibid.,* pp. 619–22.
14. *Ibid.,* pp. 627–30.

the dynamic structure itself. That moral impotence sets for man a problem which bespeaks the need of each man to seek a liberation[15] which he cannot attain on his own. The evidence for that inability to sustain development is best found within:[16] in the subject's recognition of his own inability indefinitely to withstand the demands of the tension set up by the interplay of his detached and disinterested desire to know with his attached and self-interested sensitivity and biased exclusivity. Essentially the problem lies not in some strictly theoretical realm nor in some easily rectified human situation but rather in a radical, permanent and universal characteristic of man as man. And the solution to the problem may authentically be located only in what *Insight* names a "higher integration"[17] or what Lonergan's later work will more accurately name a moral conversion. For only one's continuous struggle to overcome one's desires and fears and to allow the intelligent and reasonable demands of a radical moral conversion to become the center of one's life is an ethical stance worthy of a truly human life. But it is not the place here to discuss that ethical life further. The aim of the present analysis is a more modest one: it is merely to set the conditions for the possibility of a critical ethics by explicitating the fourth level of human consciousness in relationship to the first three and by allowing that exposition of the actual human situation to facilitate a yet more radical openness to the further questions of a possible more than human transcendence.

The Further Movement Into History: Transcendence: Religious Conversion

In terms of the basic interest of this work the two concluding chapters of *Insight*—on general transcendence (God) and special transcendence (evil)—do not play a notably direct part.

15. *Ibid.*, pp. 630–33.
16. *Ibid.*, p. 630. One should note the similarity to the analysis of the nature of original sin for Aquinas in *Gratia Operans;* cf. *G.O.* II, esp. pp. 74–82.
17. *Insight*, pp. 632–33.

For that reason, therefore, Lonergan's intricate, and in several ways, original approach[18] to these two questions will not be treated at any great length. However, the transformation of Lonergan's "universal viewpoint" on the level of proportionate being into a universal viewpoint that opens man to transcendence and closes with *intellectus quaerens fidem* must be dealt with at least summarily in order to provide some understanding of Lonergan's earliest sustained approach to the questions of the inter-relationships of philosophy, faith and theology and thereby his understanding of the peculiar nature and problems of a strictly theological method.

Hence, it would be helpful to review briefly the "inner logic" of the moving viewpoint of *Insight* in order to appreciate the structure and the exigencies of the present movement into transcendence. For if, in fact, transcendence is, as *Insight* insists, not a confrontation with some mysterious and transhuman phenomenon but the elementary matter of raising further questions, then, the very nature of *Insight*'s structure from lower context to ever further question[19] to ever higher viewpoint will provide the best entry into the thorny question of the higher viewpoint and integration (the exigence for which the chapter on *Ethics* articulated and the presence of which the final two chapters express). One may recall, therefore, that *Insight* has been written not deductively but from a moving viewpoint.[20] It began from insight as a peculiar event in human experience in order to discuss the centrality of that event, first, in mathematical knowledge and, secondly, in empirical science. It then shifted its attention from the precision and clarity communicated by the insights of mathematicians and scientists to the complex and often ambivalent functioning of intelligence in common sense

18. For Lonergan's own analysis of the originality and continuity of his approach to the question of God's existence, cf. his unpublished lecture (University of Chicago Divinity School, 1967) on his proof for the existence of God.

19. *Insight,* pp. 634–36.

20. This summary section is faithful to Lonergan's own summary of the "inner logic" of the work, *ibid.,* pp. 731–34.

and its relation to its own psychoneural basis and its objective-pole expansion into technologies, economies, politics, cultures, etc. The analysis next moved beyond all direct and inverse acts of understanding to the further question "Is it?" and to the virtually unconditioned nature of all judgments. Then (fundamentally by means of the breakthrough of "Self-Affirmation") the moving viewpoint moved beyond "Insight as Activity" to develop a strategy of encirclement and confinement for the further question of "Insight as Knowledge." Only then, on the basis of the invariant structure of human intelligence which it had explicitated was it able to articulate an explicit metaphysics of proportionate being and the general structures of an ethics of proportionate being. At the end of that search for the possibility of ethics, moreover, one finds the rationally self-conscious man ever struggling to develop, only to find himself stymied by his own inability to sustain continual reflection and his increasingly clear recognition of the need for a liberation which could carry him beyond the possibilities of his own capacities. At this limit, man gradually discovers, that he bears within himself—in fact he is—the very source of that effort to transcend whatever present limitations he might find.[21] For he is a detached, disinterested, unrestricted desire to know. And that detachment and lack of restriction to his endless questions bear him forward, by the very exigencies of his normative intelligence and reason, beyond all attachment and all restrictions of his subjectivity to the ever further demands imposed by and on his *pure* desire to know, to reject all obscurantism, however partial, and to raise all questions, however impossible a complete solution may presently seem. And yet—as the chapter on ethics has already made clear and as the restriction of metaphysics to proportionate being implied—man's unrestricted desire to know is mated

21. In his post-*Insight* work, this notion of "self-transcendence" will be further explicitated into an "intentional," "real" and "religious" self-transcendence; cf. the forthcoming work *Method in Theology* (section on transcendental method). For *Insight* itself, cf. the section "The Immanent Source of Transcendence," pp. 636–39.

to a limited capacity to attain knowledge.[22] If the question of transcendent being is raised heuristically and critically (i.e. methodically) then the possibility of reaching a careful, deliberate and slowly arrived at affirmative response to the question (pp. 641–677) becomes for Lonergan a possibility.[23] And even though present exigencies do not allow for the lengthy treatment of *Insight*'s argument for transcendent being, i.e. for God, it is within the confines of the present discussion to observe that the breakthrough to an explanatory (indeed, critical) approach to the question becomes possible. For if being is whatever can be grasped intelligently and affirmed reasonably, then being is proportionate or transcendent insofar as it lies within or without the domain of man's intentionality.[24] The possibility of transcendent knowledge, therefore, is not the possibility of experiencing God but rather—and only—the possibility of intentionally anticipating, intelligently grasping and reasonably affirming his existence. For if one has, in fact, accepted Lonergan's philosophical "position" one must stand by one's own intelligence and reasonableness as *the criteria* for *all* reality. With such acceptance (and with the correlative explicit rejection of all counterpositions) the general argument proposed by *Insight* for God's existence and carefully and gradually explicitated from proportionate metaphysics to contingence through causality[25] to being may be seen to be neither dogmatic nor incomprehensible. The

22. *Ibid.*, p. 639.

23. *Ibid.*, pp. 642–77. For a careful study of the structure of Lonergan's argument, cf. Gary Schouborg, "A Note on Lonergan's Argument for the Existence of God," *Modern Schoolman*, 45 (March, 1968), 243–48. Further critical work is yet needed on Lonergan's "argument." The present writer has difficulties with it but will not distract from the present methodological interests to discuss them here. For one example of a critique, cf. David B. Burrell, "How Complete Can Intelligibility Be? A Commentary on *Insight*: Chapter XIX" and "Response" (by Lonergan), *Proceedings of the American Catholic Philosophical Association* (Washington, 1967), pp. 250–53, 258–59.

24. *Insight*, pp. 641–44.

25. The section on causality as interpreted in the context of intelligibility is especially crucial for Lonergan's argument; cf. *ibid.*, pp. 651–57.

argument runs thus:[26] If the real is completely intelligible, God exists. But the real is completely intelligible (precisely as the unrestricted act of understanding, or the formally unconditioned). Therefore, God exists. And even if the full argument cannot find its proper place here it is not to be assumed that it is alien to the work thus far.

Indeed, a final, methodological note may be made at this point: the method employed to speak of transcendence does not differ radically from the method already employed. The upper blade of method is still the mind itself as, by critical thematization, it understands and reflectively grasps itself in its dynamism and its invariant structure. Hence the meaning of critical method is not eliminated but expanded, indeed transformed into method with respect to the ultimate, method applied to the most basic issues—including the question of transcendence.[27] For the same basic upper blade of method operative in the empirical sciences and thematized into the method of a metaphysics of proportionate being is here examined from the point of view of its possible justification of its own intelligibility—which intelligibility must either be lacking (as a mere matter of fact) or grounded in the Pure Intelligence who is God.[28] As has been seen already, the method of the empirical sciences rests on the upper-blade heuristic structure of man's desire and capacity to understand data correctly and to verify that understanding through controlled experiment.[29] Likewise the critical method employed in metaphysics allowed for both a transformation of the extra-scientific

26. For the briefest explanation of the argument, cf. *ibid.,* pp. 672–77. However, the argument in its brief form there cannot be criticized except in the context of the entire "position" developed in *Insight* and especially in the earlier sections of Chapter 19 itself.

27. *Ibid.,* pp. 684–86; cf. also the "clarification-through-contrast" with other classical approaches to the question of God (*ibid.,* pp. 677–84).

28. It is to be noted that the category *ipsum intelligere* is *logically* prior to *ipsum esse subsistens* for Lonergan; cf. *Verbum,* esp. pp. 189–90, 298–99, 212–13.

29. One may perhaps be excused for emphasizing the importance of the notion of *heuristic* for Lonergan's entire procedure. For the actual concepts, cf. the section "The Notion of God," *Insight,* pp. 657–59.

173

views of the sciences and the biases of common sense on the basis of the mind's grasp of its own nature and its "integration and implementation" of the four basic methods needed to explain the being proportionate to man's experience, understanding, and judgment—(the classical and statistical, genetic and dialectical). The same basic heuristic anticipations are employed to raise the question of transcendence. As before, so here one grasps and affirms an object (pure intelligence) as correlative to the desire (for pure intelligence). As before, so here Lonergan insists that general statements can be made about the object before it is actually understood (heuristic concepts) and that such formulations, though valid and true and helpful, fall far short of what is to be known when (or if) actual understanding is attained. In short, there is nothing inherent in Lonergan's critical method that would eliminate the question of transcendence. On the contrary, the very nature of such heuristic method and the further questions flowing from its dynamism would demand the raising of the further questions of transcendence—of general transcendence to ground the very possibility of the positions (which otherwise inexplicably remain pure contingence) and of special transcendence to ground the *de facto* possibility of holding to the positions in the face of the fact of evil. For just as the scientific method of the empirical sciences does not eliminate the notion of "nature"[30] but further specifies it as the indeterminate function to be determined (classical), as the ideal frequency from which actual frequencies cannot diverge systematically (statistical), as the genetic operator (genetic), or as the dialectical tension and opposition between the pure desire and human sensitivity, so here critical method does not eliminate the notion of "God" but heuristically formulates it as the unrestricted act of understanding and proceeds to work out its general attributes. Moreover, just as scientific method does not confuse heuristic method with its conclusions, so here critical method does not confuse this heuristic formulation of a transcendent being as unrestricted understanding with any false claims to an actual

30. *Ibid.,* pp. 36–37, 683–84, 737.

174

knowledge of everything about everything.[31] And, finally, just as the scientist is willing to abandon even his most brilliant hypotheses without abandoning his heuristic method, so too the metaphysician may, by the use of the critical method proper to philosophy, affirm the reality which the scientist seeks to know, and the fully critical thinker must further raise, viz. both the possibility and need for a development in man's heuristic notion of God as the existence of the "one and the same being to which all men refer whether they are more or less successful in conceiving him, whether correctly they affirm his existence, or mistakenly they deny it."[32]

B. HISTORY: SPECIAL TRANSCENDENT KNOWLEDGE

The problem already articulated in Lonergan's treatment on general transcendence presents itself once more in the present—and for *Insight* final—question of special transcendence. The problem, quite simply, is that present exigencies do not allow for the fuller treatment which an adequate discussion of *Insight's* famous "thirty-one" step-by-step heuristic treatment of the problem of evil demands.[33] Consequently, once again, the option has been taken to delineate the broad outlines of the heuristic approach which Lonergan applies to the question. In short, the movement of the final chapter of *Insight* is from intellect on its own to *intellectus quaerens fidem*.[34] It is, moreover, precisely that higher viewpoint and that higher integration which in fact represent the highest viewpoint *Insight* reaches. Secondly, since the main interest of the present work is its potential contribu-

31. Cf. Lonergan's reply to Burrell on this point, in *Proceedings of the American Catholic Philosophical Association,* for a concise presentation of the crucial distinction between knowing and intending (pp. 258–59).
32. *Insight*, p. 686.
33. *Ibid.,* pp. 696–729.
34. *Ibid.,* p. 731.

tion to a theological methodology, the importance of this chapter to that discussion will be raised.

The general structure of the chapter itself is easy enough to understand.

Knowledge has already been understood as transcendent in the chapter on General Transcendence (or God). As such, man has already been brought beyond the domain of proportionate being. For if it be true that there is a God (as an unrestricted act of self-understanding), He would be the first agent of every event and emergence and development. The problem set by the present chapter, therefore, is not too difficult to understand:[35] if there is a fact of evil, what solution does God offer to it? This question Lonergan names "special transcendence." His approach to the question involves establishing (1) the fact of evil; (2) the existence of a solution (viz. that God, all-knowing and all-good—Chapter 19—does exist); (3) the heuristic structure of the properties of the possible solutions (herein lie the thirty-one "steps" a general outline of which will be given below); and (4) the identification of the solution that exists. (Furthermore, strategically placed between the fifteenth and sixteenth places of (3) is a lengthy treatment of faith[36] that bears important consequences not only for the general movement to the higher viewpoint of *intellectus quaerens fidem* but also for a proper understanding of scientific methodology—on all levels—as essentially collaborative and therefore, essentially involving a commitment to the truth[37] of not merely immanently generated knowledge but also beliefs.)

The first section (the fact of evil[38]) might best be described

35. *Ibid.,* pp. 688–93.
36. For a lengthier treatment of Lonergan's approach to the question of faith, cf. David Tracy, "Analysis of Faith According to Bernard Lonergan" (unpublished paper for seminar of Rev. Juan Alfaro, Pontificia Universitas Gregoriana, 1965).
37. As in the question of hermeneutic, it is important to note that Lonergan's interest in belief lies clearly with the truth-value of the assertion. Hence, once again, the central importance to be accorded his critical analysis of judgment.
38. *Insight,* pp. 692–93.

by recalling that in the final pages of the chapter on ethics the distinction between essential and effective freedom led to a recognition of the need for liberation from man's inability to sustain his development—an inability that, in the present chapter, is concisely described: "The reign of sin, then, is the expectation of sin."[39] The existence of God, moreover (affirmed in the immediately preceding chapter), both transforms the fact of evil into a problem[40] and indicates the basic solution, viz. God himself. If the first section, then, recalls Chapter 18 and the second section Chapter 19, it is in the third section that both the peculiarity of the present chapter comes fully to light and that the relationship of the present chapter to the general "moving viewpoint" of *Insight* as a whole becomes clear. For once again, a grasp of heuristic structures allows a heuristic approach to the problem of evil.[41] For a heuristic structure is present whenever the object of inquiry admits antecedent determinations. In this chapter, then, one seeks an object of inquiry which may satisfy the intelligible unity of the actual world order given both the existence of God and the problem of evil. In the present case, moreover, the structure fails to determine a singular answer to the problem. Rather it sets forth the properties which must be observed by indicating any one of a set of possible alternative answers. Only by an appeal to the historical facts will the actual solution become clear.[42] Heuristically, therefore, it can be determined that the needed solution would satisfy certain fundamental demands:[43] it would be one; be universally accessible and permanent; be a harmonious continuation of the actual order of the universe; reverse the priority of living over the knowledge needed to guide life and over the good will needed to follow knowledge; be effected through conjugate forms that in some sense would transcend human nature; constitute a new "higher" integration

39. *Ibid.*, p. 693.
40. *Ibid.*, p. 694.
41. *Ibid.*, p. 696.
42. *Ibid.*, pp. 729–30.
43. *Ibid.*, pp. 696–703: herein abbreviated for the purposes of continuity with this work's methodological interest.

of human activity; pertain not to static system but to system on the move; and be realized with man's apprehension and consent in accord with the probabilities of world order. Finally, these conjugate forms which would constitute the higher integration would be some type of charity, of hope and of belief. But that the higher viewpoint and integration must be some kind of belief the whole dynamism of *Insight* ineluctably demands.

If the higher viewpoint is one of belief (as distinct from knowledge) the question quite naturally follows, just what is belief?[44] The answer to that question[45] will clarify, for present purposes, both the nature of the general solution offered, as well as the relevant methodological importance of belief for science.

The Notion of Belief: As Possible Higher Viewpoint and as Methodological Device

The treatment of belief in *Insight,* although in its basic lines not novel, takes an original turn from the general context of the moving viewpoint of *Insight* itself. For it should be recalled that the interest in belief is in reference to its *truth*-value, its possibility of providing a higher viewpoint consistent with the viewpoint already reached, and of showing (within the context of the role of belief in the empirical sciences and its possible role in the human sciences) the methodological importance and role of belief in any scientific approach to reality.

The basic point is clear enough: the general context of belief is established as the collaboration of mankind in the advancement and dissemination of knowledge.[46] Moreover, a careful examination of scientific procedures reveals that the evidence that counts for one's acceptance of any theory is the common testimony of all scientists that the implications of the theory have been verified in their separate and diverse investigations.

44. Cf. also Lonergan, *Analysis Fidei* (College of Christ the King, Toronto, 1952), pp. 1–19; and *De Methodo Theologiae,* esp. pp. 41–46.
45. *Insight,* pp. 703–18.
46. *Ibid.,* p. 703.

In short, the evidence that specifically counts is the evidence for a belief. This raises an important methodological issue: should each man confine his notion of truth only to immanently generated judgments or—as scientific collaboration certainly suggests—should he expand that notion to include the assents of a reasonable belief?[47] This in turn raises two further methodological issues: First, if the operation and structure of the unrestricted desire's drive to immanently generated knowledge can be thematized and exploited as a universal viewpoint, can the operation and structure of that desire's essentially similar movement to belief be thematized and thereby made available for the universal viewpoint?[48] Secondly, just as the dialectic between position and counter-position can be set up on the basis of the genetic-dialectic operation of intellect's drive to the true judgments of immanently generated knowledge, cannot a critique of belief[49] (more exactly of the believer) be established on similar lines to assure that the entry of assents into the realm of truth be maintained as a fully reasonable one? The first of these issues receives its importance from the problem set by the necessity for scientific collaboration, viz. that sustained collaboration demands belief. The alternative is not knowledge, but a primitive ignorance. And yet the practical consequences of such collaboration is a symbiosis in the minds of most men of knowledge and belief. It should be noted, moreover, that collaboration is not accepted simply as a matter of fact[50] but is itself grounded in the fact that since the criterion of truth is a virtually unconditioned,[51] any truth is not essentially conditioned by its subject and therefore includes an essential detachability from the mind in which it happened to be generated and an essential communi-

47. *Ibid.,* p. 704.
48. Hence, the need to "break" the general argument for special transcendence in order to analyze the need for and availability of the analysis of belief.
49. *Ibid.,* pp. 713–18.
50. As the "proximate and concrete" criterion for the logical possibility of belief; *ibid.,* p. 707.
51. As the "remote and general" criterion for the logical possibility of belief; *ibid.,* p. 707.

cability. For the unconditioned (precisely as such) is independent of the processes of transmission from one place or mind to another. Hence collaboration—if authentic—is merely an implementation of this essential detachability and communicability of the virtually unconditioned.

The authenticity of belief, then, can be established by determining both the general structure of belief and a critique of false beliefs. As to the first, *Insight*[52] establishes and clarifies the essential similarity of belief to intellect's search for immanently generated truth along with the important differences that must be considered (especially that the judgment in question is one of the *value* of believing another's immanently generated truth and that the final product is not judgment (as immanently generated assertion of truth) but assent (as reasonable act of believing[53]). The five stages[54] to be distinguished in belief, then, are the following:

(1) preliminary *judgments* on the value of belief in general (i.e. the necessity and nature of collaboration), on the reliability of the source for this belief, and on the accuracy of communication from the source;

(2) a *reflective* act of understanding that, in virtue of the preliminary judgments, grasps a virtually unconditioned and the *value;*

(3) the *consequent* judgment of value;

(4) the *consequent* decision of the will and;

(5) the actual assent that is the act of believing.

It might be objected that such an analysis works well enough in the empirical sciences—whose concerns seem remote from man even if their technological results change man's environment and in that sense, man himself. But does belief bear any real value for the human sciences?[55] If it does not, its importance

52. *Ibid.,* pp. 708–13.
53. *Ibid.,* p. 710. The influence of Newman's analysis of assent in his famous *A Grammar of Assent* (London, 1888) seems especially prominent, although revised in accord with the far more technical and critical attitude of *Insight* itself.
54. *Insight,* p. 708.
55. *Ibid.,* pp. 714–15.

is severely limited. For it is precisely these sciences that most need an expansion of the universal viewpoint of proportionate metaphysics and ethics to deal with man as he actually is—as before God and as faced with evil (including, indeed especially, the evil of the erroneous beliefs that besiege the mind of man). To meet this problem (and thereby to render belief more methodologically operative for the human sciences as well) Lonergan, in the light of his previous discussions of the biases of common sense, the counter-positions of philosophy, the general tendency of man to collapse mystery into myth, and the ethical impotence that man experiences in the face of his own inability to sustain his development or to remain faithful to God, initiates a critique of mistaken beliefs.[56] The method advanced, furthermore, is quite direct—and given an acceptance of *Insight*'s previous critique of error and openness to truth—relatively simple. For just as collaboration is (externally) a necessity for all men, so too every man possesses (internally) a symbiosis[57] of immanently generated knowledge and belief. That symbiosis (a lifelong acquirement) may contain several mistaken beliefs. To find one is not very difficult. But to find the reason for its origin (sources, motives, contributing judgments) is likewise not too difficult to unravel. In fact, the search for the reasons for a particular mistaken belief is simply a particular case of the already investigated general self-correcting process of learning. As in other cases, the clues, the insights, the gradually accumulating evidence lead to further clues, questions and insights until rational consciousness, true to its own demanding criteria, rests satisfied that all the relevant questions have been asked and their reasons located. The basic method employed here, in short, is the same method used elsewhere: the method of an understanding and genetic-dialectic thematization of *human knowing* itself in its possibilities and limitations of both immanently generated knowledge and belief. It is the only method, as *Insight* has continually argued, that can be truly efficacious for breaking

56. *Ibid.*, pp. 713–18.
57. *Ibid.*, p. 714.

through any extrinsicism and into the subject himself.[58] However, this critique of mistaken beliefs does not solve man's fundamental impotence in the face of the problem of evil. For the critique is a human product and cannot solve the problem of special transcendence.[59] If man's will matched the detachment and unrestricted nature of the pure desire to know, evil would not be the problem it is. As long as this is so, intellect may find methods to criticize mistaken beliefs but it cannot heal a will which does not match intellect's own unrestricted desire. In short, the critique of mistaken beliefs leads one, once again, to recognize the *de facto* condition of historical man, unable to solve the problem of evil but able (if he acknowledges the existence of God as well as the fuller expansion of truth involved in the notion of belief)—to search for a higher solution than man himself can fashion; a faith solution which man can seek and, given the facts of human history, even acknowledge as offered to him as God's gift in Christ Jesus.[60]

On the methodological plane, finally, the problem of special transcendence has quietly extended the method developed by *Insight* to include the full range of the human sciences by insisting upon an analysis of man's actual situation, of his need for a higher integration that he himself cannot attain and, of the authentic possibilities of genuine Christian conversion.[61] In a word, the intellectualist horizon of *Insight* has been opened somewhat hesitantly but really to the demands of religious and indeed Christian conversion.

58. The logical force of the argument, it should be emphasized, is the parallelism of the search for immanently generated knowledge and the advancement of a reasonable belief (the latter of which can best be clarified by a critique of an easily recognizable mistaken belief of one's own). For an expansion, cf. "A Logical Note," *ibid.,* p. 718.

59. *Ibid.,* p. 714.

60. It is important to recall that this is merely a summary of Lonergan's extended argument, *ibid.,* pp. 718–30.

61. There is a sense in which this interpretation of Lonergan's analysis of special transcendence in *Insight* is a "hindsight," yet a hermeneutically viable one, insofar as the later problematics of the human sciences-meaning-historical consciousness be employed to interpret Lonergan's earlier analysis of the question.

8. THE RETURN TO THEOLOGY: TRANSITION PERIOD: THE THEOLOGY OF THE TRINITY AND THE RISE OF METHODICAL EXIGENCE

The major achievement of *Insight* is, properly speaking, a cognitional—epistemological—philosophical one. As we have already indicated, the questions of ethical values, of God and of faith will receive more explicit and more expanded treatment in Lonergan's later work. The same might be said for the specific contribution of *Insight* to theology. However, to observe Lonergan's theological work in its actual historical development, one cannot find a more explicit example of either *Insight*'s possibilities for theology or of the emergence of the later methodological problematic than his developments in Trinitarian and Christological thought in the period immediately following the achievement of *Insight*. Indeed, the dominant question of history (more precisely of historical consciousness) becomes ever more dominant as Lonergan increases his involvement in the positive, dogmatic and systematic aspects of the Trinitarian and Christological problematics. To understand that achievement, however, it is first necessary to recall the context of those works. In the present case, that includes, above all, recalling the contribution of *Insight* to theology and the changed context of Catholic theology following the biblical, patristic and liturgical revivals and the consequent importance of clearly differentiating both a strictly positive theology and the problem of doctrinal development in dogmatic theology from the previous theological specialties.

183

A: FIRST CONTEXT: INSIGHT AND THEOLOGY

The approach that Lonergan will take to the vexed question of
theological method should be easy enough to grasp in the light
of the previous analysis of the moving viewpoint of *Insight* itself. For there it was seen that the upper blade of all method
was the actual performance of intellect as it structures itself
into a universal viewpoint of proportionate being only to find
its own self-reliance transformed when faced with the questions
of general and special transcendence. At this point then the
peculiarity and complexity of theology becomes clear. For
theology attempts to formulate the transformed universal viewpoint for the human sciences as the critical method of philosophy formulates it for the empirical.[1] Indeed, the first fruits of that
methodology are worked out in Lonergan's systematic treatises
De Deo Trino and *De Verbo Incarnato*.[2] Moreover, as the final

1. Not in totalitarian fashion, of course, but as a "higher collaboration": "To this question the remaining paragraphs of this Epilogue will
be devoted and, as the reader already has surmised, they will be written,
not from the moving viewpoint whose exigencies, I trust, I have been
observing honestly and sincerely, but from the terminal viewpoint of a
believer, a Catholic, and, it happens, a professor of dogmatic theology"
(*Insight*, p. 732).

2. It will prove helpful as more expeditious to take note here of the
chronology of the works, employed in the footnote citations of Lonergan's Trinitarian theology; for the present analysis is of four principal
works: (1) *Divinarum Personarum Conceptio Analogica* (Rome, 1957,
1959; *ad usum auditorum*); the 1959 edition is used here as essentially
unchanged from 1957 except for correction of misprints and an addition
of two short quaestiunculae (pp. 91, 297); (2) *De Deo Trino: Pars Analytica* (Rome, 1961; *ad usum auditorum*); (3) *De Deo Trino I: Pars
Dogmatica* (Rome, 1964); (4) *De Deo Trino II: Pars Systematica*. The
following abbreviations will be employed for these works: (1) *DP;* (2)
DDT (1961); (3) *DDT* I; and (4) *DDT* II. It is to be noted that (1)
and (2) are in the *ad usum auditorum* format whereas the 1964
editions (3) and (4) are regular publications of the Gregorian University Press. It is also of some note that *De Verbo Incarnato* (Rome,
1960) is in the *ad usum auditorum* format and has yet to receive the
definitive treatment of the 1964 edition of *DDT* I and II, i.e. (3) and
(4). However, the 1964 *De Verbo Incarnato* bears important additions.
(Hereafter references to *De Verbo Incarnato*, unless otherwise cited,

chapters will explain, the rise of the further relevant questions and the slow and deliberate emergence of the relevant insights led Lonergan over the years following *Insight* to begin to formulate a critical methodology for theology. This formulation, as we shall see below, received its most important breakthrough only recently and its complete formulation is yet to come. For present purposes, however, it is sufficient to show what Lonergan's thoughts on the problematic of theology were at the time of the completion of *Insight*. In the light of his more recent work those thoughts may well seem relatively underdeveloped. However, upon closer examination, they can be seen to provide a general heuristic structure by means of which the further questions, further insights and further formulations may emerge.[3]

In the "Epilogue," then, Lonergan attempts to summarily indicate some of the fruits of *Insight* for the problem of theology.

---

will be to the 1961 edition as *DVI*.) One should also recall that Lonergan's interest in the problematic of Trinitarian theology may also be found in the following publications (chronologically listed): *Verbum: Word and Idea in Aquinas* (first published from 1946–1949 in *Theological Studies;* book form, Notre Dame and London, 1968); cf. esp. pp. 183–221 of the latter; *De Sanctissima Trinitate: Supplementum Quoddam* (Rome, 1955)—Lonergan's earliest formulation of three articles which are either treated more adequately in a later formulation or not intrinsic to the methodological interests of this book and hence not analyzed in the text of this work; and the following book reviews in *Gregorianum:* (1) review: *Théologie Trinitaire chez Saint Thomas* by P. Vanier, *Gregorianum* 36 (1955), 703–05; (2) review: *The Indwelling of the Trinity* by F. Cunningham, *Gregorianum* 37 (1956), 664–65; (3) review: *Die Lehre von Gott. Bd 2: von der goettlichen Trinität* by J. Brinktrine, *Gregorianum* 37 (1956), 665; (4) review: *Les Missions divines selon Saint Augustin, Gregorianum* 44 (1963), 371. Of similar interest are two unpublished lectures of Lonergan's, viz. "The Origins of Christian Realism" (Toronto, 1961); and "Consciousness and the Trinity" (Rome, 1963). For his Christological thought, of significant interest is *De Constitutione Christi ontologica et psychologica* (Rome, 1961, *ad usum auditorum*), esp. (for methodological purposes), pp. 42–57.

3. In other words, the post-*Insight* development of the "later" Lonergan does not argue for a break in the continuity of his thought. Indeed the transcendental method of *Insight* provides the critical foundation of his later thought as well.

First of all, however, he recalls what has been named the "inner logic" of the moving viewpoint of *Insight*:[4] From a succession of lower contexts, there gradually emerged an upper context. The lower contexts were to be subject to ever further additions and revisions. The upper context was to be constituted.[5]

(1) by the invariant structures of experiencing, inquiring and reflecting;

(2) by the consequent, isomorphic structures of all there is to be known of the universe of proportionate being;

(3) by the fuller invariant structure that adds reasonable choice and action to intelligent and reasonable knowing;

(4) by the profounder structure of knowing and known to be reached by acknowledging the full significance of the detached, disinterested, unrestricted desire to know (i.e. general transcendence); and

(5) by the structure of the process which the existential situation sets for human intelligence: viz. the problem of rising above its native resources to seek a divine solution to man's incapacity for sustained development (i.e. special transcendence —Christian conversion).

And, if the highest viewpoint and integration offered to man is indeed that higher collaboration with God called faith, it then becomes imperative to know just what man's own understanding can bring to bear on his faith. In short, it becomes relevant to ask what intellectual fruit *Insight*'s discussion of man might have for man's highest intellectual possibility, viz. theology. Those contributions are principally in three fields: (1) apologetics; (2) method of theology; (3) relation of theology to the other sciences. All three contributions bear study as indicators of Lonergan's notion of the nature of theology and, at the limit, of theological method.[6]

4. *Insight*, pp. 731–32.
5. *Ibid.*
6. It is interesting to note that Lonergan's later work will not find the need to distinguish these problematics in that fashion, but will be able to include all three under the general problematic of theological method: the foundational problem and the inter-relational problem.

(1) *Apologetics or Introduction to Theology*. Lonergan observes that a Catholic thinker rejects both the exclusive rationalism of the Enlightenment and the various explosions of irrationalism that have played their by no means minor role in the history of Western man.[7] But this rejection is made only in order to make room for a more positive assertion—viz. the possibility of a synthesis of the objects and a symbiosis of the principles of reason and faith.[8] However, as a history of Catholic thought of the last two centuries makes all too clear, the "reason" of the theological synthesis has been subject to constant changes through its contacts with the different departments of science (e.g. physics, Semitic literature, biology, economics, depth psychology). Indeed, that dependence has often reached the stage where (in Lonergan's happy phrase) believers seem to be left behind in "the unenviable position of . . . arriving on the scene a little breathlessly and a little late."[9]

As a matter of fact, however, the analysis of *Insight* may speak more directly to that central question of the relationship of faith and reason.[10] For if the upper blade of all scientific method is intellect itself which can be critically thematized into a sufficiently supple and detailed cognitional theory, then the theologian may understand and articulate the positive element in rationalism without having to concede to any tempting irrationalism when the further theological questions of transcendence and belief arise. Indeed, the transformed universal viewpoint of the final chapter of *Insight* has not reversed but merely expanded and transformed that meaning into the higher viewpoint and a higher integration called Christian conversion and theology.

(2) *Method of Theology*. Here certain major areas of contribution of *Insight* to theology may be cited.

7. *Insight*, p. 732.
8. In short, one may speak of a "higher viewpoint" as in the general "moving viewpoint" of *Insight*.
9. *Insight*, p. 733.
10. *Ibid*.

First, the dialectical analysis of positions and counterpositions bears important and threefold theological application:

(a) It provides for a critical analysis of the pietist-modernist attack on dogma for just as the philosophic counterposition of empiricism appeals to experience against the truthful "yes" of rational consciousness, so too the modernist-pietist appeals to "pure" religious experience against the "yes" of an articulate, truthful (i.e. dogmatic) faith.[11]

(b) Just as dialectical analysis provides a technique to eliminate several disputed questions in metaphysics as false questions, so too a critical, intellectualist theological approach can lead to a similar elimination of several famous disputed questions of the conceptualist tradition (e.g. the Báñez-Molina problematic on freedom and providence referred to in Chapter 2).

(c) The full development of the position into an unabashed intellectualism can lend illuminating support to the statements of Vatican I on the role of theological understanding in faith, viz. as a limited but most fruitful *understanding* of the Christian mysteries both from viewpoint of the analogy of nature and of the inner coherence of the mysteries among themselves.

Secondly (and of more technical importance to theology), there is *Insight*'s differentiation of the possibility of an invariant and detailed critical metaphysics of proportionate being.[12] Hence, in his theology, Lonergan feels free to employ the generalities

11. *Ibid.,* pp. 733–34; the defense of dogma proves of key theological importance in Lonergan's Trinitarian and Cristological positions. For a brief presentation of the position, cf. "The Origins of Christian Realism" (lecture delivered at Regis College, September 8, 1961); for the continuity with his later thought, cf. "The De-Hellenization of Dogma," pp. 336–52. The Báñez-Molina dispute has already been articulated in Lonergan's *Gratia Operans* articles (cf. Chapter 2 for citations) as well as his *De Ente Supernaturali; Supplementum Schematicum* (L'Immaculée Conception, Montreal, 1946); for an excellent presentation of this issue, cf. Review: *De Deo in Operatione Naturae vel Voluntatis Operante," Theological Studies* 7 (1946), 602–13.

12. *Insight,* p. 734.

that alone are available *a priori* for a theological structuring of the supernatural elements in this world. This differentiation, then, bears two chief fruits: (a) a critical destruction of the Scotist concept of theological science by a clear espousal of the meaning of scientific theology as elaborating an understanding of this world without having to offer an explanation of other possible worlds;[13] (b) the limitation of metaphysics to the realm of proportionate being makes it clear that the theologian cannot reduce the strictly supernatural realities of the Incarnation, the Indwelling of the Holy Spirit and the Beatific Vision to purely metaphysical elements (for example, Lonergan's analogy from contingent predication as contrasted with the quasi-formal (i.e. still proportionate) causality of Rahner or de la Taille.[14]

(3) *The Relation of Theology to the Other Sciences.* The question of the relationship of the human sciences and theology may now be raised.[15] It is this question, in fact, which will receive a major emphasis in Lonergan's subsequent work. It is interesting to note, however, that he already insists that *Insight* itself was developed largely in response to this problem.[16] The problem itself, perhaps, needs clarification: the development of the empirical human sciences has created a fundamentally new problematic for theology which cannot be answered simply within the context of the medieval synthesis. For the Aristotleian notion of science which lies behind the medieval synthesis can-

13. For a further discussion of the various notions of science, cf. *De Intellectu et Methodo,* pp. 26–30.

14. For an actual thematization of this position, cf. *De Verbo Incarnato,* pp. 260–68.

15. Lonergan even suggests that this will prove the proper mode for theology to fulfill her traditional role as *"regina scientiarum";* cf. *Insight,* p. 743. Moreover, this concern is meant to continue, not eliminate the notion of theology of the conciliar and medieval (systematic) traditions, viz. via the continuity of "transcendental method" as "critical realism" with the Thomist realism of the mediaeval period; cf. the section on the "exigencies" (systematic, critical, methodical) in the forthcoming *Method in Theology* and analyzed in Chapter 9 of this work.

16. "Now it is this problem that in large measure has dictated the structure of the present work" (*ibid.,* pp. 743–44).

not express the intelligibility of the *de facto,* the contingent, the probable, and the changing which together define the goals of contemporary science. In the human sciences, moreover, (with which, after all, theology is principally concerned) the interest is not on man as he universally is or must be, but rather on man in his concrete performance[17]—a performance that manifests not only human intelligence and love but human sin, not only nature and sin but also the *de facto* need of divine grace, not only a need of grace but also of its actual reception or rejection. In short, if these are in fact the human elements that must be considered by the empirical, human sciences, then no human science can successfully analyze its object without an appeal to the specific science that handles precisely those elements, viz. theology. Inversely, if theology is to continue its historically transforming role in the changed scientific context, then theologians will have to take a professional interest in the human sciences and contribute to their methodology.[18] Finally, insofar as philosophy itself becomes more existential, it changes its relationship to theology in the same way as the human sciences do.

Theology, therefore, precisely as the transcendentally transformed universal viewpoint, has a twofold relevance to empirical human science.[19] First, it is relevant insofar as the truly scientific (i.e. pure unfolding of the scientist's detached, disinterested and unrestricted desire to understand his own field) is open to a variety of interferences (biases, counter-positions, myth, inability to sustain development, and, in the limit, sin). These latter, moreover, can ultimately be fully transformed only by accepting that higher viewpoint (viz. faith and theology) which formulates the ultimate implications of the unrestricted

17. *Ibid.,* p. 745; e.g. "In a word, empirical human science can become practical only through theology, and the relentless modern drift to social engineering and totalitarian controls is the fruit of man's effort to make human science practical though he prescinds from God and from the solution God provides for man's problems."

18. *Ibid.,* p. 743.

19. *Ibid.,* p. 745.

190

desire to know. Secondly, theology is equally relevant to the true interpretation of the results of empirical human science. For even on the so far unrealized supposition that a particular human science develops to the point where it could adequately establish the classical, genetic, dialectical and statistical laws in some area of human development, still that development would not provide a full understanding of human activity for it would try to understand but could not remedy man's problem of evil. For the solution to that problem is not within man's own resources but in his acceptance of the solution that God Himself has provided. And the systematic treatment of that solution must be theological. In other words, the empirical human sciences can only become what they desire to be—i.e. practical (constituting history and not just mediating it)[20] through theology.

There is an obverse side, however, to the question for, to use the traditional vocabulary, grace perfects nature in two senses:[21] it adds a perfection beyond nature and it confers on nature the effective freedom to attain its own freedom. Hence, theology cannot become a substitute for the empirical human sciences. Rather it remains a higher viewpoint which reveals in their fullness the concrete possibility of intelligent and reasonable solutions to human problems. For in the measure that the theologian knows that his own detached, disinterested, unrestricted desire to know is ultimately grounded in God, he will be empowered and indeed impelled to encourage scientists in their calling, to reverse those counter-positions which block the development of that spirit, and to convert "practical" men from the policies of *Realpolitik* to policies of intelligence, of reason, of responsibility and love. He will, moreover, as a fully converted man, be able to perform in an authentically religious and theoretical manner himself. In a word, he may theologize.

20 The categories "constitutive" and "mediated" meaning are post-*Insight*, yet faithful to its aim; cf. "Dimensions of Meaning," Collection, pp. 252–68.

21. *Insight*, p. 746.

B. THE RISE OF THE HISTORICAL SENSE IN CATHOLIC THEOLOGY

By now the phrases "aggiornamento" and the "return to the sources" ring somewhat hollow. To assert this, of course, is not to affirm that the truth represented by these phrases is now untrue. It is simply to affirm that the very success of their truth (best represented in the documents of Vatican II) has now become a theological commonplace. However, in the period under discussion here, the phrases were both original and, as the early struggles of the Second Vatican Council amply testify, disturbingly unacceptable to many Catholic theologians.[22] For they seemed to challenge at the root the "eternal truths" of the classicists as well as the comforting security of the theology of the "schools." And although it seemed entirely too easy an affair to ignore the charge of "extrinsicism" and "conceptualism" charged against that systematic theological tradition in the early works of a Lonergan or a Rahner, it was not so easy to ignore the problematics uncovered either by the biblical, patristic and liturgical revivals and the consequent rise of a strictly positive theology[23] or by the problematic of doctrinal develop-

22. Of the vast literature on Vatican II, cf. esp. (on the present question) E. Schillebeeckx, *The Layman in the Church and Other Essays* (New York, 1963); and Michael Novak, *The Open Church* (New York, 1963). On the post-Vatican II possibilities, cf. esp. L. K. Shook (ed.), *Theology of Renewal* I and II (New York, 1968).

23. Cf. T. Tshibangu, *Théologie positive et théologie speculative,* esp. pp. 210–93; Y. Congar, *A History of Theology* (New York, 1968). In Lonergan's own case, contrast, for example, the "rough and serviceable" distinction between positive and dogmatic-historical thought of "Theology and Understanding," *Collection,* esp. pp. 137–39, and that of *DDT* I and II where dogmatic theology takes on a dialectical character quite distinct from the strictly empirical work of positive theology (cf. esp. *DDT* I, pp. 3–14). Perhaps an analogy from Lonergan's own development may prove clarifying; as was argued in Chapter 2 of this work, Lonergan is able to employ the historical research of Landgraf, Lottin, *et al.* and still attain a synthesis of the *scientific meaning* of speculative theology for St. Thomas Aquinas in a way in which they were not; similarly the problematic here is how dogmatic and speculative theologies

ment initiated by figures like Newman and Möhler. What in fact was occurring during that turbulent period in Catholic thought was the sudden entry of a genuinely historical consciousness into the Catholic tradition. To recall how unwelcome it was, one need only recall the unhappy memories of Garrigou-Lagrange's reaction to *"la nouvelle théologie"* or the aura of suspicion cast over the careers of a Congar, a de Lubac, a Chardin—or almost any scripture scholar. That the "historical consciousness" of that period was not the full-fledged "historical consciousness" of the present scene will be the concern of the next chapter. But that the controversies of the forties and fifties of this century did represent a genuine entry of (at the very least) a widely acclaimed need for a "historical sense"[24] is by now a fact of the history of that period.

Nor was the position of Lonergan at that time uninvolved with those problematics. With the clarification of the nature of systematic theology as genuinely intellectualist[25] behind him,

---

may employ scientifically the results of positive theology without distorting those results and without abandoning the demands of their own positions.

24. It may prove helpful to distinguish the notion of "historical consciousness" in a manner which Lonergan himself does not do explicitly but does, I believe, perform. First, there is the notion of historical consciousness as the "historical sense" needed to realize that, for example, Nicea must first be interpreted in its own context, terms, etc. (viz. both positive and dogmatic theology fit this description). Then there is "historical consciousness" in the deeper and more radical meaning of the recognition of the need for the finite, historical inquirer to conduct a critique of his own possibilities of meaning and those of other cultures or epochs (viz. the problems associated with hermeneutic theory, historicity and [in Lonergan's case] the multi-dimensional levels of meaning, especially on the level of *Existenz* [cf. Chapters 9 and 10]) fit only the latter sense. The present chapter deals with the earlier meaning of the term.

25. After the study of Lonergan's Aquinas' interpretation in Chapter 2 of this work, it should not be necessary to document this. However, *inter alia*, the interested reader may note the fundamental fidelity (albeit with development) of the entire structure of Lonergan's Trinitarian theology and, content-wise, especially of *DP* and *DDT* II as well as the fidelity to the ontology and psychology of Aquinas in *De Constitutione Christi* and *DVI:* esp. pp. 181–268 (for ontology); pp. 269–312 (for

and with the possibilities for a transcendental method based on the dynamic and heuristic nature of all genuine inquiry achieved in *Insight*, it is hardly surprising that Lonergan's entry into the recently evolved Trinitarian and Christological problematics would force him to come to terms with the new theological context and to see what light the achievement of *Insight* might bring to bear on it.

In fact, however important his other contributions to the understanding of Trinitarian and Christological theologies (some of which we mentioned above), Lonergan's most important and fundamental question and contribution at this period remains his questions on the basic nature of theology itself. For, as the two editions of his Trinitarian theology elaborate, the problem is the need to differentiate and relate the three principal contemporary theological specializations: positive, dogmatic and systematic theology.[26]

First, then, a brief treatment of Lonergan's understanding of those factors would be in order here. Theology, for Lonergan, has always been thematized knowledge of God mediated by the Body of Christ. In the Catholic context of the forties and fifties, moreover, that thematized knowledge can be determined as

---

Lonergan's explicit development of Aquinas' treatment of the consciousness of Christ). The outstanding example of such development remains Lonergan's transition from his explicit treatment of St. Thomas Aquinas on the knowledge of Christ in the 1961 edition of *DVI*: pp. 333–62, to his own analysis via the historical causality of *Existenz* in the 1964 edition of *DVI*: pp. 332–416.

26. Indeed, note the opening words of *DDT* I: *"Studiis florentibus theologicis et positivis, obscurum quoddamodo atque incertum redditur quid a theologo dogmatico praestandum sit"* (p. 3). *Inter alia*, cf. *DDT* I, pp. 3–14 (on positive and dogmatic theology); *DDT* II esp. pp. 13–18 (on systematic theology). Note further that the notion of systematic theology employed here is the traditional Catholic notion (systematic categories to aid one's understanding of [principally] the dogmatic tradition), not of the notion of systematics more familiar to Protestant theologians since Schleiermacher. Indeed, that latter discipline demanded the second notion of historical consciousness (ftn. 24) (as in Schleiermacher) and is later (cf. Chapter 10) to be named "foundational" theology as distinct from systematic.

divided into positive, dogmatic and speculative theologies. Briefly, positive theology thematizes the spontaneous expression of such knowledge and their previous thematizations. It is called theology *in oratione obliqua* as it attempts an account of sources and developments in all their detail and particularity. Dogmatic theology, on the other hand, is concerned with dogmas in their genesis, content and implications.[27] It stands to positive theology as any good history of science stands to the particular studies of each of the important scientific discoveries. Finally, systematic theology, as always, tries to attain an imperfect and analogous understanding of the mysteries.[28] And

27. Note how this differs from the manuals' notion of dogmatic theology, precisely by the introduction of historical consciousness (positive theology and dialectics). Still it is perhaps worthy of attention to note that Lonergan's own theological works (*De Ente Supernaturali,* both editions of *De Deo Trino,* and *De Verbo Incarnato*) continue to employ the thesis format of the manuals—but with the significant methodological differences of the historical sense (positive and dogmatic theologies) and a critical method (to order the systematic questions). But as a result even of Lonergan's own analysis of contemporary theological method ("Functional Specialization," cf. Chapter 10 of this work), the present interpreter does not believe that even the present thesis format (e.g. *DDT* [1961] and *D.P.*) is helpful.

28. For a concise presentation of how Lonergan argues that his notion of systematic theology is in fundamental continuity with both Aquinas and Vatican I's decree in *Dei Filius,* cf. "Theology and Understandnig," *Collection,* pp. 121–42. On Lonergan's notion of systematic theology as related to the Catholic tradition, it is interesting to note that his analysis of that relationship in this period of his thought is in terms of the Aristotelean distinction of science, understanding and wisdom; it is not beside the point to indicate how Lonergan's own acceptance of the Leonine program *vetera novis augere et perficere* is itself an acceptance of this relationship, e.g. how to understand the theological achievement of the magisterium's approved theologian, St. Thomas Aquinas, and how to relate his own theological program to the determination of the nature of theology in Vatican I's *Constitutio de Fide Catholica* (Concilium Vaticanum, sess. 3., c. 4; Denzinger, *Enchiridion Symbolorum, Definitionum, Declarationum,* 1796 [DS: 3016]. Nor, as far as this interpreter can see, is this relationship to the doctrinal tradition (including the magisterial) ever omitted in Lonergan's work. For confirmation, cf. F. E. Crowe, "The Origin and Scope of Bernard Lonergan's *Insight,*" *Sciences Ecclésiastiques* 9 (1957), 263–95; cf. also B. Lonergan, "The Assumption and Theology," *Collection,* pp. 68–84, and

since those specializations find articulation in *De Deo Trino,* it will now be necessary to spell out their implications at greater length—both by a discussion of the development in Lonergan's theology of the Trinity and his Christology and of his subsequent historical and methodological work. For it is in this period above all that the methodological exigence which will be the subject of the next chapter comes to the forefront of his theological investigations.

Historical Background

In the section on Aquinas, we have presented Lonergan's understanding of the medieval achievement of a scientific theology. The present section will continue that discussion by schematizing Lonergan's understanding of the history of Catholic theology from the time of the medieval system through its breakdown until the recent rise of the positive, dogmatic and systematic exigencies referred to above. The earliest post-Aquinas period, in Lonergan's analysis, was hardly a happy one. It is best represented, perhaps, by recalling Toynbee's dictum of the bipolarity of disintegrating synthesis. For the generally conceded decadence of fourteenth and fifteenth-century Scholastician was in turn followed by the theologies of the schools (Dominican, Franciscan, Jesuit, Louvain, Roman, etc.). And, as the context of the Báñez-Molina controversy perhaps best reveals, those theologies are properly understood as not so much developments of the possibilities of strictly systematic theology as they are phenomena open to interpretation from that contemporary branch of knowledge called sociology of knowledge. In other words, they are not so much transcultural phenomena as they are adequately explained in terms of the social-economic-cultural possi-

---

Lonergan's defense of his Christology as orthodox in "Christ as Subject: A Reply," *Collection,* esp. pp. 164–65, 196–97. How that relationship is to be worked out foundationally and with the new notion of science for Lonergan is not yet in evidence.

bilities and limitations of their particular period. In terms of the categories developed in the first chapter, they represent relative rather than basic horizon factors.

Nor is the dominant sixteenth-century figure of Melchior Cano to be ignored in any attempt to understand the plight of Catholic theology.[29] For Cano's famous attempt to establish the ten places (*loci*) from which the theologian may derive his "proofs" of traditional theological theses removed Catholic thought for centuries from the medieval scientific search for understanding (and the resultant medieval theology of involvement with its culture) and impelled it into the pedagogy of the thesis and the resultant "ghetto" theology so familiar to the Catholic students of even the very recent past. Nor is the lack of receptivity afforded the rise of positive theology too difficult to understand in such a horizon. For the cumulative development of medieval decadence (exclusive concern with logic and concepts and ever-more-unlikely "disputed questions"), of the theologies of the schools, and of Cano's method gave rise (as Congar, for example, so ably analyzes the development[30]) to a dogmatic theology that consisted in ignoring as much as possible all seemingly insoluble disputed questions while affirming what is "common" to all believers and thereby all Catholic theologians. In short, the horizon of the usual Catholic dogmatic theologian of that period was no longer one of a genuinely systematic theology. As such he could not possibly understand the new concern with development or dogma nor the new issues that arose from the "return to the sources" of one's faith.

Nor—given that horizon—could one hope for any understanding of the theological possibilities of *Insight*. For, if the manualist considered *Insight* at all, he would refer its questions on the nature of science (Aristotlian and modern), the historicity of man or the techniques of critical philosophy to be at best

29. For a most helpful interpretation of Cano and his influence, cf. T. Tshibangu, *Théologie positive et théologie speculative* (Louvain, 1965), pp. 186–210.
30. Yves Congar, "Théologie," *DTC* (Paris, 1946), cols. 342–502.

further "disputed questions" and, at worst, insolent intruders on the clear, distinct and secure dogmatic horizon of the day. It might also be well to recall that (unlike the modernists) the Catholic positive theologians of that and the present day are, generally speaking, not theoretically inclined. Their position is more analogous to Cullmann's, not Bultmann's.[31] They have, perhaps, learned too well the "dogmatic" lessons of their early years and recall too accurately the misapprehension and misrepresentation accorded their earlier work to be able to enter the series of problematics exposed and developed by *Insight*. In short, the exigence of Lonergan's trinitarian theology (involving a shift to modern science, to a historical consciousness and to modern philosophy) was simply outside the horizons of both the "dogmatic" and the "positive" theologians.

Yet the very instability of the context at the time of the writing of *De Deo Trino* gave the problem and its possible resolution an opportunity to emerge. On the one hand, the method of positive studies had effectively destroyed the "proof-text" method of "dogmatic" theology. On the other, the investigations of the method of positive study had destroyed the original ambition of positive studies to communicate the intelligibility of the Christian religion to the contemporary horizon.

It is at this precise point that the earlier achievements of Lonergan and his present exigencies merge. For, as will be recalled, his earliest work involved an almost fierce rejection of the conceptualism of the schools and a consistent affirmation of the intellectualist enterprise of an Augustine, an Anselm, an Aquinas for an imperfect and analogous *understanding* of the faith. This achievement, in its turn, was employed not merely

31. In the United States it is possibly more accurate to say that American Catholic biblical scholars tend to be even closer to Albright than to Cullmann. As a specific example of such lack of theoretical interest, cf. the article on hermeneutic in the prestigious *Jerome Biblical Commentary* (Englewood Cliffs, 1968) by the distinguished scholar Raymond Brown and compare those interests (from a theoretical viewpoint) with those of, for example, James Robinson in *The New Hermeneutic* (New York, 1964).

to resuscitate the medieval attitude towards theology but to enter the modern critical problematic by grounding and criticizing modern notions in science, philosophy and, eventually, history. In the specific context of the Trinitarian problematic, moreover, it freed Lonergan to work out a notion of dogmatic theology as the reduction of the dogmas to their sources and to distinguish this work from the preparatory and basic detailed work of positive studies.

The first volume of *De Deo Trino,* then, is a theological attempt to differentiate positive and dogmatic theology and then to develop a genetic-dialectic method equal to the historical facts. It is urgent to recognize what has been achieved here. If, for example, we were to compare Lonergan's earlier theological work *De Ente Supernaturali*[32] with *De Deo Trino* the development emerges with startling clarity. For the earlier work is content with the traditional distinction between the *via synthetica* and the *via analytica.* It is not concerned to further differentiate the two tasks proper to the *via analytica.* It does not explicitate the distinctive function, the relative autonomy and thus the existence of a purely positive theology, i.e. a theology that reaches no answers that do not emerge from the text itself (dogma introduces new categories). For positive theology advances not by deductions and proofs but by a fuller scrutiny of known texts and the discovery of further texts.

Dogmatic theology, on the contrary, performs an entirely different task: it is concerned with reducing the dogmas to their sources. To perform this task correctly, of course, the interpreter must first understand the dogma itself. However, a further task is added: in order to understand the historical development of any dogma he must also understand the history of dogma. In short, the phenomenon of historical consciousness has also entered into the dogmatic field. For historical consciousness is precisely that orientation which understands human phenomena in terms of their historical development and consequently under-

32. *De Ente supernaturali: supplementum schematicum* (Montreal, 1946).

stands historical development as totally or at least formally in the intentional order.[33] In the field of dogmatics only a clear recognition of that phenomenon and a careful development of categories equal to it can help one avoid the more usual modernist or syncretist or reactionary (conceptualist[34]) tendencies that are found in so much of contemporary Catholic thought.

If we examine the first volume of *De Deo Trino* with the former methodological precepts in mind, the heuristic nature of the entire enterprise becomes clear.[35] First, the material basis for any understanding of the Christian belief in the Trinity is established, viz. the totality of documents and traditions concerned with that belief are examined and taken in their historical sense (e.g. the Trinity as found in St. Paul, the synoptics, the apostolic Fathers, Tertullian, etc.). Next, a comparative method is employed to isolate the significant points of change (especially, of course, the movement from the "economic" Trinity of the Scriptures to the "ontological" Trinity of the early councils). But that comparative method, in its turn, must yield to an explanatory account of the differences revealed by the comparisons. It is at that point that Lonergan is able to apply the genetic-dialectic explanatory method of *Insight* to Trinitarian development.[36] To state the most obvious application first: the movement most apparent in all Trinitarian develop-

33. Hence the applicability to theology of the scissors-like action of the heuristic universal viewpoint of *Insight;* cf. *Insight,* esp. pp. 312–13, 461, 522–23, 564–68, 580–81, 586–87.

34. Cf. esp. *DDT* (1961), esp. pp. 5–12, 90–115; *DP,* esp. pp. 7–51; *DDT* I, esp. pp. 5–17, 87–113; *DDT* II, pp. 7–65; *DVI,* esp. pp. 2–39.

35. However, the final result is ordinarily somewhat ambiguous: the treatises (especially *DVI*) remain incomplete in the sense that they do not expand the questions fully into the modern context but are content to achieve, first, the expansion of the *vetera* and, secondly, a careful defense of dogma and system which will allow the present problematic to become a genuine *Aufhebung* and not the destruction of the old. For an excellent example of how all these factors are operative in Lonergan's work, cf. the first thesis of *DVI* (1961) and note especially the treatment of the modern "adversaries" (pp. 5–16) as well as his development of the contemporary notion of "schemata" to defend the Chalcedonian interpretation of the New Testament (pp. 24–39).

36. For the briefest expression, cf. *DDT* I, pp. 87–112.

ment is that movement from the economic to the ontological Trinity. In any dependable comparative study, the movement is more exactly (i.e. explanatorily) defined as a movement from the *quoad nos* (i.e. the Trinitarian reality in its relationship to the believer, to his redemptive needs, to his genuine religious and Christian conversion) to the *quoad se* (i.e. the Trinitarian relationships understood in terms of those defining relationships themselves and not to the believer).[37] The same method may also allow one to understand the gradual, genetic emergence of that

37. And it is precisely the problematic of the *quoad se* which Lonergan's development of the genetic-dialectic method for dogmatic theology can resolve critically in a way the "manuals" could not; note further that such an explicitation of the implicit performance precisely as critical cannot be charged with "reading into" the historical situation anymore than an economist's use of his science as applied to an earlier period "reads into" the situation. For a later clarification of these realities, cf. Lonergan's later lecture on "Hermeneutics" (Toronto, 1962), esp. the section on communication as common sense, scientific and basic horizon; cf. also *Insight*, pp. 562–95. Note the parallelism between *Insight* and *DP*. *Insight:* if self-appropriation occurs, then a potential interpreter knows the intellectual potentialities of a particular figure or period and can reconstruct them; moreover, he can critically locate how the whole outlook is changed by varying one factor (pp. 562–95); *DP:* if the intellectualist genetic-dialectical method of *Insight* is applied to the development of Catholic doctrine and theology, the genetic movement to the *quoad se* in Nicea and Chalcedon and the further and more explicit (because scientific) medieval movement to the *quoad se* can be *critically* understood in both its genetic and dialectical moments. For a discussion of how such a critical method can eliminate dialectical aberrations, cf. *DP*, pp. 37–39, for Lonergan's critical elimination of the following dialectical aberrations from a notion of theology as primarily *understanding:* a domination of theology by philosophy (p. 37); a synthesis via juxtaposition (p. 38); all positivism (p. 38); both archaism and anachronism (both vs. *development in understanding*) (p. 38); futurism (vs. *verum intelligible*) (p. 39); rationalism and semi-rationalism (vs. the *imperfect* understanding proper to theology) (p. 39). Moreover, the close connection between the theological and the development of doctrine should be noted in Lonergan's analysis; cf. R. L. Richard, "Contribution to a Theory of Doctrinal Development," *Spirit as Inquiry*, pp. 505–30, esp. pp. 506–07; J. C. Murray, *The Problem of God* (New Haven, 1964); and F. E. Crowe, "Development of Doctrine and the Ecumenical Problem," *Theological Studies* 23 (1962), 27–46; *idem*, "Christology and Contemporary Philosophy," *Commonweal* 87 (1960), 242–47.

development by explaining the significant differences revealed by comparative method in terms of their genetic-dialectic unfolding. For example, the explanatory key to Tertullian's Trinitarian thought is his naïve realism. He has, for instance, no problem affirming the divinity of both Father and Son while still affirming the Son as temporal and the Father as eternal. Why? In Prestige's graphic term, the reason is that Tertullian believed that both Father and Son were made of the "same divine stuff."[38] In Lonergan's phrase, for Tertullian the real is "the already-out-there-now-real" and all of Tertullian's conclusions can only be properly understood from within that limited horizon of naïve realism. Similarly, Origen's Trinitarian thought can only be properly understood from within the horizon of the participation theory of Middle Platonism. Without a grasp of the confrontationism behind the cognitional theory of Platonism, and of the horizon of idealism proper to Origen's thought, all of his specific conclusions cannot be explanatorily ordered. Still more significantly, the affirmation of *homoousion* in Nicaea[39] and its classic defense by Athanasius (*whatever* is *affirmed* about the Father is affirmed about the Son except the name Father) is only properly understood within the horizon of the dogmatic realism it asserts and the unconscious conciliar shift to intellectual conversion (*quoad se*) implicit in those dogmatic expressions. In short, the real is not the "out there," nor the "in here," but quite simply the *true,* the *affirmed* (not merely the sensed, nor the experienced, the imagined, nor the understood, nor the hypothesized but the true, the real, the *it is* or *it is not* proper to the cognitional act of judgment). As such the movement of dogma beginning with Nicaea is more properly understood in terms of the entry of intellectual conversion (and the consequent search for the *quoad se*) into the basic horizon (moral,

38. Prestige, *God in Patristic Thought* (London, 1959), pp. 197–218.
39. Hence, once again, the central importance accorded by Lonergan to the role of doctrinal statements as judgmental; cf. "The Origins of Christian Realism" (Toronto, 1961), and, for a critique of a contrary position, Lonergan's review of L. Dewart's position, "The Dehellenization of Dogma," *Theological Studies* 28 (June, 1967), 336–51.

religious, Christian conversion) of the Christian community. And for Lonergan only the development of a *critical* realism (viz. *Insight*) can provide the upper blade of interpretation needed for the new genetic-dialectic task of the dogmatic theologian. For only one in possession of the critical tool of a genuinely transcendental method is able to locate the cognitional-epistemological and philosophic horizon proper to the individual under discussion as well as the genetic-dialectic unfolding of the necessary differentiations and integrations proper to that horizon's development. Nor need the positive theologian fear that there is yet another Garrigou-Lagrange waiting in the wings to "take over" and distort the results of positive theology. For it must be noted that the work of the dogmatic theologian (in the sense articulated above) can only be worked out on the basis of the data (i.e. exegesis and critical history) provided by the positive theologian. In other words, a use of the upper blade of an explanatory genetic-dialectic method made possible by the critical achievement of *Insight* need be no more an imposition or distortion of the data provided by the textual critics, exegetes, and historians than is the use of the recently developed sciences of economics or sociology upon the data provided by historians of the Roman empire. It is quite true, of course, that neither Tertullian nor Origen knew that their positions were what Lonergan's genetic-dialectic method determines them to be. Yet their performance and their explicitation of that performance in their categories, methods and conclusions can and do reveal the nature of the difficulty involved in each to the practitioner of the transcendental method. In short, only one who has himself thematized the invariant nature, structures and norms of all intelligent inquiry is in a position to grasp the hermeneutic principles behind Lonergan's analysis of the nature of doctrinal development and the interrelationships of positive and dogmatic theology.

Nor is the accomplishment of *Insight* without its fruits for the systematic theology of the Trinity. For, given the hermeneutic background of the *Verbum* articles on the psychological method of Aquinas' notion of intelligible emanations, and given further the critical analysis of consciousness in *Insight* itself, Lonergan is enabled to re-articulate Aquinas' analogy in strictly psychological terms and then structure the entire *via synthetica* in accordance with that emphasis. Anyone who has worked through the rigorous order of that latter work will agree, I believe, that it expresses the real posibilities of what was traditionally meant by a truly strict systematic theology.[40]

In conclusion, the entry of historical consciousness into the Catholic context via the rise of positive theology and the notion of doctrinal development provides the new theological context for Lonergan's post-*Insight* work. And aside from the particular philosophic categories used by Lonergan in that work, there is behind all of them the basic critical tool of transcendental method itself as it determines the upper blade for all scientific methods. Lonergan's shift, therefore, has been (as the article "Theology and Understanding" makes clear) from the medieval achievement of "reason illuminated by faith," to the contemporary achievement of "method illuminated by faith," i.e. method in Lonergan's precise sense of reason's explicit consciousness of its own norms, structures and procedures. There has been a development, not only by the entry of whole new worlds of meanings (the changed context—positive theology and development of doctrine) but also of a new critical technique to control meaning (viz. the thematization of reason's performance achieved in *Insight*). And that latter shift has made possible Lonergan's often startling developments on a

40. Cf. esp. *DP*, pp. 49–51, for the systematic structure of the work. Note especially the fruit of Lonergan's *Insight* analysis of consciousness (*DDT* II, pp. 70–92; cf. *Insight*, esp. pp. 320–28); for this development (as for those in Christology), cf. *De Constitutione Christi*, pp. 83–148; *DVI*, pp. 269–312; "Christ as Subject," Collection, pp. 164–98); for confirmation of this, cf. Lonergan's 1963 unpublished lecture, "Consciousness and the Trinity." As a second example, of strictly systematic significance, cf. Lonergan's work via his analogy from natural theology (i.e. "contingent predication") as contrasted with the analogies from created being of de la Taille ("created actuation") and Rahner ("quasi-formal causality"), *DDT* II, pp. 216–35, and esp. *DVI*, pp. 254–68.

number of particular Trinitarian and Christological problems and, yet more basically, the methodological realization that contemporary theology must differentiate the different functions of positive, dogmatic and systematic theological methods and then integrate them through a transcendental method equal to that task. The further developments involved in that final task, however, await the developments of Lonergan's later period where once again a new and deeper meaning is recognized as involved in the phenomenon of historical consciousness and a new and differentiated theological method (foundational theology) is developed to deal with that meaning.

9. THE NEW CONTEXT: THE HORIZONS OF HISTORICAL CONSCIOUSNESS

The development of Lonergan's work is consciously cumulative. To understand its most recent developments it is imperative to understand the factors already discussed which must now be taken for granted as a part of a wider horizon: the analysis of the scientific nature of theology in his work on Aquinas; the recognition of the important shift from the Aristotlian-Thomist ideal of science to the contemporary; the entry into the critical problem first in the *Verbum* articles and then definitively in *Insight;* the return to the properly theological context and the attempt to come to terms with the rise of the recent disciplines of positive theology and developmental dogmatic theology; the attempt to revitalize systematic theology in the light of *Insight*'s method and categories. It is perhaps difficult to conceive of that series of problematics as a horizon propaedeutic to Lonergan's own major work in theology. Yet, in a real sense, it is. For only after the constant temptation to conceptualism had been exposed and eliminated, only after the classical ideal had been clarified and transformed, only after a transcendental method had been developed and all the central elements in contemporary Catholic theology absorbed could the real issue of today's theology be fully pursued.

That real issue is a full and coherent acknowledgment of the phenomenon of historical consciousness. On its simplest level, that phenomenon can be described as man's realization that individually he is responsible for the life he leads and collectively

206

he is responsible for the world in which he leads it. Historical consciousness' most emphatic expression is that of those radical theologians who proclaim God's death while its most obvious manifestation is modern secularist culture, society and civilization. Nor should one too rapidly decide that the entire contemporary discussion is laden with a "subjectivism" which belies the ontological nature of the Judaeo-Christian faith commitment.[1] For the fact is that, no matter how strong Lonergan's emphasis upon intentionality, his notion of historical consciousness is not primarily knowing nor cognitional theory nor epistemological method nor a merely historical inquiry. Rather, as the *Insight* discussion of the notion of being makes clear, it is primarily a question of anthropology, ontology, metaphysics. For there is a highly important and real (i.e. true) domain of being—reality which is actually constituted by common meaning and common commitment. It is that domain which is the proper subject of the analyst of historical consciousness.

Moreover, as the emergence of the empirical approaches of Catholic positive theology have somewhat hesitantly witnessed and as the full-fledged commitment of Protestant theology since the nineteenth century bears strong and eloquent confirmation, any science purporting to deal with "revelatory events" cannot shirk the problems and the opportunities of the present intellectual context. For the divine revelation is primarily the entry of the Judaeo-Christian God not into the world of nature but into the world of meaning and history.[2] Or it is, to employ

1. For a recent example of that charge, cf. Cornelio Fabro, *The Problem of Atheism* (New York, 1968).
2. It may prove helpful to list the sources for these developments at once: (1) the two sets of notes (privately available): *De Intellectu et Methodo* (*Reportatio* of course at the Gregorian University, 1959) (St. Francis Xavier College, Rome); *De Methodo Theologiae* (notes for lectures at Gregorian University, 1962) (North American College, Rome). (2) The tapes of the institutes involved are the following: "Lectures on *Insight*" (Halifax, Nova Scotia, 1958); "Philosophy of Education" (Cincinnati, Ohio, 1959); "Lectures on Method in Theology" (Toronto, 1962). Sets of these tapes are available at Regis College, Toronto, or from the present writer's own collection. Moreover, a mimeographed outline of the lectures on mathematical logic and existentialism are available at the Thomas More Institute, Montreal, Canada. (3) The

207

THE ACHIEVEMENT OF BERNARD LONERGAN

Insight's categories, an entry into the field of interiority as conscious finality towards being. And the key categories (because the key operations) in that movement are no longer immediately metaphysical ones (as with Aquinas) nor even those derived from scientific intelligibility (as in *Insight*) but rather those categories of constitutive meaning.[3] For even after all of the

---

articles of methodological interest during this period are the following (listed in chronological order): (a) review of *The Order and Integration of Knowledge* and *Metaphysics and Ideology* (both by W. Martin), *Gregorianum* 41 (1960), 171–73; (b) "Notes from the Introductory Lecture in the Philosophy of History" (Montreal, September 23, 1960); (c) "The Origins of Christian Realism" (Toronto, September 8, 1961); (d) "De argumento theologico ex sacra Scriptura" (Rome, 1962); (e) "Hermeneutics" (Toronto, July 20, 1962); (f) "Metaphysics as Horizon," *Gregorianum* 44 (1963), 307–18 (also available in *Collection* [New York, 1967], pp. 202–21); (g) Review of *Die Gewinnung Theologischer Normen aus der Geschichte der Religion bei E. Troeltsch* (by Ignatio Alberca), *Gregorianum* 44 (1963), 369–70; (h) review of *La Crise de la Raison dans la pensée contemporaine* (by E. Barbotin, J. Trouillard, R. Verneaux, D. Dubarle, S. Bréton), *ibid.*, 372–73; (j) "De notione structurae" (Aloisianum, Gallarte); (k) "Cognitional Structure," *Continuum* 2 (1964), 530–42 (also available in *Collection*, pp. 221–40); (l) *"Existenz* and *Aggiornamento,"* *Focus*, 2 (1965), 5–14 (also available in *Collection*, pp. 240–52); (m) "Dimensions of Meaning," *Collection*, pp. 252–67. Lonergan's post-1965 lectures and reviews are included in the general bibliography but not in this chapter, as not intrinsically germane to the study of his thought up to 1965. It is anticipated that most of them will be published in a second volume, *Collection II*. (4) For the final category of lectures and printed materials the author is indebted to Father Lonergan's generosity in making available his own notes for his courses on method from 1963–65 at the Pontifical Gregorian University, at Gonzaga University (Spokane, Washington) in summer, 1963, and at Georgetown University (Washington, D.C.) in summer, 1964. Also employed are personal notes of the author's from the course at the Gregorian in 1963; the latter have always been checked against those of Father Lonergan for accuracy and not used otherwise. One may also cite F. E. Crowe, "On the Method of Theology," *Theological Studies* 23 (1962), and David Tracy, "Horizon Analysis and Eschatology," *Continuum* 6 (1968), 166–80, for a discussion of the issues of this chapter.

3. It is to be noted that Lonergan's notion of *constitutive* meaning refers to the conversions in the fourth (*Existenz*) level of consciousness and is employed to contrast with the second and third level operations of *mediated* meaning (although mediation is also present on the fourth

necessary de-mythologizing of the much-heralded "coming-of-age" of modern man, it still remains true that the contemporary consciousness is principally and most fruitfully identified with the personal recognition of responsibility which each man must have for his own worlds of meaning and for those of his society, his culture, his age. That no longer innocent consciousness likewise involves a recognition that the worlds constituted by meaning vary with the development of meaning, with the aberrations of meaning and indeed with the redemption of meaning.[4] This recognition, moreover (as Frederick Gogarten has convincingly argued), is in profound harmony with the authentically Christian consciousness.[5] For the Christian has always believed that the created world is contingent; that man's world adds the further contingencies of free acts and that redemption adds the third and redemptive contingence of God's free act for man in Christ Jesus. The challenge to the Christian theologian at the present time, therefore, is to develop categories equal to the tasks of bringing these realities of meaning to constitutive speech.

But meaning is a paradoxical term. It may not be tied down to some one universal, essential definition so beloved to the classical mind nor may its endlessly elusive character be exhausted

---

level as an integrating factor—cf. Chapter 1). Lonergan's notion of constitution, therefore, is not to be simply identified with the quite distinct Husserlian notion. For the latter, cf. R. Sokolowski, *The Formation of Husserl's Concept of Constitution* (The Hague, 1964).

4. The developments in meaning in this chapter are indebted to the sources cited in ftn. 2 as well as the section on "meaning" in the forthcoming *Method in Theology*. Father Lonergan's permission to employ the latter for this interpretation has made possible a briefer and (I hope) more intelligible manner of communicating an otherwise very complex terrain. (For the latter in its chronological development, cf. my thesis *The Development of the Notion of Theological Methodology in the Works of Bernard J. F. Lonergan, S.J.*, Chapter 4, pp. 349–462.)

5. Cf. Larry Schiner, *The Secularization of History: An Introduction to the Theology of Frederick Gogarten* (Nashville, 1966); also J. B. Metz, *Christian Anthropology* (New York, 1969); and Robert L. Richard, *Secularization Theology* (New York, 1968) as a dependable survey of the accelerating literature on Christianity and secularity.

in scientific meaning alone as the movement of Wittgenstein I to Wittgenstein II on the language of meaning has demonstrated.[6] Rather, any analyst of meaning in its multidimensional character must approach the subject as cautiously and as thoroughly as contemporary developments allow. The two basic methods of approach elaborated in *Insight* (the descriptive and the explanatory) are especially applicable here. From a descriptive standpoint, one may enumerate the realities which proceed from meaning, which are in fact constituted by meaning. From an analytic viewpoint, one may work out the constituents of meaning by determining the acts and structures in and through which meanings emerge. Both procedures obviously presuppose meaning and use it. Here we shall begin from the first (descriptive) approach in order to reveal as clearly as possible the importance and multiple nature of meaning and thereby allow the emergence of the meaningful consequents that are explained by analysis.[7]

When we speak here of meaning as constitutive, furthermore, we do not imply that it is the sole constituent of man and man's reality. For as the classical mind knows perhaps too well, many true, interesting and important realities may be examined in man without examining his meaning. One may, for example, study man as subject to the laws of physics, of chemistry, or of biology. One may even study man in terms of a strictly metaphysical psychology,[8] for metaphysically, man is still man whether he is asleep or awake, sober or drunk, in a coma or on

6. This refers, of course, to Wittgenstein's "meaning as use" and the "language games" of the *Investigations*. For the theological helpfulness of Wittgenstein's notion of meaning, cf. Dallas High, *Language, Persons and Belief* (Oxford, 1967), esp. pp. 27–70, 70–99. There remains a need for a full-length study of Lonergan's intentionality-theories of meaning similar to works recently done on Wittgenstein and Husserl.

7. This approach follows the order of Lonergan's treatment of meaning in his forthcoming *Method in Theology*.

8. Among many examples, we may cite the oft-used R. P. Phillips, *Modern Thomistic Philosophy* (London, 1935), pp. 76–137. However, one of the weaknesses of even Rahner's *Spirit in the World* would seem to be its strictly metaphysical analysis of abstraction.

LSD, intelligent or stupid. But one may also examine man from the viewpoint of his operations and worlds of meaning. For from his dream-state on through all the almost endless varieties of his conscious life—his imagining, his feeling, his knowing, his loving, his doing—man is fundamentally a creature and creator of that aspect of being called meaning. Indeed all man's highest achievements are achievements of meaning—his arts, symbols, literatures, history, natural and human sciences, families, states, philosophies, religions and theologies. For though meaning be not the sole constituent of human potentiality, it is the field in which arise good and evil, right and wrong, truth and error, grace and sin, salvation and damnation. And meaning, as we shall see in some detail below, is truly constitutive of all the symbols[9] which express our aggressivity and affectivity, our deep and irrepressible drives for transformation and integration. It is constitutive as well of all our projects, of our endless questions, of our acts and developing habits of understanding, of our explanations of possibility in mathematics or logic or fiction, of our doubts, affirmations and negations, our beliefs and opinions, convictions and certitudes. It is constitutive in fact of all our possibilities of differentiation and thereby of all possible consequent one-sidedness (e.g. classicism) as well as being constitutive of all our possibilities of integration of our many differentiated worlds (e.g. historical consciousness). At the very least, therefore, meaning is a category demanding and today receiving careful and deliberate investigation. Moreover, for the theologian who commits himself as believer to the transforming meaning of the Christian revelation, the nature, functions and varieties of meaning demand his closest attention.

Because of that latter exigence especially, we shall describe Lonergan's investigation of the phenomena of meaning in three

9. One might recall that, for Lonergan, symbol has the relatively narrow range (compared to Cassirer or Ricoeur) of always involving an image that expresses affectivity and aggressivity. Hence scientific theorems, for Lonergan, are not, strictly speaking, "symbols." For a qualification of that general principle on mathematical symbols, cf. *Insight*, pp. 17–18.

basic regions: first, the seven "vehicles" or carriers of meaning; secondly, meaning as constitutive of human living; thirdly, meaning as constitutive of human knowing. With that descriptive task behind us, we may then summarize the analytic treatment accorded meaning by Lonergan's own transcendental method.

A. MEANING: ITS MULTIPLE DIMENSIONS AND EXPRESSIONS

Lonergan's involvement in historical consciousness forced him to shift his interest from an almost exclusive concern with scientific intelligibility to study the multidimensional character of meaning.[10] But to reach that elusive element-in-being, he was first impelled to examine the many expressions of meaning. Seven such expressions will be presented here:

First, *intersubjective* meaning: Besides the intersubjectivity of action and of feeling, there are also intersubjective communications of spontaneous and natural meaning. Such communication antecedes the "I-Thou" relationship insofar as it actually constitutes the interpersonal relationship and thereby the very meaning of the relationship prior to any reflective mediation of it. In that sense, then, it antecedes all linguistic and conceptual meaning. For example,[11] a smile is not first analyzed but rather immediately communicates the human meaning present and thereby actually constitutes the human meaning-situation. It may be a smile of recognition, of joy, of sorrow, of sarcasm, of fear, of exhaustion: in any case, the meaning is immediately communicated to the sensitively aware partner and invites his intersubjective response. Such meaning may, of course, later be analyzed (as in Max Scheler's brilliant analyses of *ressentiment*

10. Contrast with the section on "Analytic Propositions and Principles" in *Insight,* pp. 304–09.
11. The example is Lonergan's own. I have been unable to trace its probable phenomenological source.

or, more generally, of *The Nature and Forms of Sympathy*[12]), but the primal, constitutive meaning is immediate and immediately communicable in the intersubjective situation itself.

Second, *incarnate* meaning: Once more the meaning here is expressed in and actually constituted by the expression. In fact, the expression *is* the actual meaning. In distinction from intersubjective communication, incarnate does not demand the presence of a *thou* to constitute its meaning. For, as Morel argues at great length, "Man *is* a symbol."[13] The actions of a man's life express and/or *are* the very meaning of his life. Heroic actions, national heroes, unconscious gestures all incarnate the meaning which a person, a culture, an epoch is. To express the clearest example of this phenomenon, one should recall that the passion, death and resurrection of Jesus the Christ are first incarnate, transforming meanings of the reality who Jesus is before any reflection, preaching, teaching of that communicable (or, with van Buren, "contagious"[14]) meaning can occur.

Thirdly, *symbolic* meaning: A symbol, for Lonergan, has a very precise meaning—it is an image of a real or imaginary object that evokes a feeling or is evoked by a feeling. Symbols are the primordial expression of that affectivity and aggressivity that relate us to our worlds of meaning. They express and reveal our fundamental attitude, stance, orientation towards that world. In Ernst Cassirer's telling phrase, "Man is the symbolic animal."[15] As employed by Lonergan, however, it should be noted that symbolic meaning does not include the wide range accorded it by Cassirer or Langer but restricts its meaning to those *im-*

12. For the former, cf. M. Scheler, *Ressentiment* (New York, 1961); and for a helpful survey of theories of the symbol, cf. Gilbert Durand, *L'Imagination Symbolique* (Paris, 1964).

13. For a specific case, cf. Morel, *Le Sens de L'Existence selon St. Jean de la Croix* (Aubier, 1960).

14. Paul van Buren, *The Secular Meaning of the Gospel* (New York, 1963).

15. In Lonergan's *Method in Theology* he attempts to transform Cassirer's analysis of symbol in terms of his own (Lonergan's) analysis of insight. The reference to Cassirer is, of course, *The Philosophy of Symbolic Forms* (I and II) (Yale, 1955).

ages (not concepts) that educe affects or patterns of affects.

Symbolic meaning exposes the great and sometimes dominant influence of affectivity in all linguistic discourse. Once persons find that they share an affinity for the same range of symbols (e.g. baroque in music, Godard in the film, Camus in the novel) they recognize their possibilities of basic meaning-ful communication on the level of Newman's *"cor ad cor loquitur."* To uncover certain basic types of sensibility and the symbols each evokes (as does Susan Sontag in *Against Interpretation*'s discussion of the "three sensibilities."[16]) is to extend the range and deepen the discourse on all meaningful human analysis. It is also to help one realize that in symbolic (as distinct from theoretic) meaning there are multiple, simultaneous and many-leveled meanings each of which is present, only to be ignored by some and "overheard" by others. Especially since the gains of the phenomenological movement, the discussion and determination of symbols (Ricoeur, Scheler, Binswanger, Gadamer *et al.*) have provided a context of meanings which the theologian may safely ignore only at the price of ignoring the basic demands of his own task (viz. to analyze the full range of Christian meanings) and of evading his responsibility to the symbol-forging-and-evoking men of his own times.

But besides the non-thematic meanings expressed in intersubjective, incarnate and symbolic meaning and exposed by contemporary analysts of symbolic meaning, there remain the dimensions of thematized meaning. That thematization need not be, of course, a scientific one. Indeed, it may first be an aesthetic or everyday or literary expression before it reaches (if it ever does or can) the level of technical expression. And those expressions too must be investigated to help one realize the fuller dimensions of meaning made so obviously present by historical consciousness and overlooked (and sometimes despised) by the classical mind.

Fourthly, then, there is *aesthetic* meaning, i.e. the conscious

16. Cf. Susan Sontag, *Against Interpretation* (New York, 1966), esp. pp. 275–304.

objectification of a purely experiential pattern of experience.[17] Our previous discussion of the aesthetic pattern of experience in *Insight* has already revealed the meaning of Lonergan's personal use of the word "pattern." But in the present context it might also profitably be noted that unlike symbolic expression, the aesthetic demands not only a certain depth of meaning but also a positive and conscious control of that meaning through the elaboration of carefully determined aesthetic forms. The artist, to be truly such, needs not only a richness of personal meaning but also the technical expertise to produce a lasting work of art (Wordsworth's "emotion recollected in tranquility"). This is not to argue that only "classical" art is truly such. In fact, as Susan Sontag convincingly demonstrates (to this non-expert at least), the "forms" of the modern and at first seemingly chaotic arts are more, not less demanding and controlled than the classical ever were. For they too bespeak (or, perhaps more accurately, "overhear") a range of meanings which technical language can no more capture than can prose express the literally mysterious power of poetry. Nor do I presume to suggest here that art has "meaning" in any "message" sense of the term. For meaning here refers not to "messages" however lofty but to reality, to being, to that human and more-than-human "isness" of things which artists as the "antennae of the race" (in Ezra Pound's apt analogy) allow the rest of us to hear. We can no more express the meaning of the Oedipus cycle or of *King Lear* by giving the plot, characters, setting and so forth than we can the meaning of the music of Beethoven or Stravinsky by outlining their scores. That they have meaning we are sure. That we can never adequately capture the fullness of that meaning through even the most brilliant critical analysis we should be equally sure.

Fifthly, there is *everyday* meaning,[18] i.e. that primary, im-

17. This analysis of "aesthetic" meaning was, of course, already treated in *Insight,* pp. 184–85.
18. This and the following ("literary") are to be found both in the tapes (1962) of the Method conference by Lonergan in Toronto and the forthcoming *Method in Theology.*

mediate, spontaneous and transient expression of meaning which our everyday words employ. It may, of course, descend to the level of Heidegger's "useless chatter" (*Gerede*), but it may also serve as simply a vehicle of that minor but necessary meaning which all of us engage in and none of us need really feel guilty about: the weather, one's health, one's lesser opinions etc. But such talk may also eventually envelope the horizon of its creator and entrap him in a "taken-for-granted" world whose limitations he simply cannot see. If pressed for exactitude or clarity, he is more liable to retreat into the annoyed repugnance of the Athenians for Socrates and simply reply, "Well, you know what I mean." The problem, of course, is, Does *he?*

Sixthly, there is a *literary* communication of meaning. In one sense, of course, this is merely a specification of aesthetic meaning but in another it requires separate treatment to clarify the distinction of everyday, literary and technical language. Literary language, then, is an objectified expression via words that is both mediated and permanent. In one of its functions, it represents an attempt to communicate through words what in ordinary language is communicated by gesture or facial expression In another, it may attempt to communicate even highly theoretic discoveries in a palatable and permanent form for the "educated layman": Plato's dialogues, for example, as contrasted to Aristotle's technical works; Augustine on Trinitarian theology as contrasted with Aquinas; Newman on judgment as compared to Lonergan. In yet another of its functions, literary language can reveal the power and sometimes the mystery of words: the reverence for the word (*"dabar"*) in the Hebrew culture; the discovery of the word "water" by Helen Keller; the search for a new "primal language" by contemporary theologians.[19] As these

19. It is hoped that the reference to the "later Heidegger" theologians as literary does not sound pejorative. It is not intended as such; in fact it simply differentiates the two approaches (e.g. on "objectifying" theological language); for the two distinct exemplary positions on the question, cf. Schubert M. Ogden, "Theology and Objectivity," *The Reality of God,* pp. 71–99 and Heinrich Ott, "The Problem of Non-objectifying Thinking and Speaking in Theology," in E. Käsemann *et al., Distinctive Protestant and Catholic Themes Reconsidered* (New York, 1967), pp. 112–135.

very different examples all suggest, words and a language which can paradoxically control them by allowing them to bespeak a reality beyond the everyday remain the primary carriers of man's meaning. Indeed, as Lonergan suggests, "It would seem that the human psyche floats with the weightlessness of images and the caprices of aggressivity and affectivity until it is able to pin things down in words."

Seventhly, there is a *technical* communication of meaning. As Lonergan's previous work has already suggested, this meaning too—exact, theoretic, controlled—is the proper technique not for more idle talk but for putting an end to all idle talk. It is the dimension of meaning proper to *theoria,* peculiar to Jasper's "axial periods" in history, and dominant in Lonergan's past and present concerns. For even though he would no longer hope to be able to determine a classical universal definition for "meaning," he is still resolved to continue the theoretic enterprise into the horizon of historical consciousness by finding technical ways (e.g. *existenziell → existenzial; le vécu → le thématique*) to study the multiple meanings of man.

Finally, the following diagram may help to indicate the important differences between the technical and the literary expressions of meaning.[20]

In conclusion, this section has briefly exposed some of the multiple meanings involved in the phenomenon of historical consciousness (intersubjective, incarnate, symbolic, aesthetic, everyday, literary, technical meanings). The following two sections will continue that discussion by indicating the centrality of meaning (in its several forms) in human living and in human knowing.

B. MEANING AS CONSTITUTIVE OF HUMAN LIVING[21]

It may be well to recall once again that meaning is not the sole constituent of human living. There are, for example, the various

20. The divisions are from Susanne Langer's *Feeling and Form.* The examples are my own.
21. A section of the "Meaning" chapter of *Method in Theology* will bear this title.

TECHNICAL EXPRESSION OF MEANING	LITERARY EXPRESSION OF MEANING
"EXPLANATION"	"DESCRIPTION"
Class concepts ("natural law")	Representative figures (Paul: First & Second Adam)
Universal Concept (justice)	SIMULTANEOUS MULTIPLE MEANINGS (Hemingway on mountains, rain, etc.)
PROOF (Logic, deduction, verification, etc.)	REINFORCEMENT: repetition, enumeration, contrast (Rhetoric: Newman's "Second Spring")
BARE NEGATION (it IS or IS NOT)	The imagination does not merely negate (Paul as wretched—exhilirated)
Single theme or level (e.g. judgment as virtually unconditioned)	Condensation of several themes (Shakespeare)
Principles, Laws (Law of Supply and Demand)	Proverbs ("You don't get anything for nothing")

physiological systems of the human animal (digestive, vascular, nervous, etc.), none of which are, strictly speaking, "meaningful" realities. But what all men instinctively mean by the distinctively human are not such functions at all but rather those meaningful realities which actually constitute human living as human.

Meaning, therefore, is constitutive of a distinctly human potentiality which becomes actual in two basic ways. In knowing it is actualized in the judgment, as the analysis of *Insight* has already indicated and as the analysis of meaning as constitutive of our knowing will explain below. For the present it will be sufficient to note that the judgmental level of human meaning is the human level of cognitive or intentional self-transcendence: the movement away from the immediate, the imagined, the conceived, to what is the case, what is true, real, actual, conceived as what *is*. That fidelity to true meaning, then, is the primary constituent of intelligent authenticity. But meaning is also realized in all one's living through all the choices, decisions, drifting, failure or willingness to confront issues which help to define the unique being-as-human of each man. One's life may in fact be a tacitly human (i.e. meaningful) one only if it is an "examined" one: the life of intelligent and reasonable decision and the consequent constitution of the self as the self. It may also be inhuman: the life of the drifter who wanders aimlessly from boredom to violence to ultimate, complete meaninglessness. Those potentialities of authentic and unauthentic individuality have been richly documented by contemporary existentialists in literature, in philosophy, in the arts, in the theater. Moreover, that such potentialities are not exhausted by the authentic individual standing alone can also be documented either by the lives of genuine communities or by such eloquent writings as Martin Buber's "The Question to the Single One."[22] For besides the admitted reality of mass-man, there is also the reality of common meaning, in a word, of community. There is always the possibility of a potential community, of those who can understand and share the meaning of others. Learning a foreign language (to use a not very existential example) is not simply learning a word for word relationship but demands rather an entry into the whole world of meaning (*Weltanschauung*) of the community in question. As any conference or committee all too clearly witnesses, the movement toward common meaning

22. Cf. Martin Buber, *Between Man and Man* (New York, 1965), pp. 40–79.

(if it is reached at all) is not the product of one or even several sittings. And as the often ambivalent attitudes of many Christian intellectuals towards the meaningful factors in the "secular" world indicate, one may live in and actually share meanings without either understanding or affirming them.

As meanings dissolve, moreover, there may occur the stratification of communities. The "masses," for example, may revolt against the complexity and abstruseness of meaning in modern technology, economy and politics. Those intermediate groups who in the past have mediated the meaning of an aristocratic society or culture from the summit to the rank and file may break down. And that latter process—as the contemporary crises of either the American or the Catholic communities bear painful witness—may well move into an open-ended period where innocence is indeed lost but a wisdom not yet evolved. In such a period, there may be found many who may find their only meaning in a meaninglessness in its hundred forms (bitterness, ennui, violence, anarchy). There may also be others who, after having tasted the bitter dregs of the collapse of the meaning of their once authentic tradition, may strive to appropriate the central authenticity of that tradition and transform it in the light of the exigencies of the sometimes frightening present and of a future as uncertain as it is impending.

In short, in any transitional crisis-period there occur not only disintegration but development in both communities of knowledge (common sense, science, philosophy , religion, theology) and communities of commitment (family, state, church, etc.). In all of them, the community remains operative as long as the meanings common to the group remain truly meaningful. But once the common store of common experience, common understandings, common judgments and common decisions has gone, the community (*pace* establishmentarian propagandists) can no longer be said to exist as it once did except as a historical memory. A new romanticism or a new anarchy may well arise to try to fill the vacuum for a world of spent meanings. But although they are able to fill the gap for a while with their new worlds of strange, spare, original, often beautiful and sometimes terrifying meanings, they too must eventually cede to the demands of intelligence and responsibility to start the constructive work of rebuilding once again. In short, man lives his peculiarly human life in meaning and is satisfied by nothing less. He founds, joins, leaves, or transforms communities for their meaningfulness and ultimately for their truth and for nothing short of that. For there exists no "Platonic" realm of "ideal" communities for which the present ones are mere replicas, for the reality of community is the reality of human meanings (at their best, *true* meanings) and there is nothing to be gained by shading over that sometimes painful fact. And if a community is in crisis, it could do worse than to re-examine the sources and carriers of the meaning which once gave it life.

C. MEANING AS CONSTITUTIVE
OF HUMAN KNOWING

In one sense, this section will not really add any new information; in another sense it is critical and inevitable. For the work of Lonergan which we have examined up to the present has been principally concerned with cognitive meaning. His later shift into the wider and deeper context of the multi-dimensional reality of meaning revealed by historical consciousness was only made possible by his study of a series of key historical developments:[23] the Romantic attack on the classical horizon of the

23. For the categories and principal concerns treated in this section, one is forced to rely on the tape-recordings of the Institute for Method in Theology, Regis College, Toronto. The references, therefore, will be kept as minimal as possible due to the difficulty of verification; all the factors treated herein can be verified in those tapes. However, as brief indications of Lonergan's interests in this period, cf. his three revelatory book reviews in *Gregorianum:* 44 (1963), 369–70 (on Troeltsch); 370–71 (on history); 372–73 (on the crisis in contemporary thought); for confirmation of the analysis (esp. on Melchior Cano and positive theology), cf. T. Tschibangu, *Théologie positive et théologie speculative* (Louvain, 1965), esp. pp. 196–213 (on Cano) and pp. 316–48 (on mod-

Enlightenment; the German discussion of the unique, meaning-laden nature of the *Geisteswissenschaften;* the largely European development of the problematics of history and hermeneutic;[24] the largely Anglo-American development of a whole range of empirical and behavioral sciences especially physics, psychology, sociology, economics and cultural anthropology;[25] and, finally, the entry of historical consciousness into the Catholic theological context through the rise of strictly empirical positive studies, of the problem of development of doctrine and all the other hopeful signs of modern Catholicism's *aggiornamento.* Yet that latter shift into the wider context of meaning does not imply a rejection of his earlier work. For knowing too (as his *Verbum* articles and *Insight* both argue) is fundamentally an intentional, i.e. meaningful reality.

One might recall, for example, that for both Aristotle and Aquinas there are four basic types of questions (*Quid sit? An sit? Cur ita sit? An ita sit?*). And it is in answer to such questions that what we call our knowledge consists. For human knowing is nothing more nor less than the matter or raising meaningful questions and answering them. For the perceptionist (including the perceptionistic interpreters of Aristotle and Aquinas) this view is too paradoxical and the epistemological problems it raises too complex to be endured. In fact, for such thinkers (as we have seen above) knowing is a far simpler

ern science and positive studies); cf. also R. Latourelle, *Introductio in sacram theologiam* (Rome, 1964), esp. pp. 35–38 (for a comparison of the scholastic and modern notions of science).

24. Fortunately, two Lonergan lectures are available not only in the tapes from the Institute but also in private form, *viz.* "Hermeneutics" (Regis College, Toronto, 1962), "History" (Regis College, Toronto, 1962).

25. For contextual literature, cf. Floyd W. Matson, *The Broken Image: Man, Science and Society* (New York, 1966), for the Anglo-American context; for the German context, amidst the vast amount of literature, a helpful and dependable survey may be found in R. E. Palmer, *Hermeneutics: Interpretation Theory in Schleiermacher, Dilthey, Heidegger and Gadamer* (Evanston, 1969).

reality: it is taking a good look. Questions and answers, then, are mere epiphenomena, mere expressions of the looking which really constitutes knowing. For the idealist, on the other hand, the perceptionist's inadequacies are spotted but not really overcome. Indeed, although the idealist is clear that mind and the categories it creates contribute greatly towards constituting our knowledge, still, at the key moment (i.e. in the analysis of judgment), he retreats from the implications of his original insight and insists that our knowledge only reaches the meant and not the true, the actual, the real.

In Lonergan's analysis, on the other hand, human knowing (precisely as distinct from animal) is a dynamic and structural process which in its final cognitional moment (the judgment) reaches a *true* meant, i.e. the real or the actual. He disagrees with both the fictional "look" of the perceptionist and with the half-hearted insistence of idealists that true meaning is not knowing the real. In terms of the horizon-categories employed throughout this work, Lonergan's view presupposes the intellectual conversions of the earlier chapters. For Lonergan, we can and must break from the world of the child, the naïve realist and the idealist to enter fully into the world mediated and constituted by meaning. That world, moreover, is not only the world of the believer and the theologian but also (as *Insight* argues at some length) of any realistic philosophy, of the natural and human sciences in their actual operation and indeed of ordinary common sense. It is that same world which teaching and learning attempt to mediate. For by provoking the student's spirit of wonder, by finding the right problem, formulating the exact question, the teacher encourages the student to relive the Greek breakthrough to *theoria* by moving from the data of his personal experience to the mediated and constituted meaning of his intelligence and his reason. By insight the data are enriched with possible meaning. By expression, definition, deduction and verification one prepares the way for judgment—for the pronouncement that the possible meaning is either true or false. In that critical sense, then, true meaning is real. For we reach the real through the true and by the elusive word "real" is meant nothing other than "true meaning."

D. MEANING: ITS THEMATIC POSSIBILITIES IN LONERGAN'S OWN DEVELOPMENT

Probably the most helpful way to indicate both the continuity and the difference which the wider context of meaning will involve for Lonergan's later work on the method and foundations of religion and theology would be to recall (but now in a thematic way) Lonergan's own development on the nature of cognitive meaning. Indeed, in the present writer's judgment, only a firm grasp of Lonergan's analysis of cognitive development in the medieval and modern periods will provide his interpreters with the conditions for the possibility of understanding his later and more contemporaneously relevant work. For the methodological and transcendant exigencies to be discussed below only emerge as genuine exigencies for Lonergan in the context of his prior differentiation of the systematic and critical exigencies both of which are developed in the "narrower" context of the meaning of cognitive meaning especially in its most strictly scientific form. For the methodological exigence, in Lonergan's precise sense of that term, is only an exigence for the genuinely critical inquirer. And the nature of the transcendent exigence for the context in which Lonergan now speaks is an exigence and a problem only for the highly differentiated consciousness of Western man.

Indeed, Lonergan's own intellectual development is perhaps best understood in terms of the four exigencies (systematic, critical, methodical, transcendent) expressing the movement from level to level of self-transcendence.[26] Since the principal

26. The categories "exigencies" and the levels of "self-transcendence" are principally employed in Lonergan's *Method*. They are used here as helpful for summarizing Lonergan's own development.

224

concern of these final chapters, however, is the work of the "later" Lonergan on method and on the nature of theology, the earlier steps of his career must be somewhat foreshortened. Indeed, Lonergan's own intellectual development represents one man's attempt to come to terms with the developments of the systematic, critical, methodical and transcendent exigencies in the Western theological tradition. First, then, the systematic: Lonergan's early work in Aquinas is familiar territory to the historian of Thomist hermeneutics. To recall this first work in *Gratia Operans* we may say that Lonergan's chief personal discovery was his realization of the possibility of a strictly theoretical approach to theology. As we have seen in the early chapters of this book, that discovery required an inquiry into the entire medieval period from Anselm's questioning spirit through Abelard's dialectics, through the medieval development of the theoretical techniques of the *quaestio* and the books of sentences up to the later medieval achievement of the *summae.*[27] For the finest medieval achievement, the *summa,* is not just a set of unrelated questions and answers but represents rather what the Germans have named a *Begrifflichkeit,* i.e. a related set of concepts, theorems, operations and techniques which may define one's theoretic horizon. In other words, the precise meaning accorded the word "theology" in the medieval period is a particular expression of a more general human—or at least Western —phenomenon. To state the problem in its simplest terms one may employ Piaget's vocabulary and say that the original and originating human consciousness is an undifferentiated one. However, the undifferentiated mind's attempts to meet the exigencies of its ever further questions can eventually result (as in fact it did in the Greek breakthrough to *logos*) in the differentiation of a purely intellectual pattern of experience. In short, one becomes differentiated in the measure that one's questions

27. Cf. Chapters 2 and 3 for specific references; Lonergan's interpretation of the medieval period is to be found principally in *Gratia Operans* and *Verbum* as well as in sections on the systematic exigence in *Method in Theology.* Hence the citations here will be minimal.

225

become precise and technical (e.g. Socrates' search for a universal definition of justice), one's demands become strictly theoretical and one's answers can be ordered into an interrelated context (e.g. Aristotle's *Ethics*). In that case, the differentiated subject no longer finds himself in one world but in two: the world of everyday common sense and the world of theory.

And precisely that is what the medieval theological achievement meant: the ability to express religious meaning theoretically through the systematic use of the categories and techniques made available by the impact of the recently discovered Greco-Arabic culture on the religious traditions of Christianity. Its finest and most rigorous achievement remains Aquinas' *Summae* with their precise and systematic (i.e. theoretic) structuring of the insights of what even anti-Thomists would now admit was a genuinely religious consciousness.

Yet the development of the systematic exigence in differentiated Western consciousness and the resultant displacement towards system serve to give rise to differing effects. On the one hand, it exposes the possibility of freeing man from the excessive creativity of his mythical and often magical imagination by the needed critique of a purely rational control of meaning in scientific definition. On the other hand, such a differentiation can and does provoke a crisis by now familiar to Western man. For besides meeting with the continuous incomprehension of undifferentiated consciousness (as, for example, in the "Augustinian" reaction to Aquinas' use of the Aristotleian categories), the differentiated consciousness gradually uncovers a problem all its own. The full thematic realization of the crises provoked by that shift does not come to expression in Aquinas himself. For even if (as Metz argues in the *Christliche Anthropozentrik* and Lonergan himself argues in the *Verbum* articles) the performance of Aquinas is truly critical (i.e. with a firm grasp of psychological fact and epistemological reality), it nonetheless remains true that the thematization of that performance in Aquinas is made in basically metaphysical, not epistemological terms. Hence, Aquinas, however anthropocentric, is neither

226

Descartes nor Kant but remains a medieval man for whom the systematic exigence finds expression in his Aristotelian-neo-Platonist-Thomist categories and with sure if unthematized intellectual and religious interiority.

In its thematic expression, therefore, the full force of the problem of relating the two worlds of common sense and theory was not a medieval problem. It could not be solved in medieval terms or within the medieval context. For that reason, Lonergan turned his attention to the full meaning of the post-Kantian critical exigence. To meet that exigence, *Insight* was written. The intellectual context with which *Insight* was concerned is, as we have seen above, exceedingly complex. But however complex those scientific, Kantian, and Hegelian origins, it will suffice for present purposes to insist upon the rise and the meaning of the critical exigence for the Lonergan of *Insight*.

In essence, then, the differentiated consciousness recognizes the existence of a problem that is simply not present to an undifferentiated one, viz. how is one to relate these two very different languages (common sense and theory) and their resultant two very different worlds (things-in-relation-to-oneself and things-in-relation-to-one-another). In a genuinely critical attempt to face this problem, one is thrown back, with Kant and the entire modern tradition, from the world of theory into the world of the subject's own interiority. For the differentiated inquirer's attempt to relate his two languages and his two worlds forces him to investigate the operations grounding both. In other words, the critical inquirer is faced with three inescapable and interrelated questions: what am I doing when I am knowing? (cognitional theory); why is doing that knowing? (epistemology) and what do I know when I do that? (metaphysics).[28] The responses of *Insight* to these questions are by now well known if still too little appreciated. For Lonergan, the possibility of the critical breakthrough is not the possibility of easy talk about intuition but only of exact speech on the appropriation of one's

28. This three-question formulation is Lonergan's own in *Method in Theology* (the chapter on transcendental method).

rational self-consciousness in its normative operations, structures and procedures. In its technical expression (self-affirmation as a virtually unconditioned) that self-appropriation resembles the world of theory. But in its own fundamental moment it expresses a quite distinct exigence. For it is the critical exigence alone which forces the subject to that level of heightened awareness present in the purely intellectual pattern of experience which can make him critically aware of his operations in their normative structures and procedures. For it recognizes that the classical control of meaning via theory must now yield place to the critical control of meaning via a thematic grasp of intellect in its normative structures, operations and procedures.

And if that critical exigence reaches the level of self-affirmation, it reveals to the critical subject the need and the possibility of yet another exigence, viz. the methodical one. For what is method in the critical meaning of that word? May it not be defined as the normative (as critical) pattern of recurrent and related operations yielding progressive and cumulative results?[29] And is not any science worthy of the name principally committed not to its results but to its methods? A critical science, moreover (i.e. philosophy), may attempt a transcendental method. Nor does that latter phrase refer to any kind of semi-magical super-method that promises to resolve all one's problems. Rather it refers to the fact that unlike other methods which exploit the opportunity of particular fields, transcendental method aims at meeting the exigencies and exploiting the opportunities of the human mind itself.

Nor is that reality as obscure as the name may at first glance seem to indicate. As a matter of fact, in one sense everyone knows and observes transcendental method. We observe it inasmuch as we are attentive, intelligent, reasonable and responsible. In short, inasmuch as we are authentic to the self-transcending demands of our personhood. In another sense, of course, it is quite difficult to be at home in transcendental method. For it is not

29. Again, the current Lonerganian formulation for *Method in Theology*.

necessarily accomplished by reading books (including *Insight*) nor listening to lectures (including Socrates') nor analyzing language (including scientific). Rather it is only achieved in its primal and originating moment, by a personal heightening of one's own consciousness and, in its second moment, by a thematization of that consciousness. It is, in its essence, something which no man can do for another but each must be willing to do for himself. In the measure that he does so, he knows precisely what he is doing when he is operating in any cognitional discipline. *Insight,* in other words, does not impose a Lonerganian system but invites the reader to achieve his own self-appropriation. That achievement, moreover, is a gradual one: in accordance with the moving viewpoint of *Insight* itself, through the earlier section ("Insight as Activity") in which (through a set of exercises provided by mathematical, scientific and common sense examples) the reader is led to experience the basic operations of consciousness as experience, understanding and judgment. Gradually too he begins to understand the unity and structural interrelatedness of his experienced experience, understanding and judgment. And then—in the central moment of self-affirmation—the reader is enabled to affirm his understanding of his experienced experience, understanding and judgment. In the fourth stage of such personal self-transcendence, he may further resolve to conform to the normative component in his operations by forcing his action to follow his knowledge.[30]

Nor need anyone fear that such an affirmation of the understood relations of the experienced experience, understanding and judgment is an escape rather than a transformation of his problem. For all he is really required to do is to heighten his consciousness and intentional operations. Accordingly, it is not

30. Note that the logic of this position on the levels of consciousness does not necessarily imply a "faculty-psychology" distinction between "intellect" and "will"—although Lonergan's own movement away from any such distinction is recent and dependent upon his deeper and more critical study of the "fourth level" (existential consciousness, especially of the morally and religiously converted).

229

possible to consider this insistence an escape from the critical problem. Indeed, it is the entry to it. For what the critical inquirer is really asked to do is to heighten his consciousness of his conscious and intentional operations. In fact one may deny the possibility of such an approach only at the price of denying the cognitional operations which that method orders, unifies and relates. But no one is ever really willing to do that (nor should he be). For no one, to our knowledge, has ever claimed that never in his life has he ever sensed anything at all; that never has he betrayed the slightest trace of intelligent inquiry or the vaguest glimmer of understanding; that never has he come to weigh the evidence for or against it; that never has he come to wonder about the truth or falsity of any statement or come to weigh the evidence for or against it; that never has he evaluated, deliberated or acted responsibly. Essentially, then, there is no escape from the exigencies of transcendental method for, "conscious and intentional operations exist and anyone who wants to be counted out has only to disqualify himself by claiming to be a non-responsible, non-reasonable, non-intelligent somnambulist."[31]

In summary, Lonergan's own intellectual development up to the present insistence upon the importance of the new context of historical consciousness reveals the possibilities and the fruits of a full commitment to the systematic and critical exigencies.[32] For unless the systematic exigence is clearly differentiated (as in the original Greek accomplishment, as in the medieval achievement of Aquinas, as in the scientific and critical revolutions of modern consciousness), the imperatives of the critical exigence will not even be experienced. And unless a truly critical exigence

31. The quotation and the context are from the chapter on transcendental method in *Method in Theology*.
32. Moreover, this can only be labeled "subjectivist" if an interpreter has already failed to grasp Lonergan's grounding cognitional theory wherein meaning is understood as an intentional category, intending being (cf. *Insight*, "The Notion of Being," pp. 348–75) and, in the act of judgment, as a virtually unconditioned reaching that partial attainment of the real-in-the-true which each judgment expresses (cf. *Insight*, esp. pp. 279–81, 377–80).

is allowed full range and the thematization of its resultant interiority completed, then the full meaning of that turn to methodology in the contemporary intellectual context cannot begin to be understood.

In its theological context, that methodological turn will be the next issue of this book. It may be well to recall, however, that the conditions for the possibility of that turn are to be located, for Lonergan, in that cognitive self-transcendence which can accurately be named "intellectual conversion." It is genuinely a conversion and not merely a development for it demands a radical turn away from what is experienced or sensed or imagined or conceived to what is rationally affirmed to be true. And that possibility, in its turn, demands a radical reorientation of the authentic subject from some little world of his own (more than likely, some dubious combination of animal faith and human error) to a world of the intelligently understood and the reasonably affirmed. It involves, in essence, the transformation of the subject from a horizon defined by his own psychological, sociological and cultural desires, fears and achievements to one that is accurately named a basic horizon, i.e. to the intelligent, the true, the good; indeed even the holy. For the transcendental imperatives "Be attentive, be intelligent, be reasonable, be responsible, develop and, if necessary, change" enforce a radical openness to the horizons of all and every true meaning: a horizon whose authentic entry for the differentiated consciousness is a radical intellectual conversion and whose further exigencies impel one to reject all obscurantism and allow the further questions to emerge. To those further questions and to the categories and the horizons which they explore, the more recent work of Bernard Lonergan is addressed.

231

10. HORIZON DEVELOPMENT: THE METHODICAL EXIGENCE IN THEOLOGY

Within the dual horizon of a prior differentiation of the systematic and critical exigencies and of the new theological context of historical consciousness with its multi-leveled dimensions of meaning, the properly methodical exigence, in Lonergan's sense, becomes the central theological problematic. Indeed, the shift of Lonergan's central category from intelligibility (insight) to meaning caused him to differentiate himself still more clearly from the European practitioners of transcendental method. That differentiation is most clearly expressed in the close of Lonergan's review of his European counterpart, Emerich Coreth:

The fact is, of course, that while I consider Fr. Coreth's metaphysics a sound and brilliant achievement, I should not equate metaphysics with the total and basic horizon, the *Gesamt- und Grundwissenschaft*. Metaphysics, as about being, equates with the objective pole of that horizon; but metaphysics, as science, does not equate with the subjective pole. In my opinion Fr. Coreth's subjective pole is under a measure of abstraction that is quite legitimate when one is mediating the immediacy of latent metaphysics, but is to be removed when one is concerned with the total and basic horizon. In the concrete, the subjective pole is indeed the inquirer, but incarnate, liable to mythic consciousness, in need of a critique that reveals where the counterpositions come from. The incarnate inquirer develops in a development that is social and historical, that stamps the stages of scientific and philosophic progress with dates,

232

that is open to a theology that Karl Rahner has described as an *Aufhebung der Philosophie*. The critique, accordingly, has to issue in a transcendental doctrine of methods with the method of metaphysics just one among many and so considered from a total viewpoint. For latent in the performance of the incarnate inquirer not only is there a metaphysics that reveals the objective pole of the total horizon but also there is the method of performing which, thematized and made explicit, reveals the subjective pole in its true and proper stature. Still, it is difficult to disagree completely with Fr. Coreth, for in my disagreement I am only agreeing with his view that, what has come from Fr. Maréchal is, not a set of fixed opinions, but a movement; indeed, I am only asking for a fuller sweep in the alternations of his dialectic of *Vollzug und Begriff*.[1]

To deal with man in the concrete, therefore, demands of the theologian that he attempt to articulate his own theological method. To that question, with increasing frequency, Lonergan has devoted his major attention from 1959 to the present.[2] Indeed, the question of method in the human sciences, in philosophy and in theology are, for many of their practitioners, the principal questions on the present horizon. As the gains of the phenomenological movement have made especially clear, the method employed is the key to all the products of any discipline. But only those who have worked through the systematic and critical exigencies have a correct notion of Lonergan's understanding of the nature of the methodological problem. For

1. Cf. "Metaphysics as Horizon," *Gregorianum,* 44 (1963), 317–18.
2. The sources for this interest are cited in chapter 9, ftn. 2; they refer to the series of courses and lectures on the problematics of meaning and method from the course *De Intellectu et Methodo* on through the forthcoming *Method in Theology.* Since it is impossible to paginate the as yet unpublished work *Method in Theology,* the analysis in this section will be from the unpublished manuscript unless otherwise indicated. From this section on, the analysis adheres fairly closely to the text itself. The footnotes, therefore, will be employed chiefly for references to other confirmatory or exemplary works rather than to the manuscript itself; on the present question, for example, one may note the greater differentiation afforded to the discussion of modern positive and historically conscious theology by the distinction between "field" and "subject" specializations.

others it tends to become a secondary or even a relatively unimportant problem. It sounds to them (as Gadamer reminds us) as if one were seeking for some new rules (usually logical) that could be followed blindly by any "hewer of wood and drawer of water."[3] Indeed, to many it sounds disturbingly like the last gasp of a dying classical culture. Now, if the contemporary search for method were in fact a search for "new" logical rules whence one may deduce one's conclusions, then that distrust would be well earned. Yet the fact is that the contemporary search for method, by and large, is nothing of the sort.

In Lonergan's case, to be more specific, the methodological search is neither for new rules nor a new "system" but for a basic pattern whence all rules can be derived. That pattern will include the logic of the classical period but must add the contemporary scientific interest in inquiry, observation, discovery, experiment, synthesis and verification. It further demands a context wherein the multi-dimensional levels of meaning (and not

3. Cf. H. G. Gadamer, *Wahrheit und Methode* (Tübingen, 1962), esp. pp. 1–7, 205–18. German interpreters, I suspect, would be tempted to ignore Lonergan's interest in methodology as yet another example of the "methodologism" of the neo-Kantian kind. This is not the context to calm such suspicions, except to remind interpreters of the critique of Kant by Lonergan (*Insight,* pp. 339–42) and the uniqueness of his notion of transcendental method vis-à-vis the Continental tradition. For further explicitations on Lonergan vis-à-vis the German tradition, cf. the essays by Frederick Lawrence and Matthew Lamb in the forthcoming volume on theological method. By way of contrast, cf. the interpretation of Lonergan in Francis Fiorenza's otherwise most helpful article, "Karl Rahner and the Kantian Problematic," p. 38. This is not to argue, of course, that Lonergan shares Rahner's Heideggerian formulation of the Kantian question but it is to insist that his position cannot be easily identified with the interpretations of either neo-Kantianism or Maréchal. (For an example of the latter difference, cf. the essay of the most authoritative contemporary interpreter of Maréchal, J. Donceel, in his Preface to the English edition of Coreth's *Metaphysics* (New York, 1968), pp. 11–12. On the other hand, the present author would agree (with Fiorenza) that Lonergan's infrequent references to the dangers of "subjectivism" in phenomenology and "existentialism" is fully inadequate to an interpretation of Heidegger (cf. especially Lonergan's 1957 "Lectures on Mathematical Logic and Existentialism" where Heidegger is interpreted as an existentialist!).

234

only scientific meaning) may find an intrinsic place in the analysis. Yet that latter inclusion need not mean that theological method can only be an "art" and not a "science." In fact, Lonergan's own development up to the time of his explicit involvement in the discussion of theological method provides an alternative view to the decreasing returns of the "art" versus "science" impasse. That alternative has already been acknowledged in the earlier chapters but its general features may be repeated here in order to aid a more immediate entry into the level of the methodological discussion in Lonergan. It might first be noted that Lonergan is not (even in *Insight*) simply analyzing in an Aristotelean manner a conspicuously successful science (viz. physics) and then judging all other disciplines as scientific or not by their degree of similarity to physics. Indeed, he has shown that he is not innocent of the gains of the *Geisteswisschenschaften* controversy nor the methodological complexities involved for anyone who recognizes the multi-dimensional horizon of historical consciousness. Lonergan's own development (in *Insight*) has been to derive a preliminary notion of method from the successful empirical sciences (classical and statistical heuristic methods) and to proceed from there to cognitional theory. There he found and thematized the invariant properties of a method that may be called transcendental in the precise sense of self-affirmation and the consequent notions of being, objectivity, reality. From that horizon he moved forward to try to determine the function of transcendental method in its relations to the particular methods of the various sciences.

Within that context, therefore, method may be defined as a normative pattern of related and recurrent operations yielding cumulative and progressive results.[4] That notion of a basic pattern is obviously the fundamental problem. And its nature must be to become a method in the generic sense given above while still maintaining its transcendental character. For basic method

4. Once again, this is Lonergan's own definition. It will be available in published form in the special "method" issue of *Gregorianum* (Fall, 1969).

THE ACHIEVEMENT OF BERNARD LONERGAN

cannot be confined categorically to any generic or specific type of result or to any limited field but applies instead to all fields where the basic transcendentals (Be intelligent, be reasonable, be responsible, develop and if necessary, change) are operative. In short, a basic method would apply to all fields where the human mind in its invariant structure, procedures and operations are operative. And unless one wishes to claim for theology that its peculiarity as a discipline consists in its being unconcerned with data, uninterested in inquiry, unimpressed by understanding, undisturbed by reflection and verification and careless of evaluation and decision, then the exigencies of the methodological problem must enter into the theological context as well.

Indeed, the problem of theology at present might best be stated as the need to move fully and coherently from classical to historical consciousness or, more explicitly still, from a notion of theology as "reason illuminated by faith" to "method illuminated by faith."[5] That latter notion of method, if we may repeat, can strive for nothing less than a transformation of classical "ratio" by revealing the invariant structures, procedures and operations of reason itself. Less than that will either trap theology into a classicism which is elsewhere dead or "free" it for the attractive but inadequate dreams of a whole group of recently arrived romantics unconcerned with the demands of reason, or *theoria,* and *a fortiori* of method.[6]

The question of method is also relevant to theology insofar as theology too has methods which attempt to mediate the Christian experience of the past and to face the exigencies of the present and the future. For however peculiar theological operations may be, theology is still the work of human minds

5. This formulation may be found in "Theology and Understanding," *Collection,* pp. 121–41.

6. For a similar emphasis in Lonergan himself, note that in a later context (on "secularity" and contemporary Christianity) Lonergan is able to emphasize this contemporary need for greater differentiation-integration (not a movement to an undifferentiated state) yet more helpfully; cf. Lonergan's essay "The Absence of God in Modern Culture." *The Presence and Absence of God* (New York, 1969), pp. 164–78.

performing the same basic set of operations in the same basic pattern of relations as common sense and the various sciences. In Lonergan's own words, "It is true that one attends, inquires, reflects, decides differently in the natural sciences, the human sciences and theology. Still there is no transition from attention to inattention, inquiry to indifference, critical to uncritical, responsible to irresponsible."[7] And those transcendental imperatives imply not some magical set of rules but a transcendental method which thematizes those imperatives. Since these transcendental notions are also unrestricted with the unrestrictedness of the pure desire to know intending but never reaching everything about everything, the objects of Christian theology (God and the God-graced world in Jesus Christ), precisely insofar as they are, are not beyond the intentional reach of transcendental method.[8] On its simplest (if most overlooked) level the problem is as basic as it is obvious: theologians are not exempt from the ordinary human encumbrance of having minds and using them. They could do worse, then, than try to come to terms with just what that means. They should, in short, face up to the demands not only of classical *theoria* but also of contemporary method.

To conceive theology in terms of method, therefore, is not to ask a second level question but a foundational one. It is to conceive theology as a basic pattern of recurrent and related operations proceeding cumulatively and progressively towards an ideal goal. But—as the earlier sections on positive, dogmatic and speculative theology implicitly argue—no single theologian can today hope to know all theology. So highly specialized has the discipline become that no one can hope to attempt more in

7. As quoted in the chapter on transcendental method in *Method in Theology*.

8. Note the importance of the qualification "intentional." Hence even Barthian interpreters need not fear that this is yet another Hegelian theological "overreaching" of faith (contrast the claims, for example, with the recent interpretation of Hegel's philosophical-theological attempt in Emil Fackenheim, *The Religious Dimension in Hegel's Philosophy* [Indiana, 1968]).

one lifetime than a mastery of the method and results of a few questions in one of the theological specializations. How, for example, may any one man hope to unite the results of biblical criticism on the knowledge of Christ with the needed philosophical or dogmatic or systematic discussion of the same question? Is there no way out of the temptations to theological totalitarianism which beset each practitioner? Moreover, as the discussions of modernism versus fundamentalism, of liberal theology versus dialectical theology, of Barth versus Bultmann, of "dogmatic" versus "biblical" theology, of the Greek versus the Hebrew mind, and so on, have made abundantly clear, a foundational problem has surfaced for any honest theologian. That problem can legitimately be named methodological.[9] In its starkest terms, the theological problem is this: can the theologian determine a basic pattern for all the patterns of related and recurrent operations involved in the theological task? Can he determine a fundamental theological method which will allow all practitioners to collaborate systematically with one another? Can he ground that pattern in a transcendental method which is not open to fundamental revision?

We have already investigated Lonergan's notion of a transcendental method. Presently we will describe the contemporary theological situation of ever further specialization and ever more meagre collaboration. From an understanding of that situation, the solution which Lonergan suggests may become intelligible.

9. A clarification would be in order here: the methodological problem is "foundational" insofar as otherwise one is left with fairly undifferentiated counter-claims as salvific for theology (e.g. it must be "purely" biblical; or it is useful *only* as a revolutionary force; or the whole tradition is to be interpreted solely in terms of the death-of-God; or the existential situations of death, guilt, etc. are no longer relevant to secular man come-of-age; and so on). On the other hand, as will be explained below, "foundational" refers to the theological-functional specialty dealing with the problem of the theologian on the level of *Existenz* (i.e. man's contemporary recognition of his time-laden finitude, his historicity) —a problem which, in various ways, practically every major theologian since Schleiermacher (including, it seems, the neo-Orthodox and the neo-Thomists, in negative fashion, to be sure) has been attempting to resolve.

238

Once again, the basic difficulty is the need to get hold of the right question.

In the present situation, therefore, one may accurately mention two fundamental types of specialization, viz. field specialization and subject specialization.[10] Field specialization divides the data to be examined: the Scriptures, the Fathers, the councils, the medieval, renaissance, reformation, enlightenment, modern, or contemporary periods. Within each of these there are further specializations: e.g. Scriptures—Old Testament, intertestamental period, New Testament; Old Testament—laws, prophets, writings, and so on. All these specializations increase their scope as the enormous amount of archeological and textual materials accumulate into ever more probably accurate critical editions. Subject specialization, on the other hand, performs a different task: it divides and studies the results to be taught in the different departments, subjects and courses. Thus it is that every complete theological curriculum must include Semitic languages, Hebrew history, religions of the Ancient Near East, New Testament theologies, the theologies of the apostolic fathers, the theology of the councils, and so on. When one recognizes both types of specialization as legitimate and indeed necessary, there gradually emerges a recognition of the need to find a way to differentiate the stages in the single process from data to results. Such a need is fulfilled for Lonergan by his development of what he names "functional specialization," i.e. a specialization which deals directly neither with data nor results but seeks to distinguish the stages in the process from data to results. Each stage, moreover, operates functionally[11] towards the next for at each stage there is a different pattern of related

10. The divisions are Lonergan's own formulation. A further clarification may be helpfully employed: Lonergan's notion of functional specialization includes field and subject specialties; field specialties divide the materials of the first phase; subject specialties divide the topics of the second phase. Finally, dialectics and foundations are least divided; research and communications are most divided.

11. The term "functional" is post-*Insight,* yet it is applicable to the levels of consciousness, each of which is functionally related to the next and higher level.

and recurrent operations applied to the results of the preceding stage. Each successive stage presupposes the results of the preceding one and complements them by moving them that much closer to the final goal. To clarify this discussion, a diagram is given below of the eightfold functional specialties which define, for Lonergan, the theological task:

Diagram: Combine two phases of theology with four levels of consciousness:

Structure of Consciousness	Mediating Theology		Mediated Theology	
deliberation	(4)	dialectic	foundations	(5)
judgment	(3)	history	doctrines	(6)
understanding	(2)	interpretation	systematics	(7)
experience	(1)	research	communications	(8)

The most obvious question occasioned by this outline is, of course, just where does this eightfold list of functional specialties come from? Perhaps a more indirect reply to the question might help before a direct one is offered. In the first place, then, any theological student will have a certain *a posteriori* familiarity with the list: for he recalls the numerous courses in textual criticism, in exegesis, in history, in what has traditionally been called apologetics (now fundamental theology), in dogmatic theology, in systematic theology, in pastoral theology. He may also recall that usually neither a balance nor an interrelatedness between the specialties is attained in any one theological school. In the Roman Catholic context, for example, if he studied at Louvain he is likely to be "stronger" in textual criticism, exegesis and history and "weaker" in dogmatics and systematics. If he studied almost anywhere in Germany or at the Gregorian in Rome, he is likely to be "stronger" in systematics and fundamental and "weaker" in textual criticism and exegesis than his Louvain counterpart. Indeed, in any theological school the alert student very quickly learns the "strong" points of the curriculum and the "weak" ones. In general, then, it is fair to say that except in those rare (and probably eschatological) places where the curriculum is balanced and the professors in each discipline highly competent in their own fields and fully conversant with the results in the fields of their colleagues, the student is left with the disconcerting impression that somehow it is up to himself alone to relate and integrate all these disciplines. Nor will he ordinarily find too much encouragement for that task from most of his professors. For he also soon discovers that most of them are so wedded to their own particular disciplines that their lack of interest in other disciplines borders on the patronizing. He may, for example, find exegetes decrying the use of any "profane" philosophy as a intrinsic violation and distortion of the pure word of God. Or he may find systematic theologians blithely using scriptural texts whose scientific exegesis has no connection at all with the systematic issue in question. Or he may find "pastoral" theologians, innocent of exegesis, history or systematics alike, insist that the sole concern of the theologian at present must be to find ways to become "relevant" to the prevailing *Zeitgeist*. Or he may find exegetes or systematic theologians contemptuous of any attempt to communicate their "purely scientific" results in a fashion relevant to the needs of any and especially contemporary culture.

In almost any major theological school, there tend to be ragged edges, very little determinateness (sometimes even internecine squabbles among the various theological fiefdoms), and usually only a rough relatedness among the various disciplines. For example, the incomprehension received by the work of Thomas Altizer from many Protestant exegetes and historians or the outright mockery sometimes accorded the sociological concerns of Harvey Cox are but two of the more recent examples of an unfortunately rather widespread phenomenon.

Yet no matter how grave the present educational situation, the problem is not just an *a posteriori* one. Rather, on a less pedagogical and more properly theoretical and methodological

241

level, we might say that the *a priori* conditions for the possibility of the eightfold functional specialties can be established. In the first place, theology operates in two phases.[12] There are various ways by which one might express those two phases. Three of them will be symbolized here: In biblical categories, one listens to the word in the first phase and bears witness to it in the second. In medieval categories, one would describe the movement as that from the *lectio* (reading) to the *quaestio* (or technical questions raised by and to the readings). In more contemporary categories, one would describe the historically conscious man as, first, encountering the past and then taking his stand towards the future.[13] The first phase, then (research-interpretation-history-dialectic), is an attempt to encounter the Judaeo-Christian past in its multi-dimensional, genetic-dialectic development while the second phase (from one's articulation of one's foundations through doctrines, systematics and communication) is one's own attempt to speak to the present and the impending future from within a basic theological horizon.

In the second place, the four levels proper to each phase are correlative to the four functional and invariant levels of consciousness uncovered and thematized by transcendental method. Those four levels of consciousness, as analyzed in *Insight,* pursue four distinct but interrelated goals. For in either the spontaneous inquiry of common sense or the methodical labor of science, the authentic inquirer always moves through four levels: he tries to establish the data (experience); he then tries to understand them (understanding); he next attempts to establish the facts

12. The division is, of course, Lonergan's own. Still, the present writer considers it basically useful for analyzing the history of theology in its various periods, as he hopes to document historically in a book on the history of theological method in the new *Catholic Theological Encyclopedia.* It is to be noted how much more developed the analysis is than the comparatively underdeveloped treatment of the *"via intentionis"* and *"via doctrinae"* in, e.g., *DDT* II, pp. 33–54.

13. Exactly how we may be said to "encounter" the past is one of the most difficult theoretical issues facing the contemporary theologian. It need not assume a romantic hermeneutic. Indeed, it is the issue assumed by exegetes, historians and dogmaticians and explicitated by the "hermeneutic" school; and by Lonergan via the functional specialty called dialectics.

(judgment); and finally, he makes his decision on what is to be done about his knowledge (decision-action). Common sense, it is true, pursues all four without sharply distinguishing among them. Scientific inquiry, on the contrary, consciously uses all four levels first in pursuit of the first end (what are the data?), then in pursuit of the second; then of the third; and then of the fourth. As the scientist moves to the second, third and fourth levels, moreover, he must allow each level to presuppose the results of the former and complement them by pursuing the activity proper to that level. Once again, but now more exactly,[14] one is involved in *Insight*'s moving viewpoint to ever higher viewpoints.

Accordingly, if the relationship of these eight functional specialties to the fourfold levels of the structure of Lonergan's transcendental method is basically clear,[15] a further clarity may be brought to bear on the discussion by elaborating the more exact meaning of each specialty in the common theological enterprise. The aim of this discussion, moreover, will not be exhaustive but suggestive, not explanatory but descriptive.[16]

First, research: the textual critic, for example, will determine with as high a degree of scientific probability as possible just what the relevant data of the Christian message and the Christian tradition are. In short, he will strive to establish (by all the scientific means available to him) critical editions of all relevant Christian texts.[17]

14. "More exactly" insofar as it is differentiated in accordance with the actually existing theological specialties rather than simply providing general heuristic norms for positive, dogmatic and systematic theology (as in *De Deo Trino*).

15. This perhaps presumptuous claim is based on the hope that the earlier chapters of this book (on *Insight*) allow for that basic clarity.

16. It is important to emphasize the descriptive and non-explanatory nature of this interpretation: indeed, in Lonergan's own forthcoming method, a general context will explain these notions more explanatorily and a separate extended section on each of the specialties will determine their nature (for Longeran) explanatorily. At the present writing, only the first four sections have been so analyzed (thus leaving the crucial "foundations" still to be done).

17. For example, Stephen Neill cites how the controversy on the authenticity of the Ignatian epistles could only be settled (in the Bâur vs. Lightfoot controversy) on the basis of exhaustive research into the texts;

Second, interpretation: the exegete will first presuppose the relevant data established by the textual critic; he will next recognize that the data in question are not simply "givens" (as in the empirical sciences) but involve and indeed are constituted by "meanings." He will then attempt to establish as accurately as possible and by means of all the scientific tools available to him (parallel texts, form criticism, redaction criticism, etc.) the precise meaning of the texts under discussion.[18]

Third, history:[19] the historian will first presuppose the mean-

cf. Stephen Neill, *The Interpretation of the New Testament 1861–1961*, p. 47.

18. It is important to recognize the limited notion of hermeneutic employed by Lonergan here—viz. dealing with the understanding of the texts and not with the myriad of problems (critical history, historicity, empathy, etc.) ordinarily associated with that discipline (e.g. in Fuchs, Ebeling, Robinson, Funk, Hart *et al.*)—and precisely because Lonergan believes it to be more helpful to treat those (for him) differentiated questions distinctly. For the fuller complexities of Lonergan's notion of hermeneutic, cf. his 1962 Toronto lecture "Hermeneutics." Whether Lonergan resolves the problems associated with hermeneutics in history and dialectics is a nice, but a further question. A specific theological example of his notion of hermeneutics would be any commentary on any work of Scripture or his own hermeneutics of Aquinas' theology of grace in *Gratia Operans*. Compare the hermeneutics lecture, for example, to the earlier formulation of *Insight* (pp. 562–95) and note both its fundamental continuity (e.g. the emphasis on cognitional theory) and the development (e.g. the emphasis on the context of the *Geisteswissenschaften* and historical consciousness and the analysis of the German discussion of hermeneutics as "to a great extent coincident with the problems of method in contemporary Catholic theology." "Hermeneutics," p. 2).

19. The problem with "history" is, of course, still more complicated than hermeneutics. Once again the section here merely indicates Lonergan's fundamental notion of where and how the specialty "history" fits into the general collaborative theological enterprise; its actual development in explanatory detail (and Lonergan's own critique of such figures as Troeltsch, Collingwood, Marrou, Becker, Heussi *et al.*) is to be attempted in *Method*. For an earlier version cf. "Hermeneutics," esp. pp. 11–12; cf. also the 1963 lecture "History" esp. pp. 2–8; and *DVI*, pp. 9–14. Note, therefore, how "history is simply an expansion of these concerns" (i.e. from "hermeneutic" (another's meaning) to "history" ("genetic-dialectic development of others' meanings). Cf. also "Notes from the Introductory Lecture in the Philosophy of History" (1961), esp. pp. 7–14.

ing established by the exegetes. On his own, he will then complement their work by using the best available historical criteria to establish just what as a matter of fact actually happened in particular events and just what was the basic movement going forward through all the varied interpretations used to communicate that event or series of events. For example, an interpreter may interpret the assassination of Julius Caesar in a way which praises Brutus or in a way which favors Caesar or in a way which concludes that both of them were simply creatures of deeper economic, sociological or cultural forces. But the historian must see to it that no one attempts to interpret that event in a manner which has Caesar killing Brutus. In other words, there remains a certain ground of historical factuality which may not be interpreted away by even the most brilliant exegesis. That ground is uncovered by the critical judgments of the authentic historian as he attempts to determine as accurately as possible (e.g. the Warren Commission Report, or Trevor-Roper on "The Last Days of Hitler") the ascertainable facts (i.e. the reality) of the event which provoked so many various interpretations. To return to a more theological context, anyone familiar with the intricacies involved in historical discussion of the meaning and/or factual status of the infancy narratives in the gospels or the far more important resurrection narratives[20] will be fully familiar with the importance of the distinction employed here. It would be well to reconsider, however, how crucial it is to differentiate the meaning element on the level of understanding-interpretation from the matter of fact, "true meaning" element on the level of judgment-history. Without such a differentiation, the theologian's need for critical historical work and, in its limit, for the historical events of the Christian tradition itself, collapse under the heavy burden of a thousand interpretations.

20. For example, one of the most startling (and to this interpreter ill-fated) attempts in contemporary theology is Wolfhart Pannenburg's attempt (it would seem) practically to ground eschatological faith in the resurrection via historical reason (as performed by the Pannenburg circle); cf. Wolfhart Pannenburg, *Jesus, God and Man* (Westminster, 1968), esp. pp. 53–115.

Indeed, the still further differentiation of this level of judgment-history from the level of a decision becomes even more crucial in contemporary theology as the *Historie-Geschichte* debate more than suggests. For as that debate developed, one witnessed a somewhat distressing scene: on the one hand, the seeming inability of several Roman Catholic and Anglican biblical and doctrinal scholars to rise to the decision-level of Bultmann's discussion of history as *Geschichte;* on the other hand, the spectacle of the incapacity of many existentialist theologians to appreciate either the discomfort of their "salvation history" or doctrinal colleagues or the epistemological ambiguities of their own decision-emphasis position.[21] In purely theological terms, therefore, the epistemological-ontological status one accords the role of judgment is crucial. It is especially crucial for a religious tradition (viz. the Judaeo-Christian) which has traditionally insisted that its religious stance is grounded in certain historical facts. In fact, if a theologian is still operating within the horizon of a Kantian epistemology,[22] then the role of judgment is considered merely synthetic and thereby not really distinct from the level of understanding-interpretation. Hence there is not a clearly differentiated functional specialty for historical study, and historical facts tend to be subsumed either by the

21. Amidst the vast literature on this question, for a clear, brief example of both positions on the Christian's stance vis-à-vis the Old Testament, cf. Bernhard Anderson (ed.), *The Old Testament and Christian Faith* (New York, 1969), the essays (*inter alia*) by Rudolf Bultmann (pp. 8–36), Alan Richardson (pp. 36–49), Eric Voegelin (pp. 64–90), Oscar Cullmann (pp. 115–24) and James Robinson (pp. 124–59). In New Testament studies the most obvious example would be the varying positions taken on Luke's "historicization" of the kerygma by either the Bultmann school (e.g. Conzelmann and Käsemann) as contrasted to either the Pannenburg (e.g. Wilckens) or the Cullmann school.

22. Hence the renewed importance of Lonergan's analysis of the nature of judgment as a "virtually unconditioned." Cf. *Insight,* pp. 279–81. For Lonergan's analysis of Kant on this point, cf. *ibid.,* pp. 339–42; for the Kantian influence on nineteenth- and twentieth-century Protestant theology, cf. James Richmond, *Faith and Philosophy* (London, 1966).

246

exigencies of straightforward exegesis ("the Jesus of history") or the more radical exigencies of existentialist decision ("The Christ of faith"). If, however, the theologian is operating within the horizon of a critically realistic epistemology,[23] the level of reflective consciousness and judgment (as a virtually unconditioned) is precisely the distinct level where truth-reality-historical fact (and the consequent functional specialty, history) emerge.

Fourth, dialectic: but the theologian's work does not cease after he has established the data, the interpretations and the historical facts and perspectives. For as every student of theology knows only too well, debates rage on every one of the prior three levels. There are, in the first place, different selections of data: Is Scripture alone the data relevant to Christian inquiry? Or does there exist a tradition which must also be studied? If the second, then what is that tradition and what is its relationship to the Scriptures? Are they really one? Or distinct and separate? Or do there also exist other, less immediately Christian data which are still relevant to Christian inquiry?

In the second place, there are many different interpretations of the same data. To name only the most obvious, there exist a Lutheran, a Calvinist, an Anabaptist, an Anglican, a Roman Catholic, an Orthodox interpretation of the same New Testament data. Each of these interpretations' histories, in its turn,

23. For example, it would seem that Schubert Ogden's Whiteheadean realism (via the "reformed" subjectivist principle) frees him from this difficulty while still allowing him to accept (as the present writer does) the major Bultmannian insistence on the need for demythologizing; cf. S. Ogden, *The Reality of God* (New York, 1966), esp. the essays "Theology and Objectivity" (pp. 71–99) and "Myth and Truth" (pp. 99–120); for a contrary interpretation on Ogden from the "hermeneutic" school, cf. Robert W. Funk, *Language, Hermeneutic and Word of God* (New York, 1966), esp. pp. 82–108. For the present writer, Ogden's Whiteheadean position provides a far more considerable development on the Bultmannian position on objectivity (and on foundations) than do the positions more usually identified as "post-Bultmannian." For two German representatives on the question of objectifying language, cf. *Distinctive Protestant and Catholic Themes Reconsidered* (New York, 1967), pp. 112–36 (Heinrich Ott), pp. 136–52 (Fritz Buri).

contains a whole history of past and present differing interpretations of the same data and an entire series of prophetic witnesses to the Christian fact. In such a context, the only way that the historically conscious contemporary theologian can remain faithful to the demands of his discipline is to operate within a genuinely ecumenical context. The age of traditional apologetics with its classical horizons and its polemical language is over.[24] The age of an authentically ecumenical theological enterprise is here to stay. And in such an enterprise there must occur a common and serious study of at least all the major interpretations, histories, and witnesses of the Christian faith in their genetic-dialectic unfolding. Now this is not to argue for what Albert Outler has aptly named the "hand-holding" stage of ecumenism as the final answer. Nor is it to suggest that the "indifferentism" which the classically minded in all our communities are forever warning us against is the only possible result of a non-apologetic but dialectical ecumenical enterprise. But it is to insist that the historical moment of polemical apologetics is spent. And that the moment for the emergence of a specific functional specialty for theology, on the level of deliberation-evaluation-decision, which will dialectically articulate and order all the major Christian positions in their significant similarities and differences must now be forged.[25]

It is, moreover, the level of dialectic which impels the theologian to a radical personal faith-decision. For with Bultmann, Lon-

24. This is not to claim that the apologetic aim is now spent. In fact, the present writer would agree with Langdon Gilkey in his observations on the subject (*Concilium* [New York, 1969], vol. 46, pp. 127–57). The simple point here is the need for post-polemical apologetics of a dialectically ecumenical kind.

25. In fact, dialectics is a technical and differentiated designation for a fairly widespread practice among contemporary theologians: recall, for example, how large a part of contemporary theological works are devoted to such articulation of significant similarities and differences (indeed, sometimes with little space left for the articulation of one's own position). For such examples of dialectics, cf. *inter alia* Van Harvey, *The Historian and the Believer* (New York, 1966), pp. 3–246; or Jürgen Moltmann, *The Theology of Hope* (New York, 1965), pp. 15–95; or Aloys Grillmeier, *Christ in Christian Tradition* (New York, 1965).

ergan insists upon the utter radicality of the Christian faith's demands and upon the historical uniqueness[26] of Christian conversion as an existential phenomenon. But more dialectically than Bultmann, Lonergan also insists that the faith-decision be made only after an in-depth study of the dialectical context wherein the various Christian interpretations, histories and witnesses have been scrupulously examined. Then the conversion experience proper to the theologian might be experienced and articulated in a wider and deeper context than the German Protestant context has thus far allowed.[27] Moreover, that dialectical discussion should be further expanded (as it is at present in the United States) to allow for the intrinsic entry of the disciplines of comparative religion[28] and, especially, the demands of the present Jewish-Christian dialectical dialogue. In such a context, he hopes, every theologian may be enabled to evaluate and deliberate more accurately and thereby decide more radically to open himself to the full demands of God's searing gift of grace in his conversion to Christ Jesus.[29] Indeed, the phenomenon of

26. For the briefest presentation of Bultmann's position, besides the "classic" texts, cf. R. Bultmann, *Existence and Faith* (New York, 1966), esp. pp. 55–58, 92–111, 298–97. The word "uniqueness" is, I realize, vague (insofar as Socrates too is "unique"). However, the present context is not the proper one to attempt to determine more exactly the *epaphax* nature of the Christian claims in a manner neither Barthian nor Bultmannian.

27. "German Protestant" context is cited since for the present writer it remains the most erudite contemporary theological tradition and, therefore, helps one to understand how it can dialectically be transformed to be both "wider" (i.e. as dialectically ecumenical) and deeper (e.g. by developing some of the secular philosophical sophistication and empirical verification demands of much of the recent American Protestant theological tradition or of the Catholic transcendental methodologists [Continental and American]).

28. For specific examples of such "dialectics," cf. the series of the "Chicago School," *Essays in Divinity* (ed. Jerald Brauer), esp. Volume II, *The Impact of the Church upon its Culture* (Chicago, 1968); and *The History of Religions—Essays in Methodology* (Eliade-Kitagawa), (Chicago, 1962). Note, moreover, the increased relevance of the "genetic-dialectic" method of *Insight* and *De Deo Trino* (analyzed in Chapters 6 and 8 of this book).

29. Hence the reinforced centrality afforded the category of "con-

conversion (intellectual, moral, religious, Christian) becomes all-important at this fourth and most existentially demanding level of the theologian's work. And nothing is really gained by clouding over that demand. For if too dazzled by the possibilities of research or interpretation or history and perhaps unconsciously fearful of the lack of security, the fear and trembling and the strange peace and joy which have always accompanied any genuinely religious spirit the theologian finds himself either unwilling or unable to move to that level of personal decision and to develop the dialectical tools proper to that level, then he should not dismiss too lightly the charges of irrelevance which any undifferentiated, perhaps, but honest generation feels compelled to hurl at him. For if he refuses to move to that level of real religious self-transcendence, he may in fact be in the unhappy state of the exegete in Kierkegaard's parable who was so busy all his life determining the exact meaning of each New

---

version" (intellectual, moral and religious) in Lonergan's later work; cf. *DMT*, pp. 3–5, and "Theology in its New Context," *Theology of Renewal* I, pp. 44–51, and Chapter 1 of this book.

Lonergan has yet to determine what for this interpreter remains a most difficult theological question for the Christian theologian, viz. the relationship between "religious" and "Christian" conversions. His Christology (*De Verbo Incarnato*), it should be recalled, was written before the emphasis in his thought on dialectics and foundations (with the exception of the last "thesis" to be written there on the *Existenz* of Christ, *DVI* [1964], pp. 332–416). His methodological work continues to attempt to work out the significant dialectical similarities and differences of religious conversion (e.g. the Lonerganian interpretation of Friedrich Heiler's "The History of Religions as a Preparation for the Cooperation of Religions," in *The History of Religions, op. cit.,* pp. 142–53) but not yet (to my knowledge) of explicitly Christian conversion. Perhaps the reason for this position is that the traditional emphasis in Catholic theology upon the universal salvific will of God and the emphasis on philosophy's role in theology rarely lead to the "exclusivity" dilemmas of the Barthian (or even the Bultmannian) positions. (The Rahner-von Balthasar exchange on "anonymous Christianity" may prove to be an important exception to this generalization.) For an interesting dialectical contrast of the Catholic and Protestant positions on "religion," cf. the Lonergan-influenced article, Joseph A. Komonchak, "The Problem of a Religious A Priori," *Dunwoodie Review* (vol. 7, pp. 199–214).

Testament text that he never had the time to ask himself the simple question, "But do I really believe all this?"

To conclude on a more positive note, the functional specialty "dialectic" is an effort towards a scientific way of dealing with the religious event called conversion from which alone for Lonergan theology may authentically speak. At that level, the theologian has the opportunity to encounter the religious situation as it is now and as it has been in a past mediated to him[30] by his dialectical involvement with the authentic Christian traditions.

At the level of decision-dialectic-conversion, therefore, the theological task proper to "hearing," to *"lectio,"* to encountering the Christian past is attempted. But still there can be no cessation of labor for the theologian for the effort of thematization of that conversion experience is yet to come. In short, it is time to initiate discussion of the next functional specialty, foundations.

Fifth, foundations: The role of foundations is to objectify conversion into a basic horizon.[31] As the category "conversion"

30. "Mediation of tradition" becomes, therefore, a crucial theological task—a factor emphasized in contemporary theology not only by such Catholic theologians as Rahner and Lonergan but also by such contemporary Protestant theologians as Ebeling and Pannenburg (via Gadamer's hermeneutic of merging horizons). The openness to the "future" mentioned by Lonergan as another task on the level of dialectics is not, to my knowledge, ever attempted by him—especially, it must be added, on the question of eschatology (which receives scant notice in Lonergan's entire work); cf., for example, the lack of such emphasis in Lonergan's recent essay "The Future of Christianity," *The Holy Cross Quarterly* (1969), pp. 5–10. Whether this need lead to a critique of Lonergan's transcendental method like that accorded to Rahner by John Baptist Metz is a further question. As I have tried to indicate elsewhere ("Horizon Analysis and Eschatology," *op. cit.*), it need not (even though Lonergan's lack of explicitation cannot be accepted); for a possibly contrary view on Lonergan and political-social realities, cf. Michael Novak. *The Theology of Radical Politics* (New York, 1969), and contrast it with his earlier "Lonerganian" work *Belief and Unbelief* (New York, 1965).

31. Hence the importance of the issue of objectivization-thematization; specifically, for Lonergan, the importance of his thematization of the invariant norms, structures and procedures of intellectual conversion

is central to the level of dialectic, so "horizon" is to the level of foundations.[32] A horizon, one may recall, is a maximum field of vision from a determinate standpoint with objective and subjective poles, each one of which is determined by and determines the other. A basic horizon, moreover, possesses a basic subjective pole (intellectual, moral, religious and Christian conversions) and an objective pole (as the thematization of those conversions). Foundational theology, then, attempts to articulate the basic horizon from within which a theologian operates. In Roman Catholic theology, the uniqueness of this conception of foundational theology might best be studied by comparing it to traditional Catholic fundamental theology. That latter discipline, with its convenient lists of various questions (inspiration, the mission of Christ, revelation, etc.) was helpful enough as a pedagogical device but never really got to the core of anything that could be called a genuinely "fundamental" theology. Its confines were both too narrow (the separate questions, the apologetic atmosphere, the failure to engage in the necessary preliminary research, interpretation, history and dialectic) and too superficial (as student malaise testifies) to allow for the development of a foundational theological horizon. Indeed the widespread retreat from *theoria* to activism among many theological students is not fully explicable in terms of a general contemporary phenomenon alone. Rather it may well expose the presence of a general, often inchoate and usually undifferentiated repugnance with the seeming lack of any fundamental intellectual, moral and religious seriousness in much of what

---

in *Insight;* and of his recent (and still incomplete) attempts to achieve the thematization of moral and religious conversion on the level of *Existenz.*

32. Cf. Chapter 1; the clearest published expression of the category remains "Metaphysics as Horizon," *Collection,* pp. 202–21. Note that the critical effort is one of thematizing the unthematic (pre-conceptual, etc.), not of Cartesian doubt; cf. *Insight,* pp. xxi–xxiii, 408–11. For Lonergan's own foundational theology, one should examine not only his former work in doctrine and transcendental method but also the sections on "religion" and the "question of God" in the forthcoming *Method in Theology.*

passes for "fundamental" theology. In effect, then, the students demand of the theologians what they might long ago have demanded of themselves: that they critically and theoretically examine and expose their presuppositions, their methods, their categories, their conversion and attempt to thematize them. That demand has forced most theologians to realize the simple historical necessity of the kind of radical theological rethinking now occurring throughout the Christian world.[33] It invites them to enter into that horizon-problematic and try to bring the Christian fact to speech again and to do so by a careful, theoretical thematization of the language and conversion-operations of their values, beliefs, faith. The only authentic entry into the contemporary theological dialectic is the entry into the level of evaluation and decision, of conversion and its thematization. And whether one's horizon be most adequately thematized in terms of the *existentialia* of the early Heidegger or the language-event of the later, of the process philosophy of Whitehead and Hartshorne or of Hegelian and Nietzschean language or of the expansion of the transcendental method in Rahner or the later Lonergan or of some other as yet untried foundation is an urgent but further question.[34] We do not propose to digress from

33. If one may repeat a needed emphasis: such radical theological thinking (whether named "death of God," secularity, etc.) is imperative at present and only those unaware of the difficulties involved with the recognition of the 'historicity' of the individual theologian can afford the luxury of surprise and "shock" at the seemingly chaotic theological situation. For a helpful summary of the meaning of "historicity" and its implications for philosophy (and, although the author does not so argue, for theology as well), cf. Emil Fackenheim, *Metaphysics and Historicity* (Marquette, 1961).

34. The crucial issue, as I interpret it, may be formulated thus: (a) how does one most adequately formulate the foundational question? (e.g. via a "transcendental" formulation on the conditions of possibility of transcendence experience and language or a Heideggerian formulation on the ontological status of the finite, historical speaker of such discourse or the Whiteheadian, etc.); and (b) what are the criteria (logical-coherence, adequacy, etc.) for the thematized conceptualities emerging from the preferred manner of thematization (e.g. Hartshorne's and Ogden's critique of the conceptuality for the God of classical theism or Lonergan's critique of the unverifiability of the Molinist *scientia media*

the present methodological problem to respond to it here. Our present aim is at once more simple, more formal and, in that sense, more fundamental than the actual working out of the thematic foundations themselves. For we wish to indicate just where and how that foundational question has arisen. We further wish to indicate that the question is not resolved either by a retreat into a classicist "fundamental" theology or by a romantic onslaught which feels free to ignore the exigencies of encountering the past (through research-interpretation-critical history and dialectic) while staking its religious and theological claims on an imagined present or future. We further suggest that that the present need is not for another *Weltanschauung* Chris-

---

theory)? Although Lonergan does not so explicitly differentiate these questions, it would seem to this interpreter that he should: otherwise they can rather easily become almost totally undifferentiated (as, for example, in much of the "death of God" position or of the activist aspect of the secular-eschatological positions). And that failure of explicit differentiation can also disallow a serious treatment of the distinct question of the logical criteria for the thematized conceptualities. (For example, I believe that one could accept the Hartshorne-Ogden critique of the logical inadequacies of classical theism without having to accept the Whiteheadian "reformed subjectivist principle," as the most helpful way to formulate the crucial issue of critically grounding transcendence language.) Moreover, on the (a) section of the question, Ricoeur's emphasis (esp. in "Existence et herméneutique" (*Interpretation der Welt* [Wurzburg, 1965]) that one must not (he is criticizing Heidegger) move immediately to philosophical reflections without dealing with the hermeneutics of the different human and empirical sciences seems to me entirely correct. In terms of the "foundational" question that insistence (expanded by Ricoeur in *Histoire et vérite* [Paris, 1955]) should seem to impel Lonergan to develop his distinction between "relative" and "basic" horizon more fully than he has at present and thus to clarify how the human sciences are related functionally to theology on the level of foundations as well as communications.

If, however, one's position is fundamentally fideist (as, for example, in some of the theological uses of Wittgenstein), then, of course, the whole issue of these questions seems folly. But if we will not choose the intellectual escape of fideism then one cannot flee from the foundational issue—nor from a recognition of the truth in Schillebeeckx's insistence "that the present-day crisis in faith is essentially a crisis in metaphysics"; cf. Edward Schillebeeckx, *God the Future of Man* (New York, 1968), p. 47.

tianity but for a basic horizon Christianity which can mediate to and, if need be, transform any *Weltanschauung*. That believers must find ways to communicate Christ to any culture or to any epoch is an obvious but methodologically later task (viz. communications). But that they should first attempt to understand him as either those who wrote the New Testament or those who communicated that New Testament belief to later generations did should seem at least equally obvious. The theologian must, therefore, first commit himself to the rigor of research, interpretation, history and dialectics. That he should also attempt to thematize his conversion-understanding through a basic horizon language or languages is a perhaps less obvious but certainly fully compelling need.

Sixth, doctrines: one should note, first of all, that doctrine only becomes a proper theological question after the work of the first five theological specialties has already been accomplished. One must have developed from data through interpretation, history, dialectics and foundations before the basic horizon is explicated whence one may understand that movement toward doctrine and system involved in the Christian community's development from the *quoad nos* of the Scriptures to the *quoad se* of the councils.[35] Secondly, the several Christian doctrines each demand an analysis by the properly qualified textual critics, exegetes, historians, dialecticians, and foundational theologians. On the foundational level, moreover, the pressure of a thematized intellectual conversion is essential for understanding the nature of the doctrines.[36] Thirdly, the placement of the specialty "doctrines" on the third level of consciousness is also of

35. This has, of course, already been treated in Chapter 8 on the nature of dogmatic theology; note, however, how the present differentiation is able to functionally relate that discipline to all the other theological disciplines.

36. It is possible, for example, that the ambiguities of the neo-Orthodox tradition on the earlier question of the relationship of philosophy (or historical reason) to faith in theology led to some of the difficulties involved for that tradition in interpreting the meaning and possibilities of the conciliar period.

some importance.[37] For as with the "facts" of history, doctrines are placed by Lonergan not on the level of experience or understanding or decisions but of judgment.[38] In other words, doctrines *affirm* incompletely but truly (i.e. really) certain essential features of the Christian belief. Within the foundational horizon proper to the Christian theologian, doctrines provide the minimal judgments and affirmations proper to the Christian's belief. For, even granted the limitations and present inadequacies of the classical hellenistic categories of the conciliar, patristic and medieval periods, it still remains true that the Greek movement to *theoria* (in present categories, the movement to and from intellectual conversion) allowed the Christian community then (as it does now) to make certain clear affirmations of its basic beliefs. The transposition, for example, from the nature-person categories of Chalcedon to the person as presence-in-the-world categories of a Rahner or a Schillebeeckx is a transposition which only occurs within a basic continuity with those affirmations which Christians (beginning with the New Testament "Jesus is Lord") have always made. Once again, therefore, the importance of Lonergan's analysis of judgment for his handling of the related problems of history and doctrines cannot be overemphasized.

Seventh, systematics:[39] the nature of systematics for Lonergan has already been articulated in the second chapter of this book. For there it was argued that the exact nature of the medieval achievement was its articulation of a strictly technical language and of rigorously theoretical techniques aimed at clarifying and explaining the scriptural and doctrinal beliefs of the Christian community. So Père Bouillard, for example, has argued that if

37. Cf. Lonergan's critique of L. Dewart for lack of same in "The Dehellenization of Dogma," *The Future of Belief Debate* (New York, 1967), pp. 69–91, esp. pp. 71–73.

38. Hence the renewed importance of the critical realism of *Insight* and the insistence upon realism as foundational for the Christian; cf. the unpublished 1961 lecture "The Origins of Christian Realism."

39. Cf. Chapter 2 of this book, and *inter alia* cf. *Verbum*, pp. 206–21; and *GO* IV, pp. 572–78.

Aquinas had known the anti- Semi-Pelagianist decrees of the Council of Orange, he might have been able to resolve his early struggles with the theology of grace far more rapidly. In short, it is imperative for the theologian at the systematic level of discussion to search out a technical language that might express as clearly and distinctly as possible the nature of the realities he affirms as believer. And even if the classical categories of an Aquinas or a Calvin are no longer adequate to that systematic task, this does not exempt the contemporary theologian from the effort to achieve in the new scientific context what they achieved in theirs.

Eighth, communications: at this final level, the problem named "relevance" emerges. Indeed here the disciplines variously named catechetics or religious education or pastoral theology must find their contemporary transformation. Only certain central factors intrinsic to that transformation may be noted in this brief discussion. In the first place, the question of communication emerges as a properly theological question only after each of the first seven functional specialties has played its proper role. For no more than intuitionist theories can save the epistemological day, can leaps from Jesus to the fabled man in the street save theology. In short, simpliste solutions solve nothing in the long run for they only require the eventual re-emergence of the original and originating problem. In the second place, vague calls for a renewed "pastoral" theology will not suffice. Instead the theologians must learn to collaborate with the methods and results of theoreticians and practitioners in the field of communications theory, of linguistics, of comparative literature, of political theory, of psychology, of sociology, of cultural anthropology and of the rest of the whole range of recently developed and developing human sciences.[40] Otherwise even very good theology may continue to crash against the charge of irrelevance from non-theologians (or even from other theologians—as in Cox's sociological critique of Bultmann or Metz's political-historical

40. Note, therefore, that this functional specialty also remains a strictly *theoretical* discipline.

THE ACHIEVEMENT OF BERNARD LONERGAN

critique of Rahner). In the third place, there can be no pretense that any one theologian can master the methods of all seven previous specialties much less that he can become an expert in all the various sciences which the level of communications includes. But he can learn (as Cox or Metz or Callahan show) to collaborate with human scientists, first in a genuinely theoretical way (by learning the science in its accepted methods, procedures and results) and only then with theological applications. That such an interdisciplinary task can be achieved in a university setting is at present more a hope, I suspect, than a reality. But one may continue to hope (especially in the light of the "proleptic" anticipations of that possibility in figures like Cox, Metz, Callahan, Berger, Gilkey *et al.*) that this crucial task will also someday be attempted in a genuinely collaborative way.

A. POSSIBILITIES OF FUNCTIONAL SPECIALIZATION[41]

The most obvious advantage of the methodical approach which Lonergan develops is its ability to order the different theological tasks. Moreover, that ordering is not merely a matter of necessary convenience as are the various field specialties (too much data for one man) or the various subject specialties (too great a growth in all subjects for any one man to master them all). For the functional specialties are determined as such by their specifically different tasks: different ends, different means, different methods. The methodical theologian must constantly distinguish those eight separate tasks and keep them separate. In one form or another, all eight of those tasks demand the theologian's attention. But once theology reaches the contemporary

41. The listing of these possibilities is fundamentally faithful to Lonergan's own analysis in the *Gregorianum* article on functional specialties. The point is more adequately determined in the section of *Method in Theology* on religion; the further possibilities of functional specialization, moreover (especially the interrelationship of the two phases; most especially of the third and fourth levels of each phase), will also be extensively discussed there.

stage of development its two phases and the four functions of each phase become clearly differentiated.

A second advantage may also be determined, viz. that theology may be unified without retreating into deductivism. No function is deduced from any others. Rather each presupposes the earlier and complements it in some clearly differentiated way. The whole process, moreover, possesses the intrinsic unity of the dynamism of human consciousness itself: from an undifferentiated state (the original faith experience) through differentiation and specialization (doctrines, systematics and increasing specialization) to the integration of the various specialties (viz. by the dynamic, self-structuring integration of the eight functional specialties themselves).

A third advantage also recommends itself: viz. that functional specialization can reveal the genuine need of the contemporary differentiated consciousness for a theology. In fact, the needed differentiation between religion and theology can be apprehended adequately only by a differentiated consciousness. For only the man who has himself appropriated the theoretical and critical tradition of the West can begin to appreciate that movement towards theology which began in the apostolic Fathers, continued through the conciliar, patristic, medieval and reformation periods and must be continued today for the still more differentiated consciousness of twentieth-century man. Otherwise, the living religious spirit which must ground all genuine theology (dialectic-foundations) will become ever more suspect as the theology intended to illuminate religion increases its competence in field and subject specialties but actually decreases its possibilities of integration and communication. It is true, of course, that wherever consciousness is not differentiated, theology as a theoretical exercise with eight functional specialties becomes incomprehensible. In fact, in that situation it is not really needed. For all the worlds of the human horizon (profane-sacred; interior-exterior; common sense-theory[42]) are

42. Cf. Chapter 1 of this work. Also the reader may agree with the present writer that Lonergan's own critical grounding of the sacred is less than adequate.

already unified for the undifferentiated mind and the possibilities of symbolic expression prove fully adequate to its religious needs. But whenever consciousness becomes highly differentiated, then one's former childlike apprehension of religion appears childish or at best esoteric and marginal to one's intellectual life. One soon finds oneself joining the eternal "cultured despisers" of religion. In such a context, the possibly evangelical features of the contemporary theological task become clear: either religious faith is abandoned or a highly rigorous and sophisticated theology is learned. Accordingly, unless the truly contemporary adult prefers to "differentiate" his religious life only by allowing the memories of a childhood happiness to evaporate into the adventitiousness of an undifferentiated religious "atmosphere" (to which he returns only when the emotional uplift of the "God of the gaps" is desired), then the adult's need to make the religious values of his life cognitively accessible becomes ever more imperative. In short, he needs a theology. It is true that the differentiation between theology and religion should occur primarily to allow a deepened return to the life of religious self-transcendence (communications-experience). But without that prior scientific differentiation the later return tends to become empty-handed and peremptory.

In that context, then, Lonergan's own earlier work on theory, on system, on science, on cognitional analysis becomes ever more relevant to contemporary theology. For as Bonhoeffer has reminded us all in a manner we dare not forget, it is capricious and ultimately irresponsible for the contemporary man who affirms religious values to retreat into anything less than full involvement with the scientific, philosophical and even technological advancements of our day.[43] And, as Eric Vögelin further reminds us,[44] it is imperative for the contemporary analyst of the religious phenomenon to investigate and, if possible, appropriate not only the whole range of religious phenomena which Max Weber so brilliantly analyzed but also the two which he

43. How full that involvement was may be recognized in the recent impressive biography by Mary Bosanquet, *The Life and Death of Dietrich Bonhoeffer* (New York, 1969).
44. Eric Voegelin, *The New Science of Politics* (Chicago, 1952).

did not—the Greek philosophers' study of religion from the viewpoint of *theoria,* and the medievals' analogous application of *theoria* to Christian interiority.

It would be well to clarify another possible source of misrepresentation: Lonergan's notion of theology as an eightfold methodically ordered structure does not impose some new Lonerganian "system" upon theology but allows it to explicate the essentially open and heuristic structure which theology already is. That heuristic openness, furthermore, must be present on every level of theology's development: research is always open to further relevant data; interpretation to deeper penetration; history to firmer affirmations and wider narrative perspectives; dialectic to expansion and more accurate clarification of the real similarities and differences between positions; foundations to more exacting thematization; doctrines to greater development; systematics to more rigorous technical expression; communications to the discovery of new fields (e.g. McLuhan *et al.*) and the improvement of the already existing human sciences. Moreover, each level is also open to further development insofar as each is functionally related to all the others and thereby reciprocally dependent on them. For example, interpretation is obviously dependent on research but the reverse is also true: a new method of interpretation can bring about different determinations of the original data. Dialectics is obviously dependent on research, interpretation and history but once again the reverse is true: for example, as the ecumenical dialectic widens and deepens the level of discussion exemplified in the Hans Küng-Ernst Käsemann exchange on the New Testament foundations of "early Catholicism"[45] will demand more probing research, interpretation and history on the first three levels. Or, as the problem of communications accelerates, there is bound to emerge a John A. T. Robinson or a William Hamilton to raise issues and demand clarifications that should force anyone oper-

45. Ernest Käsemann, *Essays on New Testament Themes* (London, 1964), pp. 63–95, 95–108; *idem., Distinctive Protestant and Catholic Themes Reconsidered* (New York, 1967), pp. 14–28; Hans Küng, *The Living Church* (London, 1963), pp. 233–74.

ating in any of the first seven functional specialties to more exacting labors. As such functional interrelationship develops, each specialist may learn to curb his own temptations to omniscience as he listens to and learns from his colleagues in the other specialties. And if theologians can begin to collaborate in that functional way, then the whole series of unnecessary impasses (dogmatic vs. biblical theology; "relevance" vs. theory; "dialogue" vs. foundations) which have tended to dominate much of the theological horizon since the entry of historical consciousness into theology may finally become past history. In its unmourned place, a truly collaborative and contemporaneously scientific theological enterprise might be initiated.

Finally, a second kind of reciprocal interdependence should be noted, viz. the dependence of the two phases on one another. It is hardly necessary, I suppose, to insist upon the dependence of the second phase ("mediated theology") upon the first ("mediating theology") but it might prove helpful to spell out that dependence in greater detail. The first phase, then, mediates theology by transforming the field specialties into functional specialties which, on the level of dialectic, finally mediates the Christian conversion that grounds for Lonergan the theological Christian horizon. All first phase questions must be met not by any appeal to the second phase as an *a priori* (e.g. Aquinas' use of Aristotelian categories in his commentaries on the scriptures or, at times, Bultmann's use of the Heideggerian *existentialia* for his hermeneutic) but out of the resources of the first phase itself.

On the other hand, the second phase must obviously be dependent on the first. Otherwise, the difficulties all-too-familiar to those who have endured the "proof-text" methods of the manuals or even the inspiring but scientifically somewhat capricious "spiritual" hermeneutics of Alexandria or, more recently, Karl Barth[46] will again emerge to fashion theologies with too

46. A fascinating example of the kind of impasse occasioned by such misunderstanding may be found in the recently published Barth-Harnack exchange, *Continuum* 7 (1969), 195–213.

tenuous a connection with their Christian sources. But once that dependence is clearly established then the exigencies represented by the prophetic *and* theological demands of a Barth that theology be concerned with God and all things in their relationship to God can be met without falling into Barth's theological disdain for the earlier exigencies of the historico-critical method (phase one). For those former exigencies are properly resolved only by the full development of the second phase as it descends from the horizon of thematized Christian conversion through doctrines and systematics to communication.

Such interdependence of the two phases, moreover, is especially crucial on the third and fourth levels. On the third level (judgment-history-doctrine)[47] there is always an intrinsic interdependence between the specialist in doctrines and the specialist in doctrinal history (as, for example, in Lonergan's own work on the doctrines of the Trinity and of Christology). To employ a non-theological example, it is easy enough for anyone to grasp that one dare not write a history of physics unless he already understands present physical theory. Conversely, he cannot fully understand contemporary physical theory unless he has made some study of the history of its development. Similarly, as the recent controversies in the Roman Catholic world on transubstantiation testify, one cannot hope to understand the doctrines as other than verbal formulae unless one first understands the history of their emergence.[48] But understanding that history demands some prior apprehension of the doctrines themselves. For example, if the theologian did not already possess some understanding of the notions of process, relation and person, he could not hope to write a history of Trinitarian development

47. It is on this level that most of the Catholic discussions on "development of doctrine" have been conducted. For a useful survey of same, cf. Charles N. Bent, *Interpreting the Doctrine of God* (New York, 1968); for specific examples, cf. *Lo Sviluppo del dogma secundo la doctrina catholica* (Rome, 1953); for a similar approach from a Protestant author, cf. Jaroslav Pelikan, *Development of Christian Doctrine: Some Historical Prolegomena* (Yale, 1969).

48. For a clear summary and example of same, cf. Edward Schillebeeckx, *The Eucharist* (New York, 1968).

THE ACHIEVEMENT OF BERNARD LONERGAN

that could avoid the pitfalls of entirely missing certain key factors, of overemphasizing minor points and, in general, confusing rather than clarifying that complex issue.

On the fourth level, moreover, there is a yet more radical interdependence between the specialties, dialectics and foundations. For the foundational theologian attempts to objectify authentically Christian conversion as it emerges from dialectical discussion. And while there may well be more than one account of authentic conversion, still dialectics may hope to reveal certain fundamental similarities among the differences. That revelation, in its turn, may tend to reduce the multiplicity exposed in the earlier stages of dialectic and eliminate merely polemical and apologetic tendencies. Hence, the thematization proper to foundations will not be left to the caprice of a *Weltanschauung* or the merely private religious experience of the foundational theologian. In fact, may not the attempts of Bultmann and Tillich and those who followed them be legitimately interpreted as major efforts to break out of the religiously rigid confines of the Barthian dialectical system? And was not their limited but real success due to their attempts to establish deeper contact with what we have called the level of conversion-dialectic? Does not Bultmann's exegetical work reveal a deeper realization than Barth ever possessed of the theologian's need for fidelity to the first three functional specialties? Or does not Tillich's dialogue with the contemporary human sciences reveal a greater sensitivity to the pressing need for what we have called the functional specialty "communications"?[49] Admittedly, both Bultmann's and Tillich's theologies can now be recognized as inadequate. But that is not really the point at issue here. Rather both their partial success and their distinct failures serve to illustrate the nature of theology conceived as functional specialization. Their

49. The example of Tillich in his attempt to resolve the totality of the theological enterprise strikes this reader as unparalleled among theologians for the ambitiousness of the task he was willing to undertake—up to the final lectures where he seems willing to revise his entire notion of systematics in the light of his study of the history of religions! Cf. *The Future of Religion* (New York, 1966).

partial success reveals the genuine integrity of their realization of the need to attempt some kind of integration of what we have called field (phase one) and subject (phase two) specializations on the level of dialectics and foundations. For the collapse of all classical theological systems or even the ultimate failure of the modern Barthian, Bultmannian and Tillichian attempts at theological integration do not argue for the impossibility of any attempt at integration. To be more specific, their failure should not argue against careful attention by all theologians (in whatever discipline, of whatever tradition) to the possibly more sophisticated if at present purely formal principles of theological integration afforded by Lonergan's notion of theology as comprised of eight functional specializations. For the dynamic unity and the integrating power of functional specialization is composed of the interaction of those two phases and those eight functional specialties which, as a unitive whole, define contemporary theology. Moreover, that notion of theology finds its basic heuristic structure verified in the transcendental method of *Insight* and thus allows for the dynamic, self-structuring method of functional specialization. Finally, it demands and makes methodologically possible the intrinsic interaction of religion and theology (dialectics-foundations) and the same kind of interaction between theology and the world (the first seven specialties and communications).

In conclusion, the major advantages of Lonergan's peculiar notion of theology as an eightfold functional specialization may be stated as frankly as possible. In the present writer's judgment, that method goes beyond but does not cancel out the genuine achievements of field specialization and subject specialization. For field specialization provides the theologian with the ideas and categories of a biblical, a patristic, a medieval, a reformation, a modern and a contemporary theology. And subject specialization provides him with his properly theological self-identity as involved with the science of God and all things in their relation to God as known under the light of revelation and faith (e.g. Aquinas or Barth). Functional specialization, on the other hand, precisely as faithful to the exigencies of historical consciousness and to its own grounded possibilities in transcendental method, can promise to unite both field and subject specialties into a higher integration. In fact, it brings the two together by means of the heuristic, methodical and functionally integrating structure of the theologian's own consciousness. It also demands the necessary differentiations: for each phase and each functional specialty in each phase must be allowed its full role and significance without being allowed to neglect the role of the other phase (or of any function in that phase). Finally, Lonergan's method allows for the clear differentiation of theology from religion without an abandonment of either the demands of a genuinely religious conversion (dialectics) or its communication (communications) or the demands of the strictly scientific approach proper to an authentically theological stance toward the Christian and religious phenomena. In Lonergan's own theological development, moreover, it allows the breakthrough towards which all his prior work had been aiming and in the light of which his former work seems relatively unintegrated.[50] That the possibilities of functional specialization are as yet untried is quite true.[51] That those possibilities are genuine ones, however, —indeed, possibly epoch-making ones for theology—is all that the present chapter has tried to communicate.

B. CONCLUSION

Lonergan's specification of theology as a method involving an eightfold functional specialization may provide a new turning point for contemporary theology. At the very least, it may al-

50. One should compare this development, for example, not only with the early and very general methodological precepts of the 1959 *De Intellectu et Methodo* but also with the more refined but still unintegrated concerns and categories of the 1962 *De Methodo Theologiae* or the 1964 Georgetown lectures on method.

51. And that the present chapter has been merely descriptive, not explanatory of them, is likewise true.

low for a collaborative enterprise which at present is almost desperately needed in the certainly creative but somewhat chaotic situation of contemporary theology. One may, of course, hope for even more than that. But at the present juncture it would, I believe, be too sanguine to expect more. For the facts remain that Lonergan's past work is still widely either unknown or misunderstood and his present work is at the critical stage of facing some of the most fundamental questions in the new context of historical consciousness for contemporary theology. Such questions include those upon the nature of religion and of speech about God. Since these later positions have not yet been published, the present writer does not feel at liberty to discuss them here except to indicate that the articulation of Lonergan's position on religious conversion (or, if one prefers, the "problem of God") receives deepened and, in certain significant ways, revised formulation as a direct result of his analysis of the new context of theology and his methodological reply to that context, especially his signal specification of the fourth level of dialectics and foundations. Indeed, the transcendent exigence argued for in *Insight* within the context of the category of intelligibility receives its later formulation from the viewpoint of a transcendental notion of values and religion in the position to be worked out in *Method In Theology*. At that time Lonergan's work may connect more immediately to the exigencies of the recent debates on hermeneutic, history and radical theology. For those latter debates are, I believe, on the level of what we have called dialectic and foundations and their resolutions are yet to be discovered. It is hoped that this exposition of Bernard Lonergan's published works may allow his forthcoming work in dialectic and foundations the contextual understanding, if not the agreement, which such a project demands.

As for his past work, perhaps the finest tribute which one may pay to that is to state the obvious: that Lonergan's work over the years is a significant, indeed great, body of work precisely because it stands up to the demanding criteria for theoretic and critical rigor which Lonergan has consistently and often eloquently argued for. Indeed, in my judgment, his work represents a single and in many ways singular achievement: the articulation of the authentic scientific possibilities realized throughout the changing contexts of Christianity's relationships to various cultures—the conciliar, patristic, medieval, modern and contemporary. I realize that the exigencies of contemporary culture can often prove so demanding that the already realized if now inadequate possibilities of theology's developments in previous cultural contexts may bear only slight interest for today's theologians. But it may be well to point out that one by no means minor aspect of the phenomenon of historical consciousness is the contemporary recognition of the need to study one's own and one's culture's history well before proceeding to transform it. This becomes especially imperative if the theologian, as committed Christian, continues to believe in the constitutive and transforming possibilities of the Christian revelation and the constitutive and mediatory possibilities of theology to any and all cultures.

Nor do I wish to suggest that the full complexities of the contemporary theological situation can be readily resolved if only theologians would understand and appropriate the Lonerganian method. Such an appropriation would certainly prove extremely helpful but it would serve primarily not to close questions but to show a new mode of entry into the whole series of fundamental theological questions crying for resolution: the questions of comparative religion, of the radical theology debate, of the secularization discussion, of the hermeneutic problem, of the constitutive nature of Christian eschatology, and so on. Still, it may be well to point out, for this one last time, that Lonergan's enterprise does not impose a new classical system, however rigorous and attractive, but promises rather a new possibility of open scientific inquiry based upon certain invariant dynamic and structural elements in human consciousness. Those elements found their thematic emergence in Lonergan's work in Aquinas, their specification in his *Insight* and their expansion and application to the contemporary task of theology in his notion of functional specialties.

Finally, it may prove helpful to speak more directly to the American context towards which this work is principally addressed. For one way of interpreting Lonergan's achievement is to note how, without abandoning the genuine accomplishments of our European predecessors, he has quietly managed to bring into the theological enterprise some of the most valued characteristics of the Anglo-American intellectual tradition: that tradition's demand for empirical verification, its distrust of all "impeccable" systems, its openness to the modern experience, especially to the scientific demands of our period, its emphasis on development and process and its insistence on the ethical imperatives now put upon us to transform nature and, if possible, man himself. But since the other side of the Anglo-American experience too often reveals the darker possibilities aptly expressed in Herbert Marcuse's phrase "the totalitarianism of tolerance," I trust I will not be misunderstood as polemical or arrogant if I close with the hope that Lonergan's past and present work will be met with full and rigorous criticism but not with the kind of totalitarian tolerance which would effectively destroy the very exigencies he insists upon. For any truly critical work can withstand neither ideological totalitarian rigidity nor totalitarian tolerance. It demands rather an audience willing to live up to the transcendental exigencies: Be attentive, be intelligent, be reasonable, be responsible, develop and, if necessary, change. If the latter prove to be the case, one need not fear that Lonergan's work will receive both the attention and criticism it deserves.

BIBLIOGRAPHY

A. PRIMARY SOURCES: LONERGAN'S OWN WORKS

The works listed below are the major sources employed for this book and of relevance to Lonergan's notion of theological method. There are some minor semi-popular articles of Lonergan's not cited here which may be found in the bibliography of Lonergan's works provided by F. E. Crowe in *Spirit As Inquiry* (pp. 544–49). The order here follows that of Crowe's with the addition of those later works and of tape-recordings employed for this book.[1]

1. Regarding the order of F. E. Crowe's bibliography in *Spirit As Inquiry* (pp. 544–49) the following observations should be made: "Bracketed items are works that have not been made available to the general public through commercial channels: notes mimeographed for students, lectures recorded and issued in some similar form, etc. Some of these have been issued more than once in the same or different houses of study, but only the first issue is listed here; likewise, translations in this category are omitted, the principle of their inclusion at all being merely their necessity for an adequate picture of Lonergan's work as an author. The size of these notes may be anywhere from foolscap to half foolscap, but the number of pages is given anyway to provide at least some idea of the length of the work.

"Order is chronological, but later editions are grouped with the original, except for revisions and translations which have their own place in the list according to the date of their appearance. Printed lectures are included according to the time of the lecture rather than that of the printing" (*ibid.*, p. 544).

270

Section A. Principal Sources

1. Review: *The Problem of Error, From Plato to Kant. A Historical and Critical Study,* by L. W. Keeler. *Gregorianum* 16 (1935), 156–60.

2. Doctoral Dissertation: *A Study of the Speculative Development in the Writings of St. Thomas of Aquin* (dissertatio ad lauream in facultate theologica Pontificiae Universitatis Gregorianae, 1940).

[3. *De Sacramentis in genere: Supplementum.* L'Immaculée-Conception. Montreal, 1940–41. 26 pp.]

4. "St. Thomas' Thought on *Gratia Operans,*" *Theological Studies* 2 (1941), 289–324; 3 (1942), 69–88; 375–402; 533–78.

4a. *Gratia Operans: A Study of Speculative Development in the Writings of St. Thomas Aquinas* (Excerpta ex dissertatione ad lauream in facultate theologica Pontificiae Universitatis Gregorianae). Montreal, 1946. (The 4th article of n. 4, with two pages of introduction added.)

5. Review: *Marriage,* by Dietrich von Hildebrand. *The Canadian Register,* Quebec edition, May 23, 1942, p. 5.

6. "Marriage," *ibid.,* June 6, 1942, p. 9. (A letter in reply to a letter of correspondent on n. 5.)

7. "Marriage," *ibid.,* p. 9. (Reply to another letter of same correspondent on n. 5.)

8. Review: *The Living Thoughts of St. Paul,* by Jacques Maritain. *Theological Studies* 3 (1942), 310–11.

9. "The Form of Inference," *Thought* 18 (1943), 277–92.

10. "Finality, Love, Marriage," *Theological Studies* 4 (1943), 477–510.

[11. *De materia confirmationis: Supplementum.* L'Immaculee-Conception, Montreal, 1943–44. 4 pp.]

[12. *De notione sacrificii.* Notes for lectures at L'Immaculee-Conception, 1943–44. Regis College, Toronto, 1960. 18 pp.]

13. Review: *A Realistic Philosophy,* by K. F. Reinhardt. *The Canadian Register,* Quebec edition, Feb. 17, 1945, p. 8.

14. "The Concept of *Verbum* in the Writings of St. Thomas Aquinas," *Theological Studies* 7 (1946), 349–92; 8 (1947), 35–79; 404–444; 10 (1949), 3–40; 359–93.

15. Review: *De Deo in Operatione Naturae vel Voluntatis Operante,* by E. Iglesias. *Theological Studies* 7 (1946), 602–613.

[16. *De ente supernaturali: Supplementum schematicum.* L'Immaculee-Conception, Montreal, 1946. 83 pp.]

17. Review: *Mediaeval Studies.* Vol. VIII. *Theological Studies* 8 (1947), 706–707.

18. Review: *The Ground of Induction,* by Donald Williams. *Thought* 22 (1947), 740–41.

19. Review: *The Eternal Quest,* by William R. O'Connor. *Theological Studies* 9 (1948), 125–27.

20. "The Assumption and Theology," in *Vers le dogme de l'Assomption* (Journées d'études mariales, Montreal, 12–15 aout, 1948), 411–24. Montreal, 1948.

21. "The Natural Desire to See God," *Proceedings of the Eleventh Annual Convention of the Jesuit Philosophical Association* (Boston College, April 18, 1949), pp. 31–43. Woodstock, Md.

22. Review: *Man's Last End,* by Joseph Buckley, and *La sagesse de Senèque,* by Andre de Bovis. *Theological Studies* 10 (1949), 578–82.

23. "A Note on Geometric Possibility," *The Modern Schoolman* 27 (1949–50), 124–38.

24. Review: *Certainty: Philosophical and Theological,* by Dom Illtyd Trethowan. *The Modern Schoolman* 27 (1949–50), 153–55.

25. Review: *Being and Some Philosophers,* by Etienne Gilson. *Theological Studies* 11 (1950), 122–25.

[26. *De scientia atque voluntate Dei. Supplementum schematicum.* College of Christ the King (now Regis College), Toronto, March 23, 1950. 48 pp.]

27. "A New Dogma," *The Canadian Messenger of the Sacred Heart* 61 (1951), 11–15.

28. Review: *Ueber Schicksal und Vorsehung,* by Eduard Stakemeier. *Theological Studies* 12 (1951), 259–60.

29. Review: *Sciences ecclésiastiques.* Vol. III. *Theological Studies* 12 (1951), 292–93.

30. "Le role de l'université catholique dans le monde moderne," *Relations* 11 (1951), 263–65. (Cf. Erratum, *ibid.,* p. 320.)

[31. *The Mystical Body of Christ* (Conference, College of Christ the King, Toronto, Nov., 1951). Regis College, Toronto, May, 1960. 5 pp.]

32. "Humble Acknowledgement of the Church's Teaching Authority," *The Canadian Messenger of the Sacred Heart* 62 (1952), 5–9.

[33. *Analysis fidei*. College of Christ the King, Toronto, March 8, 1952. 19 pp.]

34. Review: *Théologie du verbe: Saint Augustin et Saint Thomas*, by H. Paissac. *Theological Studies* 13 (1952), 121–25.

35. Review: *De Deo creationis finem exsequente*, by E. Iglesias. *Theological Studies* 13 (1952), 439–41.

[36. *De conscientia Christi*. College of Christ the King, Toronto, fall term, 1952. 8 pp.]

[37. *De ratione convenientiae eiusque radice, de excellentia ordinis, de signis rationis systematice et universaliter ordinatis, denique de convenientia, contingentia, et fine incarnationis. Supplementum schematicum*. With appendix: *Aliqua solutio possibilis*. St. Francis Xavier College (Gesu), Rome, 1953–54. 14 pp.]

38. "Theology and Understanding," *Gregorianum* 35 (1954), 630–48. (On J. Beumer's *Theologie als Glaubensverständnis*.)

[39. *De Sanctissima Trinitate: Supplementum quoddam*. Gregorian University, Rome, March 7, 1955. 50 pp. (Three articles, of which first and second are printed with slight changes as Appendices I and II in n. 49.)]

40. Review: *Les dimensions de l'etre et du temps*, by J. Chaix-Ruy. *Gregorianum* 36 (1955), 137–38.

41. "Isomorphism of Thomist and Scientific Thought," *Sapientia Aquinatis* (Communicationes IV Congressus Thomistici Internationalis, Rome, 1955), Rome (1955), 119–27.

42. Review: *Théologie trinitaire chez Saint Thomas d'Aquin*, by P. Vanier. *Gregorianum* 36 (1955), 703–705.

43. Review: *El Yo de Jesucristo*, by B. Xiberta. *Gregorianum* 36 (1955), 705–706.

44. *De constitutione Christi ontologica et psychologica*. Gregorian University, Rome, 1956. 150 pp. (Ad usum auditorum.)

44a, 44b, 44c. Second, Third and Fourth Editions. 1958, 1961, 1964. Unchanged.

45. Review: *The Indwelling of the Trinity*, by F. L. B. Cunningham. *Gregorianum* 37 (1956), 664–65.

46. Review: *Die Lehre von Gott*. Bd. 2: *Von der Goettlichen Trinitaet*, by J. Brinktrine. *Gregorianum* 37 (1956), 665.

47. Review: S. Thomae Aquinatis: *In octo libros de physico . . .* (D'Auria). *In . . . libros peri hermeneias et posteriorum analyticorum . . .* (Mariette). *In librum de causis . . .* (Marietti). *Gregorianum* 37 (1956), 691.

48. *Insight: A Study of Human Understanding.* Longmans, Green & Co., London; and Philosophical Library, New York, 1957. xxx & 785 pp.

49. *Divinarum personarum conceptio analogica.* Gregorian University, Rome, 1957. 302 pp. (Ad usum auditorum.)

49a. Second edition, 1959. Unchanged, except for correction of misprints and addition (pp. 91, 297) of two short *quaestiunculae.*

[50. *Mathematical Logic & Notes on Existentialism* (Notes for lectures at Summer School, Boston College, July, 1957). Thomas More Institute, Montreal. 50 pp.]

51. "Philosophic Difference and Personal Development," *The New Scholasticism* 32 (1958), 97. (Synopsis of paper to be given at meeting of American Catholic Philosophical Association. But the paper listed under n. 52 was given instead.)

52. *"Insight:* Preface to a Discussion," *Proceedings of the American Catholic Philosophical Association* 32 (1958), 71–81.

53. *Insight: A Study of Human Understanding.* Second (students') edition, revised (but pagination unchanged). London, 1958.

53a, 53b, 53c, 53d, 53e. Third, Fourth, Fifth, Sixth, and Seventh printings. 1961, 1963, 1964, 1965, 1967. Unchanged.

[54. The Redemption. (Lecture at the Thomas More Institute for Adult Education, Sept. 25, 1958; text from tape-recording.) Thomas More Institute, Montreal. 14 pp.]

55. Review: *Tractatus de Verbo Incarnato: I & II,* and *Enchiridion de Verbo Incarnato: Fontes . . . ,* both by B. Xiberta. *Gregorianum* 40 (1959), 155–56.

56. Review: *Le mystere du Dieu vivant,* by Bernard Piault. *Gregorianum* 40 (1959), 156.

57. Review: *Saint Augustin et le néoplatonisme . . . ,* by M. F. Sciacca, and *Existe-t-il une philosophie chrétienne?* by M. Nedoncelle. *Gregorianum* 40 (1959), 182–83.

58. "Christ as Subject: A Reply," *Gregorianum* 40 (1959), 242–70.

59. Review: Plotinus: *The Enneads.* Translated by Stephen McKenna, revised by B. S. Page. *Gregorianum* 40 (1959), 389–90.

[60. *De intellectu et methodo* (*Reportatio* of course at the Gregorian University, 1959). St. Francis College, Rome. 72 pp.]

61. Review: *The Order and Integration of Knowledge,* and *Metaphysics and Ideology,* both by William O. Martin. *Gregorianum* 41 (1960), 171–73.

62. *De Verbo Incarnato* dicta scriptis auxit B. Lonergan. Gregorian University, Rome, 1960. 750 pp. (Ad usum auditorum.)

62a. Second edition, 1961. 546 pp. Retyped, but text unchanged.

63. "Openness and Religious Experience," *Il Problema dell'esperienza religiosa* (Atti del XV Convegno del Centro di Studi Filosofici tra Professori Universitari, Gallarate, 1960), 460–62. Brescia, 1961.

[64. *Notes from the Introductory Lecture in the Philosophy of History* (Text from tape-recording). Thomas More Institute, Montreal, Sept. 23, 1960. 14 pp.]

65. *Intelligenza. Studio sulla comprensione dell'esperienza.* Alba, 1961. 826 pp. (Translation by Carla Miggiano di Scipio of n. 53.)

66. *De Deo Trino: Pars analytica.* Gregorian University, Rome, 1961. 326 pp. (Ad usum auditorum.)

[67. *The Origins of Christian Realism* (Lecture at Regis College, Toronto, Sept. 8, 1961; text from tape-recording). Regis College, Toronto. 8 pp.]

[68. *De methodo theologiae* (Notes for lectures at Gregorian University, 1962). North American College, Rome. 60 pp.]

[69. *De argumento theologico ex sacra Scriptura* (Notes for lecture to professors of Gregorian University and Biblical Institute). Gregorian University, Rome, 1962.]

[70. *Hermeneutics* (Notes for lectures during Theology Institute, Regis College, Toronto, July 20, 1962). Regis College, Toronto. 16 pp.]

71. *Consciousness and the Trinity* (Lecture at North American College, Rome, 1963). North American College, Rome.

72. "Metaphysics as Horizon," *Gregorianum* 44 (1963), 307–318. (On E. Coreth's *Metaphysik.*)

72a. "Metaphysics as Horizon," *The Current* (Harvard-Radcliffe Catholic Club) 5 (1964), 6–23. (Reprint.)

73. Review: *Die Gewinnung Theologischer Normen aus der Geschichte der Religion bei E. Troeltsch,* by Ignacio Escribano Alberca. *Gregorianum* 44 (1963), 369–70.

275

74. Review: *Le lieu théologique, "Histoire,"* by Jean-Marie Levasseur. *Gregorianum* 44 (1963), 370–371.

75. Review: *Les missions divines selon Saint Augustin,* by Jean-Louis Maier. *Gregorianum* 44 (1963), 371.

76. Review: *In opera Sancti Thomae index seu tabula aurea eximii Doctoris F. Petri de Bergomo. Gregorianum* 44 (1963), 371–72.

77. Review: *La crise de la raison dans la pensée contemporaine,* by E. Barbotin, J. Trouillard, R. Verneaux, D. Dubarle, S. Breton. *Gregorianum* 44 (1963), 372–73.

78. "La Notion de verbe dans les ecrits de saint Thomas d'Aquin," *Archives de Philosophie* 26 (1963), 163–203; 570–620 (à suivre). (Translation of n. 14; minor revisions by the author.)

79. *De Deo Trino. I: Pars dogmatica* (Editio altera et recognita). *II: Pars systematica* (Editio tertia et recognita). Gregorian University, Rome, 1964. 308 & 321 pp. (Part I is a revision of n. 66, Part II a revision of n. 49.)

[80. *De notione structurae* (Lecture at the Collegium Aloisianum, Gallarate, March 7, 1964; text from tape-recording). Aloisianum, Gallarate. 7 pp.]

81. *De Verbo Incarnato.* Gregorian University, Rome, 1964. Third edition, revised. 598 pp. (Ad usum auditorum.)

82. "Cognitional Structure," *Continuum* 2 (1964), 530–542.

83. *"Existenz* and *Aggiornamento,"* Focus (Regis College theological journal) 2 (1965), 5–14. (Notes of a lecture at Regis College, Toronto, Sept. 14, 1964.)

84. *Collection: Papers by Bernard Lonergan, S.J.* Herder and Herder, New York, 1967. xxxv & 280 pp. (Collection of previously published papers and an unpublished lecture. Because of its ready availability for verification, all references in this thesis to these papers and lectures have been made to this work. Hence the usefulness of citing those articles anew as they are to be found in *Collection.*)

"The Form of Inference," 1–15 (n. 9).

"Finality, Love, Marriage," 16–53 (n. 10).

"On God and Secondary Causes," 54–67 (n. 15).

"The Assumption and Theology," 68–83 (n. 20).

"The Natural Desire to See God," 84–95 (n. 21).

"A Note on Geometric Possibility," 96–113 (n. 23).

"The Role of a Catholic University in the Modern World," 114–120 (n. 30).

"Theology and Understanding," 121–141 (n. 38).

"Isomorphism of Thomist and Scientific Thought," 142–151 (n. 41).

"Insight: Preface to a Discussion," 152–168 (n. 52).

"Christ as Subject: A Reply," 164–197 (n. 58).

"Openness and Religious Experience," 198–201 (n. 63).

"Metaphysics as Horizon," 202–220 (n. 72).

"Cognitional Structure," 221–239 (n. 82).

"Existenz and *Aggiornamento,"* 240–251 (n. 83).

"Dimensions of Meaning," 252–267 (Lecture given at Marquette University, Milwaukee, May 12, 1965. Previously unpublished).

85. *Verbum: Word and Idea in Aquinas.* Edited by D. Burrell. University of Notre Dame Press, Notre Dame, 1967. xv & 300 pp. (n. 14).

86. "Dehellenization of Dogma," *Theological Studies* 28 (1967), 336–351. Also available in G. Baum (ed.), *The Future of Belief Debate.* Herder and Herder, New York, 1967. 69–91.

87. "Response," *Proceedings of the American Catholic Philosophical Association.* Catholic University of America Press, Washington, 1967. 254–259.

88. "Transition from a Classicist World View to Historical Mindedness," *The Role of Law in the Church Today.* Helicon, Baltimore, 1967. 126–133.

89. *Verbum: Word and Idea in Aquinas.* Darton, Longman & Todd, London, 1968. (N. 85, unchanged, except for correction of misprints.)

90. *The Subject.* Marquette University Press, Milwaukee, 1968. 35 pp. (Lecture given at Marquette University, March 3, 1968.)

91. "Molina, Luis de," *Encyclopedia Britannica,* 15 (Chicago, 1968), 665–66.

92. "Natural Knowledge of God." (Unpublished lecture given at the June, 1968, meeting of the Catholic Theological Society of America, Washington, D.C., to appear in *The Proceedings of the Catholic Theological Society of America,* 1968.)

93. "Theology in its New Context," in L. K. Shook (ed.), *Theology of Renewal I.* Herder and Herder, New York, 1968. 34–46.

94. "Absence of God in Modern Culture," *The Presence and Absence of God*. Fordham University Press, New York, 1969. 164–178.

95. *Method in Theology*. (To appear.)

Section B. Lectures Delivered Since 1964 But Not Yet Published (Some or all may be included in a possible volume entitled *Collection II*)

96. "The Future of Thomism," Lecture at Pittsburgh, 1967.

97. "Belief: The Contemporary Issue," Lecture at New York and Pittsburgh, 1967.

98. "The Future of Christianity," Lecture at Holy Cross College, Worchester, Mass., 1969.

99. "History." Lecture at the Catholic University of America, Washington, D.C., 1969. (An adaptation of the section on history is in the forthcoming *Method in Theology*.)

Section C. Sets of Tape-Recordings (Available at Regis College, Toronto, or from present author)

100–01. *Mathematical Logic and Notes on Existentialism* (Lectures given at the Summer School, Boston College, July, 1957).

102. *Lectures on Insight* (Lectures given at St. Mary's University, Halifax, Nova Scotia, 1958).

103. *Philosophy of Education* (Lectures given at Xavier College, Cincinatti, Ohio, 1959).

104. *Lectures on Method in Theology* (Lectures given at Regis College, Toronto, Summer, 1962).

105. *Lectures on Method in Theology* (Lectures given at Boston College, Summer, 1968).

B. SECONDARY SOURCES

The secondary sources principally employed for this book fall into two general categories: a first section (A) deals with those

278

articles either on Lonergan or heavily influenced by him which the present author has found the most helpful for interpreting Lonergan; a second section (B) deals with those general background works read and footnoted throughout this book in the various sciences with which Lonergan's work deals (primarily, of course, in theology). Neither list is intended to be exhaustive: there are a number of articles on Lonergan's work (e.g. those of E. MacKinnon or most of the reviews of *Insight*) which the present writer did not find helpful for understanding Lonergan's work. Consequently, they are not listed herein. There are, moreover, a great number of other works in the history of theology consulted but not referred to here as less directly relevant to a study of Lonergan's own interpretation. An excellent bibliography on theology as a science may be found in: T. Tshibangu, *Théologie positive et théologie spéculative* (Louvain, 1965), pp. xiii–xxxix.

Section A. Background Articles on Lonergan and/or on Other Thinkers from a Perspective Influenced by Lonergan's Own Thought

1. *Spirit as Inquiry: Studies in Honor of Bernard Lonergan, S.J. Continuum* 2 (1964), 305–552. (Since this work represents the first *Festschrift* on Lonergan's work, the articles are all listed below as they appear there.)

Walter Burghardt, S.J., "From a Theologian," 308–310.

Frederick C. Copleston, S.J., "From a Historian of Philosophy," 311–313.

R. Eric O'Connor, S.J., "From a Mathematician," 313–315.

Frederick E. Crowe, S.J., "The Exigent Mind: Bernard Lonergan's Intellectualism," 316–333.

Patrick A. Heelan, S.J., "A Realist Theory of Physical Science," 334–342.

Edward M. MacKinnon, S.J., "Cognitional Analysis and the Philosophy of Science," 343–368.

Ernan McMullin, *"Insight* and the *Meno,"* 369–373.

Philip McShane, S.J., *"Insight* and the Strategy of Biology," 374–388.

Michael Novak, "Lonergan's Starting Place: The Performance of Asking Questions," 389–401.

Joseph Thomas Clark, S.J., " 'The Form of Inference'—Revisited," 402–408.

William A. Stewart, S.J., "Abstraction: Conscious or Unconscious?" 409–419.

Dom Sebastian Moore, "The Discovery of Metaphysics—One Man's War," 420–424.

Jean Langlois, S.J., "The Notion of Being According to Lonergan," 425–433.

David B. Burrell, C.S.C., "Analogy and Judgment," 434–446.

Emerich Coreth, S.J., "Dialectic of Performance and Concept," 447–454.

Andrew J. Reck, "Interpretation," 455–463.

Justus George Lawler, "The Poem as Question," 464–470.

Paul Vanier, S.J., "Towards an Effective Philosophy of Education," 471–479.

Henri Niel, S.J., "The Old and New in Theology," 480–488.

P. Joseph Cahill, S.J., "A Primary Affirmation," 489–496.

Michael J. Lapierre, S.J., "Redemption in the Understanding of Faith," 497–504.

Robert L. Richard, S.J., "Contribution to a Theory of Doctrinal Development," 505–527.

Bernard Lonergan, S.J., "Cognitional Structure," 530–542.

2. *Other Interpretative Works:*

Burrell, David B., C.S.C., "A Note on Analogy," *New Scholasticism* 36 (1962), 225–32.

————, "Indwelling: Presence and Dialogue," *Theological Studies* 22 (1961), 1–17.

————, "Aquinas on Naming God," *Theological Studies* 24 (1963), 183–212.

————, "Aristotle and Future Contingencies," *Philosophical Studies* 13 (1964), 37–42.

————, "Kant and Philosophical Knowledge," *New Scholasticism* 38 (1964), 189–213.

————, "C. S. Pierce: Pragmatism as a Theory of Judgement," *International Philosophical Quarterly* 5 (1965), 521–40.

————, "God: Language and Transcendence," *Commonweal* 85 (1967), 511–16.

————, "How Complete Can Intelligibility Be? A Commentary on *Insight:* Chapter XIX," *Proceedings of the American Catholic Philosophical Association.* Catholic University of America Press, Washington, 1967. 250–253.

————, "Faith and the Nature of Mind as Inquiry," *The Future as the Presence of Shared Hope.* Edited by M. Muckenhirn. Sheed & Ward, New York, 1968. 130–47.

Crowe, Frederick E., S.J., "Index," *Insight* by Bernard Lonergan. Longmans, Green & Co., London, 1957. 749–85.

————, "The Origin and Scope of Bernard Lonergan's 'Insight,'" *Sciences Ecclésiastiques* 9 (1957), 263–95.

————, "Complacency and Concern in the Thought of St. Thomas," *Theological Studies* 20 (1959), 1–39; 198–230; 343–95.

————, "Complacency and Concern," *Cross and Crown* 11 (1959), 180–90.

————, "St. Thomas and the Isomorphism of Human Knowing and Its Proper Object," *Sciences Ecclésiastiques* 13 (1961), 167–90.

————, Development of Doctrine and the Ecumenical Problem," *Theological Studies* 23 (1962), 27–46.

————, "On the Method of Theology," *Theological Studies* 23 (1962), 637–42.

————, *De Verbo Dei cum hominibus communicato.* (Mimeo notes for class.) 1962–63. 109 pp.

————, "Introduction," *Spirit as Inquiry: Studies in Honor of Bernard Lonergan. Continuum* 2 (1964), 306–07.

————, "The Exigent Mind: Bernard Lonergan's Intellectualism," *Spirit as Inquiry: Studies in Honor of Bernard Lonergan. Continuum* 2 (1964), 316–33.

————, "Bibliography of the Writings of Bernard Lonergan," *Spirit as Inquiry: Studies in Honor of Bernard Lonergan. Continuum* 2 (1964), 543–49.

————, "Neither Jew nor Greek, but One Human Nature and Operation in All," *Philippine Studies* 13 (1965), 546–71.

————, *The Doctrine of the Most Holy Trinity.* (Mimeo notes for class.) 1965–66. 198 pp.

————, "Development of Doctrine: Aid or Barrier to Christian Unity?" *Proceedings of the Twenty-First Annual Convention of the Catholic Theological Society of America.* Catholic University of America Press, 1966. 1–20.

————, "Aggiornamento," *The Canadian Messenger* 77 (1967).

————, "Bernard Lonergan," *Modern Theologians, Christians and Jews.* University of Notre Dame Press, 1967. 126–51.

————, "Christology and Contemporary Philosophy," *Commonweal* 87 (1967), 242–247.

————, Editor. *Collection: Papers by Bernard Lonergan, S.J.* Herder and Herder, New York, 1967.

————, "Indices," *Verbum: Word and Idea in Aquinas,* by Bernard Lonergan, S.J. Edited by David B. Burrell, C.S.C. University of Notre Dame Press, 1967. 221–300.

————, "Insight," *National Catholic Encyclopedia* 7. McGraw-Hill Book Co., New York, 1967. 545b.

————, "Intuition," National Catholic Encyclopedia 7. McGraw-Hill Book Co., New York, 1967. 598b–600b.

————, "Theological Terminology," *National Catholic Encyclopedia* 14. McGraw-Hill Book Co., New York, 1967. 37b–38b.

————, "Understanding (*Intellectus*)," *National Catholic Encyclopedia.* McGraw-Hill Book Co., New York, 1967. 389a–391b.

————, "Christologies: How Up-to-Date Is Yours?" *Theological Studies* 29 (1968), 87–101.

————, "Development of Doctrine," *American Ecclesiastical Review* 159 (1968), 233–47.

————, Review: *Revelation and Theology,* by E. Schillebeeckx. *Theological Studies* 29 (1968), 339.

————, Review: *Revelation and Theology I.* by E. Schillebeeckx. beeckx. *Theological Studies* 29 (1968), 779–81.

————, *A Time for Change: Guidelines for the Perplexed Catholic.* Bruce Publishing Co., Milwaukee, 1968.

————, "The Trinity," *A Catholic Dictionary of Theology* IV. Edited by Joseph Crehen. (To appear.)

Hart, James G., *Theories of Consciousness: Lonergan and Some Contemporaries.* (Unpublished M.A. thesis. Catholic University of America, Washington, Jan. 1965.)

Heelan, Patrick, *Quantum Mechanics and Objectivity: A Study of the Physical Philosophy of Werner Heisenberg*. Martinus Nijoff, The Hague, 1965.

————, "Horizon, Objectivity and Reality in the Physical Sciences," *International Philosophical Quarterly* 7 (1967), 375–412.

Johnson, Donald, "Lonergan and the Redoing of Ethics," *Continuum* 5 (1967), 211–20.

Komonchak, Joseph A., "The Problem of a Religious *a priori*," *The Dunwoodie Review* 7 (1967), 199–214.

Lamb, Matthew, Review: *Verbum: Word and Idea in Aquinas*. *Continuum* 5 (1967), 425–31.

MacKinnon, Edward, "The Transcendental Turn: Necessary But Not Sufficient," *Continuum* 6 (1968), 225–231.

McShane, P., "The Hypothesis of Intelligible Emanations," *Theological Studies* 23 (1962), 545–68.

Murray, J. C., *The Problem of God*. Yale University Press, New Haven, 1964.

Novak, Michael, "Bernard Lonergan: A New Approach to Natural Law," *Proceedings of the American Catholic Philosophical Association*. Catholic University of America Press, Washington, 1967. 246–49.

Richard, Robert L., *The Problem of an Apologetical Perspective in the Trinitarian Theology of St. Thomas Aquinas*. Rome, 1963.

————, "Lonergan's Contribution to the Present-Day Theological Dialog," *Philippine Studies* 13 (1965), 524–45.

Sala, G. B., "L'analisi della conscienza umana in B. Lonergan," *La Scuola Cattolica* 94 (1966), 200.

————, "Oltre la neoscolastica, verso una nuova filosofia. Quale?" *La Scuola Cattolica* 4 (1968), 291–333.

Sanders, James W., "A New Approach to a Catholic Philosophy of Education," *Jesuit Educational Quarterly* 24 (1961–62), 88–108, 133–150.

Schouborg, Gary, "A Note on Lonergan's Argument for the Existence of God," *Modern Schoolman* 45 (1968), 243–8.

Tracy, David W., "Analysis of Faith According to Bernard Lonergan." (Unpublished paper for seminar of Rev. Juan Alfaro, Pontificia Universitas Gregoriana, 1965.)

283

————, "Holy Spirit as Philosophic Problem," *Commonweal* 89 (1968), 205–213.

————, "Horizon Analysis and Eschatology," *Continuum* 6 (1968), 166–180.

————, Review: *Jesus, God and Man* and *Revelation as History*, both by Wolfhardt Pannenberg. *Catholic Biblical Quarterly* 31 (1969).

Section B. Background Articles on the Problematics of Theology and Science: Principally Catholic Context

Beumer, J., *Theologie als Glaubensverständnis*. Echter-Verlag, Würzburg, 1953.

Bonnefoy, J.-F., *La Théologie comme science selon Saint Thomas d'Aquin*. J. Vrin-Ch. Beyaert, Bruges-Paris, 1939.

Bouillard, H., *Conversion et grace chez S. Thomas d'Aquin. Étude historique*. Coll. Theologie, I, Paris, 1944.

Burns, John V. *Dynamism in the Cosmology of Christian Wolff: A Study in Pre-Critical Rationalism*. Exposition Press, New York, 1965.

Butterfield, Herbert, *The Origins of Modern Science* (Revised Edition). Macmillan Co. (Free Press), New York, 1966.

Chenu, M.-D., *La théologie comme science au XIIIᵉ siecle*. J. Vrin, Paris, 1959.

Colombo, C., *"La methodologia e la sistemazione teologica," Problemi E Orientanenti Di Teologia Dommatica I*. Milano, 1957. 1–56.

Congar, Yves, "Théologie," *Dictionnaire de Theologie Catholique* 15. Librarie Letouzey et Ané, Paris, 1946. col. 342–502.

————, *A History of Theology*. Doubleday & Co., Inc., Garden City, New York, 1968. (English translation of above with revisions.)

Denzinger, *Enchiridion Symbolorum, Definitionum, Declarationum*. Edited by K. Rahner. Herder, Freiburg im Breisgau. (31st edition, 1952).

Dillenberger, John, *Protestant Thought and Natural Science*. Abington Press, Nashville, 1960.

Doms, H., *Die Gnadenlehre des sel. Albertus Magnus.* Müller & Seiffert, Breslau, 1929.

Eldarov, G. M., *Presenza della teologia.* Il Messaggero di S. Antonia, Padova, 1954.

Gagnebet, R., "La théologie de saint Thomas, science aristotélicienne de Dieu," *Acta Acad. Pont. S. Thomae Aquinatis* 11 (1946), 203–228.

Gardeil, A., *Le donné révélé et la théologie.* J. Gabalda & cie., Paris, 1932.

Geiger, L. B., Review: *"Verbum* Articles," *Bulletin Thomiste* 8 (1952), 477–79.

Gilson, E., *La philosophie au moyen age, des origines patristiques à la fin du XIVe siecle.* Payot, Paris, 1944.

————, *Réalisme Thomiste et critique de la connaissance.* J. Vrin, Paris, 1939.

Heidegger, Martin, *Sein und Zeit.* Erste Hälfte. *Jahrbuch für Philosophie und phänomenologische Forschung* (Halle) 8 (1927).

Heinz, R., *Französische kantinterpretation im 20 Jahrhundert.* Bouvier, Bonn, 1966.

Hoenen, P., "De origine primorum principiorum scientiae," *Gregorianum* 14 (1933), 153–84.

————, "De philosophia scholastica cognitionis geometricae," *Gregorianum* 19 (1938), 498–514.

————, "De problemate necessitatis geometricae," *Gregorianum* 20 (1939), 19–54.

————, "De problemate exactitudinis geometricae," *Gregorianum* 20 (1939), 321–50.

————, *La théorie du jugement d'après S. Thomas d'Aquin.* Analecta Gregoriana XXXIX. Rome, 1946.

Holz, H., *Tranzendental-philosophie und Metaphysik.* Matthias-Grünewald-Verlag, Mainz, 1966.

Jaki, Stanley L., *The Relevance of Physics.* University of Chicago Press, Chicago, 1966.

Jaspers, Karl, *Psychologie der Weltanschaungen.* Springer, Berlin, 1925.

Kuhn, Thomas A., *Structures of Scientific Revolutions.* Phoenix Press, University of Chicago, 1962.

Latourelle, Rene, *Introductio in sacram theologiam.* Rome, 1964.

————, *Theologia scientia sacra.* Pontificia Universitas Gregoriana, Romae, 1965. (Ad usum auditorum.)

Lottin, O., *La théorie du libre arbitre depuis Saint Anselme jusqu'a Saint Thomas d'Aquin.* Saint Maximin, 1929.

————, "Liberté humaine et motion divine," *Medievale* 7 (1935) 52–69; 156–173.

Mansion, S., *Aristote et S. Thomas d'Aquin.* Publications universitaires, Louvain, 1957.

Matson, Floyd W., *The Broken Image. Man, Science and Society.* Doubleday & Co., Garden City, New York, 1966.

Metz, J. B., *Christliche Anthropozentrik.* München, 1 1962.

Muck, O., *Die tranzendentale Methode in der Scholastichen Philosophie der Gegenwart.* Verlag Felizian Rauch, Innsbruck, 1964. (ET) *The Transcendental Method.* Herder and Herder, New York, 1968.

Nachbar, Bernard A. M., "Is it Thomism?," *Continuum* 6 (1968), 232–35.

Newman, John H., *The Grammar of Assent.* Longmans, Green, & Co., London, 1888.

O'Connell, Matthew, "St. Thomas and the *Verbum:* An Interpretation," *Modern Schoolman* 24 (1947), 224–34.

Ogden, Schubert M., "The Challenge to Protestant Thought," *Continuum* 6 (1968), 236–40.

Palmer, Richard E., *Hermeneutics.* Northwestern University Press, Evanston, Illinois, 1969.

Peghaire, J., *"Intellectus" et "Ratio" selon saint Thomas d'Aquin.* Publications de L'Institut d'Etudes Medievales d'Ottawa VI. Ottawa-Paris, 1954.

Pirotta, A.-M., "De methodologia theologiae Scholasticae," *Ephemerides Theologicae Louvaniensis* 6 (1929), 405–38.

Preller, V., *Divine Science and the Science of God: A Reformulation of Thomas Aquinas.* Princeton University Press, Princeton, 1967.

Rahner, Karl, *Geist im Welt: Zur Metaphysik Endlicher Erkenntnis bei Thomas von Aquin.* Kösel, München, 1957. (ET) *Spirit in the World.* Herder and Herder, New York, 1968.

————, *Hörer des Wortes: Zur Grundlegung einer Religionsphilosophie.* Neu beakbeited von J. B. Metz. Kösel-Verlag,

München, 1963. (ET) *Hearers of the Word.* Herder and Herder, New York, 1969.

———, *Theological Investigations, IV.* Darton, Longman & Todd, London, 1966.

Reck, Andrew J., "Bernard Lonergan's Theory of Inquiry vis-a-vis American Thought," *Proceedings of the American Catholic Philosophical Association.* Catholic University of American Press, Washington, 1967. 239–45.

Richmond, James, *Faith and Philosophy.* Hodder and Stoughton, London, 1966.

Rothacker, E., *Logik und Systematik der Geisteswissenschaften.* Bonn, 1947.

Rousselot, P., *L'intellectualisme de saint Thomas.* J. Vrin, Paris, 1924.

Roy, L., Review: *"Verbum* Articles," *Sciences Ecclésiastiques* 1 (1948), 225–28.

Schillebeeckx, E., (ET) *Revelation and Theology I, II.* Sheed and Ward, New York, 1968.

Schupp, J., *Die Gnadenlehre des Petrus Lombardus.* Freiburg, 1932.

Tshibangu, T., *Théologie positive et théologie spéculative.* Publications de l'Universite Lovanum, Paris-Louvain, 1965.

van Ackeren, G., *"Sacra Doctrina." The Subject of the First Question of the "Summa Theologica" of S. Thomas Aquinas.* Officium Libri Catholici, Rome, 1952.

van Riet, Georges, *Thomistic Epistemology I, II.* B. Herder Book Co., St. Louis, 1963, 1965. (Translation of *L'Epistémologie Thomiste.* Editions de l'Institut Superior de Philosophie, Louvain.

van Steenberghen, F., *The Philosophical Movement in the Thirteenth Century.* Thomas Nelson and Sons Ltd., Edinburgh, 1955.

Wyser, P., *Thomas von Aquin. Bibliographische Einführungen in das Studium der Philosophie.* Berne, 1950.

Xiberta, B. M., *Introductio in Sacram Theologiam.* Instituto Francisco Suarez, Madrid, 1949.

NAME INDEX

Descartes, R., 27, 91 (n9), 227
Dewart, L., 29 (n5), 149 (n39), 202 (n39), 256 (n37)
Dillenberger, J., 284
Dilthey, W., 10 f., 119
Doms, H., 285
Donceel, J., 29 (n5), 234 (n3)
Dubarle, D., 208 (n2)
Dunne, J., 1
Durand, G., 213 (n12)

Ebeling, G., 6, 6 (n1), 244 (n18), 251 (n30)
Eddington, A., 122
Einstein, A., 73, 98, 113, 130 f.
Eldarov, G., 285
Eliade, M., 16

Fabro, C., 25–27, 207 (n1)
Fackenheim, E., 237 (n8), 253 (n33)
Fiedler, L., 4
Fiorenza, F., 234 (n3)
Freud, S., 18, 117, 118 (n34), 119
Fuchs, E., 6, 6 (n1), 244 (n18)
Funk, R., 11 (n14), 244 (n18), 247 (n23)

Gadamer, H.-G., 6 (n6), 8, 11, 158 (n55), 214, 234, 251 (n30)
Gagnebet, R., 25 (n3), 285
Galileo, 95 f., 98, 108, 110
Gardeil, A., 25 (n3), 285
Garrigou-Lagrange, R., 193, 203
Geiger, L., 26 f., 54 (n6), 285
Gilbert de la Porrée, 35
Gilkey, L., 4, 248 (n24)
Gilson, E., 25–27, 58, 59 (n12), 81 (n36), 149 (n38), 285
Gödel, K., 150 (n40)
Gogarten, F., 209
Grabmann, M., 25, 32, 37
Grillmeier, A., 248 (n25)

Hamilton, W., 261
Harnack, A., 262 (n46)
Hart, J., 135 (n5), 282
Hart, R., 6 (n6), 244 (n18)
Hartshorne, C., 140 (n20), 253, 254 (n34)
Harvey, V., 248 (n25)
Heelan, P., 8 (n9), 10 (n13), 143 (n27), 279, 283
Hegel, G., 6, 12, 18 f., 30, 50 (n4), 91, 94 f., 97 f., 120, 126 (n55), 140 (n20), 237 (n8)
Heidegger, M., 6, 6 (n6), 7, 10, 16, 91 (n9), 158 (n55), 216, 234 (n3), 253 f., 285
Heiler, F., 250 (n29)
Heinz, R., 28 (n5), 285
Heisenberg, W., 143 (n27)
Herzog, F., 5 (n2)

Heussi, K., 244 (n19)
High, D., 210 (n6)
Hoenen, P., 40 (n13), 285
Holz, H., 28 (n5), 285
Hume, D., 91 (n9), 96, 139
Husserl, E., 7 (n7), 8, 19, 57, 123, 140 (n20), 158 (n55), 210 (n6)

Jaki, S., 10 (n12), 90, 285
James, W., 153
Jaspers, K., 18 (n25), 118 (n34), 217, 285
Johann, R., 17
John, Helen James, 11 (n15), 23 (n2)
John of St. Thomas, 24
Johnson, D., 165 (n3), 283
Joseph, J., 91 (n9)

Kant, I., 27–30, 53 f., 91–97, 103, 134, 149 (n38), 158 (n55), 227, 234 (n3), 246 (n22)
Käsemann, E., 216 (n19), 246 (n21), 261
Kepler, J., 95 f.
Kierkegaard, S., 250
Komonchak, J., xv, 250 (n29), 283
Kopkind, A., 4
Kuhn, T., 10 (n12), 285
Küng, H., 261

Lamb, M., xv, 234 (n3), 283
Landgraf, A., 25, 32, 192 (n23)
Langer, S., 47 (n2), 213, 217 (n20)
Langlois, J., 144 (n29), 280
Lapierre, M., 280
Latourelle, R., 25 (n3), 222 (n23), 285
Lawler, J., xv, 1, 280
Lawrence, F., xv, 234 (n3)
Leibniz, G., 27
Leo XIII, 22
Locke, J., 28
Lombard, P., 35, 43
Lottin, O., 25, 32, 37, 192 (n23), 285 f.

MacKinnon, E., 278 f., 283
Macquarrie, J., 6 (n6)
Mansion, S., 25 (n3), 286
Marcuse, H., 269
Maréchal, J., 27–29, 91 (n9), 93, 158 (n55), 233, 234 (n3)
Maritain, J., 26 f., 58, 59 (n13)
Marrou, H., 244 (n19)
Martin, W., 208 (n2)
Marx, K., 119
Matson, F., 222 (n25), 286
May, R., 3 (n1)
McLuhan, M., 18, 261
McMullin, E., 279
McShane, P., 112 (n20), 280, 283

SUBJECT INDEX

Abstraction: and consciousness, 77; and empirical residue, 108; as enrichment, 46; involved in scientific explicitation, 94 f.; notion of, for Lonergan, 109; problematic for Hegel, 94; "three degrees" of, 76

Alienation, Hegelian, 94

"Already-out-there-now-real," 65 (cf. Confrontation theory of knowing)

Analytic viewpoint, and meaning, 210

Anthropology and historical consciousness, 207

Apologetics, 186

Appropriation, of rational self-consciousness, 159 (cf. Self-affirmation)

A priori intuition, 93

Aquinas: abstraction, notion of, 76; actual grace, 32, 36; analogy of intelligible emanations, 23, 79, 204; on Aristotle's scientific ideal, 57 f., 90, 103; Augustinian interiority, and psychological analogy, 60 f.; cognitional approach, 49; conceptualist dangers to interpretation, 38, 40 (n13), 48; critical performance, 75, 153, 226; and critical problem, 48; "distinguish-in-order-to-unite," 27; God-language, 78; influence on Lonergan, 91 f.; "inner word," 78; and intellect, 62; interpretation by Lonergan in *Verbum* articles, 2, 9, 22 (n1), 30, 59; inverse insight, 107; knowledge by identity, 60 f.; and medieval horizon-shift, 10, 16 f.; metaphysical language of, 75, 208, 226, 262; methodological dilemma, response to, 38; science, notion of, 85, 206; speculative theology, scientific meaning of, 192; theorems on grace, 32; theorems on transcendence, 23, 32, 79; theoretic atti-

tude, 48; Thomist revival, 24–31; Trinitarian theology, 31, 57

Aristotle: Aristotelian act to Thomist *esse*, 58, 106; formulation of heuristic structure, 123; grasp of dynamic structure of knowing, 163; interrelated contexts of his ethics, 226; Lonergan's critical interpretation of, 153; notion of theory, 57 f.; science, understanding and wisdom, 195 (n28); shift in notion of science, 84–91, 103; Aristotelian-Thomist notion of science, 189, 206; "wonder," 140

Aufhebung (sublation): and the Latin treatises, 200 (n35); for Rahner, 18; and relativism, 90

Augustine: *De Trinitate*, 17, 59; illumination, 60; "inner word," 59; interiority, 60 f.; and "presence," 101 (n14)

Awareness, 14 (cf. Presence)

Báñez-Molina dispute, 31 f., 188, 196

Basic horizon, 133–182; in contrast to relative horizon, 197, 201 (n37); and Coreth, 232 f.; expansion of, 164–182; as explanatory, 141–163; and foundational theology, 252 f., 253–254 (n34); insight as entry to, 133–163; and intellectual conversion, 143 f., 231; language of, as foundational, 255; as moral, religious, Christian, and intellectual conversion, 202 f.; methodical entry into, 155–163; self-affirmation as entry into, 133–163

Begrifflichkeit: Gratia Operans as development of, 37 f.; related set of concepts, theorems, operations, techniques defining one's horizon, 36, 225

Being, 144–163; *esse* in Aquinas,

291

SUBJECT INDEX

meneutics, 244 (n18); of interpretations, 247; modern notion of, 199; movement into transcendence and religious conversion, 169–175; of science, 195; of theology, 242 (n12)

History (third functional specialty, on the level of judgment, 240), 242, 244–247, 250, 252, 254–256, 261; historico-critical method, 42, 201 (n37), 263; level of truth-reality-historical fact, 247; no single functional specialty for study of history, 246; presupposes the meaning established by exegetes, 244 f.; and special transcendent knowledge, 175–178

Horizon, 9 f., 92, 203, 231, 233, 266; Aristotelian theory as Aquinas' horizon, 57; Augustinian interiority as Aquinas' horizon, 59; basic horizon, 19–21, 133–163, 197, 254 (n34), medieval horizon of theory, 22–44, merging horizons, 251 (n30), methodical entry into, 155–163, self-affirmation and, 133–141; and *Begrifflichkeit*, 36, 225; as central category, 151 f.; cognitional, epistemological, philosophic, 203; definition (technical), 12–21, 49 f.; descriptive entry, 9–12; as developing (Piaget), 15; as grouping experiences, 150; idealism as, 202; manualist, 51; origin in Husserl, 7 f.; relative horizon, 19, 197, 254 (n34); and "worlds" of man, 259

Horizon analysis, 1–21, 87 (cf. Horizon); and extrinsicism, 8; as heuristic and schematic possibility, 7; and idealism, 9; and intentionality analysis, 7; and positivism, 9; and pragmatism, 9; and shift in notion of science, 10; as theoretic *Begrifflichkeit*, 36, 225

Human sciences, 189–191, 233, 237, 254 (n34), 257, 261; as constituting history, 191; as empirical, 189, 190 (n17), 191; theology and, 184

Husserl, E.: mediation, 19; and "bracketing," 123; notion of constitution, 208 (n3); origin of horizon, 7 f.; shift from absolute to conditional necessity, 140 (n20)

Idealism: as horizon, 202; and judgment, 223; in knowing, 223; transcendental method and phenomenology, against, 9

"Inner word," as Augustinian intelligible emanation, 59, 78

Inquiry: as different from "looking at," 102; as heuristic, 111; inquiring subject, 98; scientific vs. descriptive, 111

Insight: basic (universal) characteristics, 105–113; and conceptualization, 125; empirical residue, 107 f., significance of, 108; and heuristic anticipation, 112 f., via classical empirical method, 113, via statistical empirical method, 113; inverse insight, 107; movement to concept, and intellect, 67; into phantasm, and intellect, 65, 67; and theology, 184–191; into "things" and "bodies," 121 f.

Insight: and belief, 178–182; as entry into basic horizon, self-affirmation, 133–144; expansion of basic horizon, 164–182; structure, 104–132; thematization of reason's performance, 204

Intellect: for Aquinas and Aristotle, 62 f.; confrontation theory, 60; distinction between knower and known, 71; insight into phantasm, 63; movement, insight to concept, 67

Intellectual conversion, 143, 223, 255; and basic horizon, 202, 231; as cognitive self-transcendence, 231; exigency of, 231; as shift to *quoad se,* 202

Intellectualism, as theological approach, 22, 188, 201 (n37)

Intelligence: clarity of, 100; questioning as "upper blade" of, 126; as source of ever higher viewpoints, 123

Intelligibility: de facto, and modern science, 86; and Lonergan's shift to meaning, 232

Intelligible emanation, 23, 49, 68–70; as analogy to Trinitarian process, 50; as analysis of subject pole, 50; in Aquinas, 203; as different from natural causality, 69; as "inner word" of Augustine, 59

Intelligible relationships, 84; in modern science, 87

Intentionality, 149, 207; as awareness of object, 14; as constitutive of object, 57; definition, 14; and horizon analysis, 7; as infinite, 74; intention of being not "subjectivist," 230 (n32); intentional operations, 229 f.; intentional self-transcendence, 219; and knowing, 222, 230 (n32); and pure desire to know, 237; and Rahner, 7 f.

Interiority, 91–103; authentic, and the *Verbum* articles, 61–81; Augustinian, 60; as conscious finality towards being, 208; and critical

296

214; illative sense, 73; influence on Lonergan, 91 (n9); on judgment, 127, 180 (n53), 216

Newton, I.: classical empirical method, 113; on motion, 107; systematic laws, 95 f.

Nicea, 193 (n24), 202; genetic movement to *quoad se*, 201 (n37)

Notion, 145; heuristic notion of being, 145–147; of objectivity, 148–151; understanding of term for Lonergan, 145

Object: agent object, 76; constitution by intentionality, 57; as operative in Aquinas, 58; shift from formal object to field, 87; terminal object, 76

Objective pole, 87, 92, 115, 232 f.; definition, 14; as thematization of the basic conversions, 252

Ontic concern, as ground for ontological, 98

Ontology: and historical consciousness, 207; and ontic, 98

Operations, intentional, 229 f.

Orange, Council of, 257

Pannenberg: hermeneutic of "merging horizons," 8; and historical reason, 245 (n20)

Patristic theology and symbolic spirit, 45 (n1)

Patterns of experience: as analysis of common sense, 116–120; definition, 116; and possibility of bias, 117–120; types, artistic, 116, biological, 116, "dramatic," 117, intellectual, 116, 122

Perceptionist, and knowing, 222

Performance, 190, 203; Aquinas', as critical, 226; critical examination of, as defense of scientific ideal in *Insight*, 96; dialectic between system and performance of the system, 152; and empirical human science 190; of subject pole as inquirer, 232; thematization of performance as control of meaning, 204

Perspectivism, 89

Phases of theology, 240, 242, 258, 263, 265 f.; interdependence of phases, 258 (n41), 262; mediated theology, 262; mediating theology, 262

Phenomenology: and intentionality analysis, 7 f.; and method, 233; and proportionate being, 154; and transcendental method, 7 f.; vs. idealism, 9; use in theology, Schillebeeckx, 89

Philosophia perennis, requirements for, 153

Philosophical method, and scientific method, 158–163

Philosophy: conditions of possibility, 91–93; and critical analysis of human consciousness, 93; critical interiority, 91; as necessarily an appropriation of one's rational self-consciousness, 159; philosophical influences on Lonergan, 91–92 (n9); realist tradition and Maréchal, 93

Piaget, Jean: use of by Lonergan, 15; and undifferentiated consciousness, 153 (n48), 225

Platonism, as confrontationist cognitional theory, 65, 202

Pluralism, 89

Pole: objective, 87, 92, 115, 232 f., definition, 14, as thematization of the basic conversions, 252; subjective, 87, 92, 115, 232 f., 252

Polymorphism, in latent metaphysics, 153, 155–158

Positivism: anti-positivism of Lonergan, 40 (esp. n12)

Positive theology, 192, 194, 195 (n27), 195, 197, 199, 203, 206, 237, 243 (n14)

Position: vs. counter-position, 151–155, 159, as Lonergan's "chief tool," 151; Lonergan's, 152 f.; requirements for philosophical, 152

Pragmatism, lack of critical foundations, 9

Presence: definition, 12 f.; empirical, 101; inner word, 59; material, 101; self-presence as ground, of all other modes, 101 f., for understanding Trinity, 59 f.

Proportionate being: and human knowing, 154 f.; and metaphysics, 154, 188

Proportionate good, as object of ethics, 166

Protestant dialectic, shift to historical consciousness, 4

Psychology, and ontology in Aquinas, 194 (n25)

Quasi-formal causality vs. contingent predication, 189, 204 (n40)

Question, 125; and anticipation of unknown as known, 126; *docta ignorantia,* and higher viewpoint, 104; originating drive of human spirit, 70; *quaestio* as method, 125; radically new question posed, 5; role of, in consciousness, 138, questions for inquiry, 125–128, 138, questions for reflection,

235; as transformation of classical *ratio*, 236
Transcendental notion, of value, 267
Trinitarian theology: analogy for processions, 50; Augustinian interiority, 57; "economic" (*quoad nos*) to *quoad se*, 56; and manuals, 55 f.
Truth: and meaning, 224; and the real, 71
Truth-value, of belief, 178–179
"Turn to the subjective," 8, 12

Understanding: direct, 100; flight from, 100; as level of consciousness, 124, 229, 240; reflective, 100; vs. semi-rationalism, as imperfect understanding, 201 (n37)
Universal viewpoint: as heuristic, *Insight*, 200 (n33); as higher collaboration, 184 (n2); of human sciences, 184; theology as, 184, 187
Unknown: heuristic anticipation of, 110; known unknown, 9; unknown unknown, 9
Unrestricted desire to know (cf. Desire to know): and being, 144; as the ground of all intelligent activity, 137; as *the* moving viewpoint, 104; as the notion of being, 145
Upper blade, 173; and *Insight*, 155 f., 203; and lower blade methods, 161; questioning as, 126; of scien-

tific method is intellect, 187; thematized as cognitional theory, 187

Vatican I (*Dei Filius*), 188, 195 (n28)
Vatican II, 5, 192
Verbum articles, 2, 9, 23, 30, 45–81 (cf. Interiority, Theory)
Verification, judgment as demand for, 70
Virtually unconditioned, 146; and belief, 180; as nature of judgment, 128–132, 246 (n22), 247; self-affirmation as, 100, 228

Wisdom, and judgment, 74
Wittgenstein: notion of meaning, 210; use of "language games," 210 (n6)
Wolff, Christian, 92, 134; conceptualist, 53; logic and possible being as poles of horizon, 14; rationalism, 28
World: "common sense," theoretical, 16; of immediacy, 15; integration, 17, elimination, 17, mediation, 18 f., oscillation, 18, synthesis, 18, transposition, 18; interior-exterior, 17; of meaning (*Weltanschauung*) and community, 219; mediated by language, 15; as objective pole of horizon, 14; sacred-profane, 16; six worlds based on three possibilities of human consciousness, 15, 211, 213

302